SING FOR YOUR LIFE

ALSO BY DANIEL BERGNER

*What Do Women Want?: Adventures in the Science of
Female Desire*

*The Other Side of Desire: Four Journeys into the Far
Realms of Lust and Longing*

*In the Land of Magic Soldiers: A Story of White and Black
in West Africa*

*God of the Rodeo: The Quest for Redemption in
Louisiana's Angola Prison*

Moments of Favor: A Novel

SING
FOR YOUR
LIFE

A Story of Race, Music, and Family

DANIEL BERGNER

A LEE BOUDREAUX BOOK
LITTLE, BROWN AND COMPANY
NEW YORK BOSTON LONDON

This is a work of nonfiction. Names have been changed for three minor characters: Barry, Trevor, and Terrence Coleman.

Lee Boudreaux Books / Little, Brown and Company
Hachette Book Group
1290 Avenue of the Americas
New York, NY 10104
littlebrown.com

First Edition: September 2016

Lee Boudreaux Books is an imprint of Little, Brown and Company, a division of Hachette Book Group, Inc. The Lee Boudreaux Books name and logo are trademarks of Hachette Book Group, Inc.

The publisher is not responsible for websites (or their content) that are not owned by the publisher.

The Hachette Speakers Bureau provides a wide range of authors for speaking events. To find out more, go to hachettespeakersbureau.com or call (866) 376-6591.

The author is grateful for permission to reprint lyrics from "Ol' Man River" from *Show Boat*. Lyrics by Oscar Hammerstein II. Music by Jerome Kern. Copyright © 1927 Universal-Polygram International Publishing, Inc. Copyright renewed. All rights reserved. Used by permission. Reprinted by permission of Hal Leonard Corporation.

A portion of this book originally appeared, in different form, in the *New York Times Magazine*.

ISBN 978-0-316-30067-4

LCCN 2016930855

10 9 8 7 6 5 4 3 2 1

RRD-C

Printed in the United States of America

For Natalie and Miles,
the music that saved me

SING FOR YOUR LIFE

ONE

Ryan Speedo Green did not belong here. He didn't belong in the hotel room they had booked for him, where the headboard was high and plush and the light was faintly gold. There was more gold in the lobby, lots of it: the shimmering antique frame of the huge mirror beside the elevators; the austere silk curtains that rose three stories toward the vaulted ceiling; the velvet of the deeply curved couches; the abstract sculpture at the turn of the stairs.

Each time he left the lobby, passing under the hotel's marquee and facing Lincoln Center, in the middle of New York City, he felt even less at home. He climbed the broad steps to the Lincoln Center plaza and was surrounded by towering white stone columns that made him think of ancient stadiums—Olympians competing for Zeus's pleasure and gladiators battling one another for survival. At the far side of the square stood the opera hall. This was the home of the Met, the greatest opera company in the country. The building looked as grand and remote as the White House.

As he started to traverse the plaza, the fountain ahead

of him was almost inaudible. But as he neared the circular pool, the countless silvery plumes of shooting water created not a loud trickle or a concentrated splash: the heavy plumes produced a crescendo of sound that compounded the anxiety or thrill he felt on any given crossing of the square. It was a crossing he made repeatedly during those few days—in the early spring of 2011—leading up to the semifinals of the contest.

Behind him, the clamor of the fountain hushed swiftly. In front of him were the giant poster stands, the posters announcing the season's productions, lead singers photographed in dramatic shadow, and the opera house—the series of archways, the excess of glass, the vast murals with their airborne goddesses, their harp, cello, violins, horns. Beyond the windows hung an array of chandeliers with their pinpoints of pale gold light, and beyond the chandeliers was an aura of darker gold.

Backstage, awaiting his turn to sing, Ryan definitely did not belong, but there he was on the Sunday of the semis. This was the most revered competition in America for would-be opera stars. Twenty-two singers had made it this far after the district and regional rounds. Ryan was slotted eighteenth of the twenty-two for his minutes in front of the judges. He listened to the others; he couldn't escape their voices as he sat in the common area outside the dressing rooms, where their performances were piped in. But it wasn't only the voices themselves that confirmed how misplaced he was. It was the backgrounds of the other semifinalists. One had begun vocal training at seven, another at eight. His rivals brandished the invisible badges of having studied at the country's most prestigious conservatories, at Curtis or the Academy of Vocal Arts or Juilliard. They not only belonged—for years they had been destined for this moment here at the Met.

Ryan's home, in southeastern Virginia, was as much a shack as a house, with bullet holes above his mother's bedroom window. Before that, he'd grown up in a trailer park; before that, in low-income housing. Along the way, he spent time locked up in Virginia's institution of last resort for juveniles judged to be a threat to themselves or to everyone around them.

And Ryan was black. There was one other African American among the selected twenty-two, but she'd had a much different upbringing. A part of him—a driven, half-conscious part—sang to make race disappear.

♌

He was twenty-four years old. Waiting, he listened to Philippe, who had a low voice like his own, a bass-baritone, and the looks of a teen idol, with curly blond hair and fine expressive lips and a wisp of a nose. They had struck up an unlikely friendship during the past few days. Philippe was relentlessly confident. Walking through the corridors of the Met, he crooned out lines of Sinatra—"Fly me to the moon; let me play among the stars"—as if he'd bypassed awe and deference and took for granted his place in this house. Never mind if famous singers and conductors heard him in the hallways.

With his turn several singers away, Ryan heard Philippe perform an aria by Wagner, probably the art form's most daunting composer. Philippe was one of the youngest contestants; they were all required to be between twenty and thirty. In the first round the previous fall, twelve hundred artists had sung in cities from Seattle to Philadelphia, Houston to Cincinnati to Boston. Ryan's journey through the competition had started in Denver. He had a job, at seventeen hundred dollars per month, driving between Colorado towns with a small troupe and putting on drastically abridged operas in schools and community centers.

The contest had been inaugurated back in 1935, broadcast nationally by NBC radio and sponsored by the Sherwin-Williams paint company. "The largest paint and varnish maker in the world takes pleasure in presenting the Metropolitan Opera Auditions of the Air!" the nasally MC declared. Winners were guaranteed a Met contract. But gradually things had changed. The contest no longer had a corporate sponsor; it was no longer an advertising vehicle; it was funded by opera-loving benefactors. And it no longer gave out Met contracts. Even for the winners—and the judges usually named a few, depending on how they rated the talent when the final round was over—a thriving career was far from certain. Yet there were winners from eras past who occupied opera's pantheon, and some recent victors were ranked among the best opera singers in the world, and the Met made it known that the competition was a crucial way of finding promising artists to keep tabs on, so the prospect of being chosen seemed like the beginning of a fairy tale.

Philippe's voice, full of gravity yet capable of elevating effortlessly, floated to a high plateau. He sounded, to Ryan, as though spirits had blessed him, lifted him.

Ryan heard Deanna, a soprano, carry out coloratura

acrobatics. She did a tightrope walk with flourishes and flips, never so much as teetering. And Nicholas, a bass, offered the judges an entire lake of sound on his final note, a flawlessly smooth and seductive expanse.

By the time he was told to get to the edge of the stage, Ryan felt like he was evaporating. He stood six feet five and weighed over three hundred pounds. He wore size seventeen shoes. His biceps were about three times as big as an average man's. But he felt like his body was almost gone. It didn't help that to walk from the dressing area to the wings meant pushing through doors striped yellow and marked "Do Not Enter." It didn't help that he had to pass through a long desolate space of rough wood and raw metal, the opposite of everything on the Met's public side. Multiple stories of backstage apparatus and nothingness loomed crushingly above him. With a couple of other singers, he waited in a tight, scarcely lit spot between a stage monitor's booth and a set of immensely tall black curtains, three or four strides from the exposed part of the stage.

In his gray suit, he drew a few steps back and tried doing jumping jacks to calm his nerves. Three hundred–plus pounds of him, tremendous muscle and soft belly, jumped and reached, jumped and reached. He tried running in place. He quit running and touched his toes. When that failed, he attempted to deep-breathe his body back into being.

He prayed silently, *If this is meant to be it's meant to be. Let me sing to the best of my ability. Let me share my voice.*

He told himself, *Don't cheat yourself.*

He warned himself, *Take full breaths.*

He blew air through his closed lips, flapping them, hoping to keep the muscles around his mouth from freezing up.

He schooled himself, *Don't follow the piano, let the piano follow you.*

He recited the lyrics of his aria in his mind:

Studia il passo, o mio figlio!
Usciam da queste tenebre.

Watch your step, oh my son!
Let us leave this darkness.

***

His father had promised that if he made it through this round, he would come to hear him sing in the finals. His father, Cecil Green, who had given him his middle name and whom he had spent time with on just a handful of occasions since he was four, said he would get himself to New York from Bakersfield, California. Ryan had reached him there by phone some days earlier and told him about the contest and how well he'd done so far.

Usciam da queste tenebre.

Ryan had chosen Banquo's aria from Verdi's opera of Shakespeare's *Macbeth*. The king of Scotland has just been stabbed to death, and Macbeth has claimed the throne. But three witches have suggested to Banquo, a nobleman, that his son will somehow rise to displace Macbeth and rule the land. All feels anarchic and ominous. One night, as Banquo stands with his son outside the king's castle, he has a premonition that they are about to be murdered. Sensing the killers near, he sings protectively to his child.

To learn and prepare the aria, Ryan had done what opera singers do these days: study the renditions of renowned artists on YouTube. He had a range to pick from, but quickly he hit on a video of Nicolai Ghiaurov, a Bulgarian bass, playing Banquo at Italy's historic house, La Scala, a decade before Ryan was born. It became his favorite, and he watched and listened to it over and over, as Ghiaurov delivered the opening lines with his head bowed and his hands tenderly on his young teenage son, one palm on the boy's back and the other on his chest. Then, singing about the menace hovering close around them, the father clutched the child fully to him, to his warrior's breastplate; Ghiaurov opted completely for sentiment, hugging his son, gripping him, fingers digging in, cheek pressing against the boy's head. *"Di terror,"* he sang, and kissed the boy with an urgent look of love seconds before the cloaked villains swarmed. He pushed his son into flight and surrendered himself, martyred himself, so the boy would not be caught.

℘

Ryan knew little about his father, and there were lots of times growing up when he didn't want to know anything, yet the limited things he did know had a special clarity, and when he wasn't spurning these details he clung to them. One was that his father, who stood no taller than five seven, had been a bodybuilder as a young man. Ryan had an old scratched photograph of him, posing. The picture's background was black; maybe the snapshot was taken during an amateur competition of some kind, or maybe his father was in a photographer's studio and fantasizing about being in a contest. He wore a tiny red swimsuit. His expression was all determination. He flexed his arms while squatting with one leg extended to make the most of his quads. His oiled pecs shone in the flash.

Another thing Ryan knew, or recalled hearing and believed to be true, was that his father had once met Arnold Schwarzenegger somewhere, that his father had been touched by greatness in this way, and that he'd also met Lou Ferrigno, the Incredible Hulk. He knew no specifics of these meetings but remembered that his father worshipped Schwarzenegger and that he'd watched *Terminator 2* with his father during one of their times together. Ryan had been seven or eight. Battling the horrifying T-1000, Schwarzenegger rescued the ten-year-old boy who was destined to be the savior of humanity. Since then, Ryan had seen every Schwarzenegger movie. His most-watched was probably *Kindergarten Cop:* Schwarzenegger, as a tough detective, went undercover, became a beloved kindergarten teacher, vanquished an evil drug dealer, and saved the dealer's son.

℘

Ryan walked toward the black piano at the center of the Met stage. The piano was the only accompaniment in this round; below him the empty orchestra pit plunged like a canyon. No one sat in the orchestra level of the house except the judges behind their laptops, their seven luminous white faces almost lost yet godly amid the endless rows. This was among the largest theaters for opera anywhere, a space that threatened to take any voice and swallow it. His mother was someplace up in a balcony with the families of the other contestants. He kept his eyes on an uninhabited point between the tier where she sat and the territory of the judges.

His eyes were big and espresso brown, and his face was gently tapered, gracefully shaped. His features, both handsome and childlike, had a vulnerability that contrasted with the contours of his body. His emotions seemed to live, most of the time, in his wide eyes, and on his forehead below his closely shaved head, and on his animated mouth. Whenever Ryan smiled, people took notice, and often his feelings of distress were unmistakable. But at the moment his face was opaque.

Beginning an aria felt, to him, like getting on a roller coaster despite having a dire fear of heights. The car climbed inexorably, *chuck chuck chuck chuck,* and if you handled your dread during those initial seconds, the rest of the ride might go all right. You might be swept along. But if you lost control early, if your nerves started to surge, you would quickly be left wailing, your brain and throat giving way irreversibly to chaos.

Now the pianist played the opening rumble of notes, the low, tremulous introduction, and then, while the piano went silent, Ryan intoned his first lines, his recitative. And soon the two, piano and voice, were joined; he was past the initial treacherous bars. Yet his face remained rigid. His body was stiff, motionless. His feet in their polished black shoes didn't shift an inch on the wood of the stage; they were angled awkwardly apart. The size of his voice was striking, and his sound held intimations of hidden layers, a wealth of barely revealed tones. Yet his singing was robotic.

The stiffness of his body and sound were not only due to his own fear. Nor did these failings stem mostly from his wish to evoke Banquo's apprehension, though that was part of it. There was a third reason, a choice he had made.

He wanted his performance to be pure. He wanted it to be devoid of any acting, or any embellished drama in his voice. All the emotion should come directly from his adherence to Verdi's score. He would honor Verdi's composition; he would rise to the demands of the piece. Working on the aria, he had formulated this abstract goal and grown fixated on the notion of purity. And he had wrapped this idea into the understanding he developed about Banquo's character. He focused on Banquo's noble rank and royal stature. He decided that Banquo's dignity thoroughly overrode any other feeling and that the piece was above all about Banquo's regal, unflinching acceptance of death.

After picking the most sentimental version to study on YouTube, a rendering that blended the theatrical heavily with the vocal, a rendering that put Banquo's gripping fingers and fatherly love at the heart of the performance, Ryan all but eliminated the dramatic and jettisoned the paternal feelings, purging them without pausing to think about how far his decisions were taking him from the portrayal that spoke to him.

Partially, his emphasis on Banquo's nobility and on paying strict tribute to Verdi was compensation for the way he felt among the other singers. The day before yesterday, another contestant had asked what he would perform. When

Ryan told him, the young man, who had already been awarded a training fellowship with a major opera company, murmured "Oh" and named the more challenging aria he would sing. Now, onstage, Ryan made his delivery stately. And his performance, though strong and deft enough vocally, fell flat. With every noble-sounding measure, he seemed to progress further toward the impassive; every bar seemed to mark a further disappearance of self, of anything that might have made his minutes unique to the judges. He sang his way toward forgettable.

TWO

ABOVE AND UNSEEN, in an ivory-colored dress with floral brocade, Ryan's mother, Valerie, sat a few miles from the Brooklyn housing project where she'd spent some of her girlhood. Next to her high-rise complex was another, made famous by the hip-hop mogul Jay Z, who had grown up there. He advertised having shot his older brother when he himself was twelve, because his brother had stolen some of his jewelry. He rapped about dealing crack as a teen and announced that he'd been shot at, from a distance of six feet, that three bullets had been fired and he'd gotten away unscathed.

> Check the four corners of the earth I'm a man of
>   respect
> Marcy Projects motherfucker I'm the man of respect

In 2014, three years after the semifinals, at the corner of Tompkins and Myrtle, at the boundary of Valerie's childhood project, two cops were shot in the head as they sat

14

in their patrol car, assassinated in revenge for the deaths of two black men killed by police—and, indirectly, in revenge for the aggressive, racially fraught policing that had been employed, in recent years, on these streets and in neighborhoods like this one across the country.

But Valerie didn't remember the area in a way that mirrored its reputation, possibly because crack hadn't arrived to carry out the worst phases of destruction around her project until after her family moved away. She recalled sweet things as we walked through the cluster of city-run brick towers where she'd lived. "They would have block parties in this inner area," she said, standing between the tightly placed buildings that were home to three or four thousand. "Coca-Cola would sponsor them. With different artists. People would yell, 'The Coca-Cola truck is here!' We had Kool and the Gang come and play."

Every Christmas brought a competition among the eight towers: which one could create the best holiday lights. Valerie's father, who worked in a foundry, pouring scalding liquid metal into molds, took charge of their building's entry each year. Starting before Thanksgiving, he canvassed the residents for ideas. He and the helpers he recruited bent wire hangers into stars and animals, and wrapped strings of lights around the wire. He crawled out a neighbor's window and somehow managed to mount the twinkling displays to the facade.

Her father had grown up near the Georgia-Florida border with fifteen or sixteen siblings, natural and adopted. He was part Seminole on one side of his family and part white on the other. *His* father, Ryan's great-grandfather, Valerie said, was well along in years when he married and began producing children in a frenzy. Ryan's great-grandfather had been born into slavery, though his skin was so pale that he'd been raised for a time within the master's family.

"My father," she said, "he was a handsome man. The profile of the Indian on the nickel? That was his silhouette. If he walked me to school in the morning, later that day the women would come up to me. 'Ooo, is that your father?' His nose was straight, and his hair was wavy, and he wore it combed back."

The concerts in the project courtyard, the Christmas lights, the father who came home from work and, still in his foundry uniform, read her the newspaper funnies— these were her memories. But her recollections existed on a margin between the sweet and the harsh. When we walked up to the entrance of her building, thinking we would peek in at the lobby through the plexiglass of the front door, or maybe press a superintendent's buzzer with the hope of being let in, we found, as we neared, that the plexiglass was completely missing and that the lock had been removed. The low-ceilinged, unlit lobby was like an open cave. We went in, and though the outside air mingled with the indoor atmosphere, the acrid smell of urine curled at the backs of our nostrils. "It smells the same," she said.

We turned into the elevator to ride up to her old floor. The door closed, the odor thickened; she found a cloth in her coat pocket and covered her mouth and nose. The button for her floor was broken. From the floor above, we walked into the dim stairwell and down the steps, which were gouged, as if an addict had tried, in an act of lunatic need, to score by chiseling off and selling chunks of concrete. "People killed themselves on that elevator," she remembered, lowering the cloth from her face. "They was on whatever drugs they was on in that era."

We knocked repeatedly at the door that had once been her family's. A woman opened it several inches, then quickly bolted it again. We continued down the ravaged steps and outside along a path, passing under a series of sycamore trees whose branches were covered in discarded plastic bags, black sacks from corner stores, hundreds of them whisked up in the wind, caught in the limbs, and quivering like monstrous leaves.

Valerie's older brother was sent away for robbery as a teenager, she mentioned, and at some point, either before that first incarceration or later, he started using, shooting up. Eventually purple blotches and bloody lesions appeared and spread on his skin, the skin his family had called "clean" in the winters and "dirty" in the summers because his complexion stayed light through the cold months and turned darker when he was out in the sun. Eventually he died of AIDS.

℘

Each contestant performed two arias in the semifinals. The singer picked the first. The judges listened, conferred among themselves for about ten seconds, and chose the second piece from a short list of repertoire that the semifinalist had submitted. "'Madamina,'" one of the judges called up to Ryan. He drank from a bottle of water and remembered to unbutton his suit jacket, which he'd planned to do if this aria was selected. He revealed a bright and glossy scarlet vest.

17

In the aria, from Mozart's *Don Giovanni,* Ryan's character, who is Giovanni's manservant, gleefully torments one
of Giovanni's lovers by telling her about all the women his
boss has seduced. The music is full of mischief, the lyrics
full of comic hyperbole. The singer has hardly any option
except to be theatrical, to be playful, to ham, and Ryan
didn't resist. He swayed his shoulders as he pronounced the
sensuous syllables of the word *"Ispagna"*—in Spain alone,
he sang, his boss had claimed no fewer than "a thousand
and three!"

When he gave his upper body a twist to one side and the
other, his jacket flapped wide open. "Country girls, cham-
bermaids, city girls"—he celebrated Giovanni's conquests,
his red vest looking like a sign declaring unlimited lust.
"Baronesses, marquises, princesses." His resonant voice
filled the far reaches of the theater, and as he ran on with
his list he exuded every bit of Mozart's unhinged exuberance. "Women of every rank, of every shape, of every age."
He swept his hands profligately through the air. "He likes
them plump when the winter sets in." Ryan sang the Italian
lyrics—*"Vuol d'inverno la grassotta"*—with relish. "But
in the summer he likes them slim."

He fluttered his fingers manically. He tilted his hefty
torso to one side. "He is not choosy, be she ugly, be she
beautiful." He shimmied and grinned. "Even the old ones
he conquers." On the climactic notes, he did a single quick
gyration with his hips, leaned back with his elbow on the
piano, and beamed.

℞

The competition's director, Gayletha Nichols, told the singers to line up. An hour and a half had crept by since Ryan's "Madamina"; four more contestants had taken their turns, and then the judges had hidden themselves away and debated. Everyone was crowded in an area between the red-carpeted stairs curving down to the lobby and the bank of windows overlooking the plaza: singers, family, Met patrons, voice teachers, in-house photographers, a hundred and fifty people through whom Nichols navigated, her large, pillowy body draped in patterned fabric. With her round face and little glasses and ready laugh, she was the maternal figure of the contest; her soft weight seemed to absorb and slightly reduce the desperation surrounding her. Decades ago, she herself had set out to sing opera. She had trained at a top conservatory. But she'd been rescued from her ambition by the chance to discover talent that wasn't her own, first with a regional company, then with the Met. "Sometimes there will be a tug," she had told me. She would hear a young singer perform something that had once been part of her own repertoire. "I'll remember what it was like to make that music." But the feeling didn't go any further. "There isn't the impulse to run home and find that score. Not anymore." She smiled ruefully. "To train to be an opera singer takes as much time as to train to be a physician. And the odds of success are frightening." Prevailing in the contest merely allowed a singer a toehold on a new ladder to be climbed.

Plenty of winners wound up scraping away at the edges of the profession, a cruelty that waited most often for those with low voices like Ryan's and for women whose voices had a particular power. For them, the risk of futile effort, of vain devotion, was greatest, because for them, everything that was physical and ineffable, everything in the anatomy and the mind, was known to take longer to evolve and settle, to meld and emerge into the artist's true timbre and intensity. "Big voices take longer to cook," Sondra Radvanovsky, a Met superstar with a substantial sound who'd won the contest in 1995 and who'd been a regional judge this year, said to me. Unlike with coloratura sopranos, whose level of lithe talent was clearly perceptible in their twenties, the potential of a voice like Radvanovsky's or Ryan's could be unknown till early middle age or later. For such singers, it was easy to keep thinking back to the prediction of the judges, to keep telling themselves to be patient. For them, it was easy to keep trying for too many years.

Gayletha didn't have to raise her voice to gather the semifinalists in a row. The singers and spectators were loud with nervous chatter, but every contestant's ears awaited any signal that the selection had been made, that the winnowing was done. Ryan lurched away from his mother. Opposite Gayletha, twenty-two bodies, in their suits and gowns, were aligned in an instant, silent and still.

"We have eight finalists this year."

Ryan's eyes scanned her face. He forgot manners, forgot pride; guilelessly he searched her features for some hint of whether he would be named. He fixed his eyes on hers. His hands were fists in his pockets. He kept staring.

She read out the finalists, singer by singer, pausing for applause after each one, pronouncing the names with excitement but not with so much fanfare as to punish the others who, name by name, were hearing their chances diminish, dwindle.

She announced, first, a soprano. Next a baritone. Then a bass-baritone. Ryan kept count of the voice types. Only so many low voices were likely to be chosen. That was two. Gayletha named another soprano. Four finalists to go. His chances were cut in half. The clapping died down, but it was difficult for him to hear. Had she just announced a second bass-baritone—a third low voice? She had. He clenched his chest, constrained his breath; it seemed that if he inhaled too loudly he could miss his name, forfeit his spot. Yet the reality, he knew, the near certainty, was that the judges had picked at least one higher-voiced man, a tenor. The reality was that it was over.

A soprano came sixth. A bass was seventh. His fists stayed tight, but it was finished.

When she spoke his name—with just a bit of buildup: "And last but *not* least..."—his fists burst from his pockets. He squatted down and sprang upward, his three hundred–plus pounds exploding into the air.

THREE

"THEY CALLED ME Kindergarten Dropout," Valerie said, laughing, as we walked around her housing project. "Because I got skipped past kindergarten. Went right into first grade."

Later, she showed me a letter from one of her elementary school teachers. She'd received it after she graduated from high school and wrote him to say that she'd enlisted in the military. She and the teacher had corresponded occasionally over the years since grade school. He had recognized something special in her back when she was a young girl, she believed. In his brief letter, he gave his approval: with the military, she would be seeing the world.

The letter, from this man who had known her for nine months when she was a child, was like a fragile relic from the far side of a divide, a scrap that she treasured. The divide was defined by the period of enlisting and training, of being sent to California and South Korea. Before then, in high school, she had played on the basketball and volleyball teams, competed in track and field. She had kept her grades up even after her father suffered a debilitating heart attack, and even while she worked the cash register at a grocery store. She had joined the junior ROTC and risen to squadron commander, and she had applied to the Air Force Academy.

As she told it, she was accepted; she could have gone. In return for eight years of service afterward, during a time when the country seemed likely to stay out of war, she was given the promise of a Bachelor of Science degree— for a girl whose mother, from a Virginia hamlet called Saint Stephens Church, hadn't reached as far as seventh grade, and whose father hadn't made it to ninth. Right out of the academy, she would be appointed to the rank of second lieutenant. She would be promoted from there. But at seventeen, she didn't like the idea of committing herself for such a long time, and she had no one to guide her. Signing up, instead, for boot camp and the Air Force's bottom rungs seemed to make more sense. She would be free to leave after half as long. She would be keeping her options open.

She was stationed in San Bernardino, east of Los Angeles, at the border of the Mojave Desert, and there, on the base, she did what the Air Force trained her to do: handle paperwork for the personnel department. She was a low-level secretary. Hangars and sheds and squat houses sprawled across the base, where the stretches of pavement led nowhere, stopping at fenced boundaries or at the ends of runways.

She met Cecil at a club nearby. He was from San Bernardino. His destiny, he told her, was to become a chef, and in the meantime, he worked at a local battery plant.

She was five feet ten and beautiful, with a sleek, high-on-top hairstyle that made her yet taller, and with elegant features and a strong, honed body. He was three inches shorter, stubby, muscly, a jokester. He clowned and attached himself to her.

The dance floor was his habitat. He knew every move—not only knew, but had mastered. He moonwalked, making the floor look frictionless and his feet look like they were tugged by an unseen puppeteer. He pop-locked, undulating and suddenly paralyzing his shoulders, causing them to bend and jerk and seize in high-speed patterns that seemed inhuman, alien. Standing straight, he was short, but dancing, his height didn't matter. He took on all sorts of contorted forms, his limbs by turns rigid and rubberized, his torso angling in multiple directions simultaneously, his neck a spring.

"He could have been a professional. He could have been one of those Michael Jackson video–type dancers. He could spin on his head, he could do the worm, but it was more than that. He was so smooth." She said, "Cecil was always the life of the party. And we became fast friends. But I was not in love with him, and he knew it from the get-go."

He proposed, and she told him no. He waited and asked again, this time in front of his parents. Thinking back, she felt he had trapped her with this ploy of having his mother and father in the room; she adored his parents; he left her no choice but to say yes. Suppressed anger took hold of her voice as she recounted this. Her mouth tightened, her tone sharpened; rage sat low in her throat. She added, with bitterness and bewilderment, "I was nineteen. Twenty. I had nothing else to do."

𝒢

She gave birth to Adrian and then to Ryan. A few years later, after a reenlistment, the Air Force decided that she was needed for secretarial duties in Korea. Adrian, two and a half years older than his brother, was already in school; she left the boys with Cecil, living on the San Bernardino base, while the military took her for a stint on the other side of the planet.

The first sign of trouble was that her checks, written off their joint account, began to bounce. Cecil, ever the clown, gave goofy, dismissive explanations or cooed apologies when she asked about the missing money. It happened again and again; the salary she earned in Asia, and sent home "to take care of my two boys," was getting spent in ways that she felt helpless to figure out at a distance of six thousand miles. Because her checks were bouncing where she was stationed, a sergeant got involved, reprimanding her but eventually helping her to set up a separate account and telling her to deposit just what she thought her husband needed in the account he could access. Shortly after that, the military mail delivered divorce papers. She read Cecil's demands for custody and child support, and guessed some of what was going on.

"Needless to say, they had to sedate me, because I was ready to swim across the Pacific. I mean sedate as in *put me under*. But my heat was still on high when they let me leave. I got me back to California, and I got me a room on base, because I needed to collect myself. I took a nap, and I got dressed, back into my uniform. I had my key. That was *my* home. I put *my* key in my door, and the latch was on. So I had to knock.

"'Who is it?' That's what he said. And when I heard that! I told him, and he tells me, 'Just a minute, just a minute.' And after a minute, he opened the door. He reached out for a hug, and I moved him out of the way. I went to the back room. That was my boys' room. They were sleeping. I had bought them one of those trundle beds, and the mattress from the trundle was out on the floor, away from the bed, and some strange child, about Ryan's age, around four, was laying on it, and my two boys, my two babies, was sleeping together.

"I woke them up. They was excited to see Mommy, but they was still sleepy. I put them back down. I shut the door, and my husband, he was there in the hallway area. Adrian and Ryan's room was off to one side, and then there was the master. He was blocking my way to the master. 'Tell her to come up out of there.' 'Ain't nobody here.' 'What you talkin' about?' 'Ain't nobody here.' 'Whose kid is that?' 'That's the babysitter's son. She left him here 'cause he was asleep.' 'Do you think I'm stupid? Do you think I'm stupid?'

"That's when Cecil and me started tussling, and I kicked the master door off the hinges. We tussled, and I got into the bedroom. She was in the closet. Cowering. I told her she had thirty seconds.

"None of this was because I loved him. I didn't. It was because he was playing house with some other woman with some other child in my home. Well, she grabbed her kid and took her leave, which is when the tussling really started.

"I roughed him up. We was in the living room–kitchen, and there was a door there, to my left. We shut that door behind us. I roughed him up, and I went to do open heart surgery on him. I snapped. How are you going to be in my home with my children with somebody else? It was like I blacked out. He liked to think he was a chef, and we had a lot of knives. I took one of those big knives, and I was standing right there with it, ready for open heart. That's when Ryan opened that door, crying. He said, 'Mommy, Mommy.' I had that knife in my hand."

 ℒ

The morning after the semifinals, the eight remaining singers wended through a maze of Met passageways and gathered in a rehearsal room. The final round was next Sunday, six days away. It would be a formal concert. The theater would be packed from the front row to the upper boxes; the singers' photos would be in the *Playbill*. The days between now and then would be spent with the concert's guest conductor and the Met's own coaches. The finalists would absorb their wisdom. They would race to incorporate the alterations they were advised to make, to lace them into their arias, note by note, so that, when next Sunday came, the audience would cry out and the judges would feel their voices burned into their minds.

And for this week, the chosen eight could imagine themselves part of the Met's world. They could enter the building through the stage door. With the special passes they'd been given, they could glide by the guard in his interior security booth and through a waist-high wooden gate, the same gate that Luciano Pavarotti and Maria Callas and Ferruccio Furlanetto and Anna Netrebko had pushed open and strode through on the way to their dressing rooms.

The Met's rear halls were not at all glamorous. One hallowed corridor leading beyond the gate—and the gate itself was chipped and scratched—was lined with black metal lockers. Another passage was almost barricaded off by a pile of decrepit cardboard boxes, the bottom box crumpling under the weight of whatever long-disused props or paraphernalia the others held. Detritus cropped up constantly along routes blearily lit by fluorescent bulbs. A theme of disregard ran throughout the sections of the building that only insiders ever saw, making the point that to perform in this house, or to be in any way involved in the splendid offerings that blossomed on the front side of the stage, was to have no need of any other affirmation. To walk here, to work here, to sing here was to be at one of the world's pinnacles in the most exacting of art forms.

To reach the rehearsal room for their meeting on the morning after the semis, the finalists squeezed past the costume department. A cavern of designers and seamsters stooped over tables and created the royal garments of kingdoms spanning from sixteenth-century Spain to ancient China. The tables were strewn with gauze and beads. Lamé shimmered. Metal clothing racks lined the hall. The racks were jammed, the garments crushed together. Elaborate collars and velvet trains were smashed. Here was more of the Met's excess, more of its indifference. Satin bodices gathered dust.

The cinder block room where the singers assembled was spare and windowless. Large mirrors were framed haphazardly in unfinished plywood. A leak from the ceiling was channeled into a strip of tubing and dripped into an old watercooler keg. Gayletha Nichols sat at a fold-out table beside Camille LaBarre, a Met patron and the chief fundraiser for the competition. They congratulated everyone, went over the week's schedule in detail, and asked if anyone had any questions before the preparations for the finals began.

"Yes," Ryan said. "Where can I do my laundry?" He hadn't packed for a stay lasting past the semis. He smiled at Nichols and LaBarre, but the price of the hotel's laundry service had been weighing on him since he'd found out yesterday that he would be here for another week.

With the location of a nearby laundromat sorted out, the meeting moved on. Though most of the coming week would be devoted to artistry, to understanding and giving deeper expression to music, for the next couple of hours everyone concentrated on what the contestants would wear. LaBarre reviewed the singers' tuxedos and gowns. She was in her sixties, with an impeccable haircut and a petite figure and tailored ensembles that emanated a modest flair.

Deanna, the soprano with high-wire vocal agility, modeled a dark dress with restrained adornments. It showed off her slim body in an unshowy way; it left uncovered only a splash of upper chest. She won immediate approval from LaBarre.

Philippe, the bass-baritone who trailed phrases of Sinatra as he traveled through the building, danced while Deanna modeled. With his prow of blond curls and his skinny hips, he executed a sequence of Astaire-like spins, the twirls apropos of nothing going on at the meeting except his own wish to dazzle, a desire so unbridled it was endearing.

"I'm considering a second tuxedo," he said when LaBarre turned toward him.

She told him there was no need, that his tux was lovely.

"No, no." He went on dancing. "I'd like to change tuxedos between my first and second arias."

"Absolutely, Philippe. We don't want to take any chances. We don't want anyone to forget you."

He gave her his teen idol smile; she put her fingers to her temples in mock dismay.

Michelle was next. She was the one other African American who'd been in the semis. The gleaming undulations of her voice had won her a spot in the finals. Her father was a thriving pastor in Houston, and after she'd stumbled onto a telecast of *Madama Butterfly* as a young girl and sobbed while watching on the living room sofa, her parents had begun subscribing to Houston Grand Opera, a premier regional company. Her teenage years had been saturated in spirituals and arias, and now, at twenty-eight, she was in her last year as a graduate student at the Academy of Vocal Arts.

Her body was the opposite of Deanna's and far from the birdlike build of the third woman left in the contest. Michelle was all bust and backside, and her dress, scant on top and clinging below, put her on exhibit. LaBarre, rarely flustered, wasn't sure how to respond. There was no rule against sexiness in opera; in fact, it was increasingly prized. But with every step Michelle took, her hips and butt seemed to announce not only sensuality but blackness, and the element of race stirred a subtle yet palpable uneasiness in the white room.

"Maybe," LaBarre started, then lost her words before blurting out: "Is there just a bit too much jiggle factor in that outfit?" She hurried to clarify that she didn't want anyone to be distracted from Michelle's gorgeous singing.

Michelle listened with composure and soon returned, for another inspection, in a gown with more coverage and floral blooms stitched to the garment's lower half, obscuring her body below the waist. LaBarre declared that this was much better, and Michelle said she agreed. But she told me afterward, "That was culture clash. In my opinion, the first dress goes very well with my character, the woman in one of my arias. She longs for passion; she longs to be desired. And the first one also suits *me*. I'm curvy, and I love my curves." She sounded unsettled, as if something had been stolen.

With the attire of the seven other finalists resolved, LaBarre focused on Ryan. He owned no passable tuxedo, and in any case, having had no expectation of moving on to this round, he hadn't brought the badly worn, ill-fitting one he did own. LaBarre set about making the problem go away. Not to worry about the money, she told him. That would be all taken care of.

"The only challenge is going to be finding what we need in your size."

"Sometimes that can really be a challenge," he replied, happy to be in LaBarre's hands, and his sonorous laugh mingled with her lighter one.

"Let me go back to my office and make a few phone calls."

Promptly she had things figured out and escorted him to Brooks Brothers' main New York store. With Philippe along for the outing, they entered between stone pillars and beneath an American flag. Ryan was surrounded by a display of fancy umbrellas, their wooden handles burnished, and by a sea of dress shirts in powdery shades, and by an area dedicated to people who might be spending some upcoming time on a yacht. There were silver sailing trophies, cobalt-blue luggage trunks, mannequins in white trousers, and pairs of plaid boating sneakers or white bucks arranged at the mannequins' feet.

Philippe, whose father was a radiologist, wasn't affected by any of this. As they continued upstairs to the formal wear department, past equestrian sculptures on antique tables, Philippe spilled forth, mostly to LaBarre and me, about his repertoire, about the career he anticipated, about how magical the art form was because you had to control the nuances of the voice less through voluntary physical adjustments than through "the hypothetical, the illusory, the metaphorical, the imaginary." Within this speech came a prediction, uttered at prestissimo speed, that he would be one of the winners next Sunday. His self-assurance was more befuddling to Ryan each time he heard it, though he didn't feel it was unjustified. Where did anyone get so much certainty? How did anyone get so far beyond intimidation?

The formal wear floor was designed to resemble a men's club. A full-size pool table with leather pockets stood beside a bar whose stools were emblazoned with the early nineteenth-century year of Brooks Brothers' founding, and this way and that were wood-paneled sitting rooms and libraries with leather-bound books. A calfskin-encased grooming kit and white gloves rested next to a silver tray laid out with a selection of polished cuff links. Horse statuettes were everywhere.

"He's having his debut at the Metropolitan Opera in a competition," LaBarre informed a salesman, who had approached with the reserve of a head butler.

The salesman stepped away, then produced something appropriate. "This is a hand-tailored tuxedo."

Ryan entered the vestibule between the fitting rooms. He reappeared, minutes later, to LaBarre's effusions and the salesman's shoulder-smoothings and an elfin tailor's scrutiny. The salesman raised the question of whether to opt for a cummerbund or a vest, and he enumerated the pros and cons. Ryan slipped into a vest, slid the jacket back on, and stood again in front of the mirror.

What he saw looked extremely good.

All was done, or almost done. The shirt he'd put on, with a size eighteen and a half neck, fit too well—it would be too snug for singing. He should wear a nineteen.

Preferably with a piqué front, LaBarre told the salesman, and he went off to search. But the store had no such size in stock, not in piqué or pleated.

Together, LaBarre promised Ryan, they would find exactly what he needed.

FOUR

I looked down and he was there to my left. 'Mommy, Mommy,'" Valerie recalled. He took in what was in front of him: his mother with the knife, his father. "Then somebody must have called the authorities, must have been the neighbors from all the noise, and they showed up. They saw me in my uniform. So they asked me what was up, and they took Cecil outside. They gave him a beating. You could hear it. When he came back in, his shirt was torn. He was crying and apologizing."

And then he was gone, gone with the babysitter, who became his second wife, and with whom he soon had another son. He'd already had a boy with a woman before Valerie, when he was eighteen, a son he didn't see from when the child was two till a chance encounter when the boy was nine. Counting the stepson who'd been sleeping on the mattress from the trundle bed, Cecil now had five boys.

The Air Force dispatched Valerie back to Korea to finish her tour. She stowed Adrian and Ryan with her mother, who, after Valerie's father's death, was living in Florida. The service moved Valerie, next, to a base outside Tampa, but in short order she quit the military in a fury. She wasn't treated fairly, she felt. When Ryan had an allergic reaction to a vaccine—"I forgot that he couldn't have any of those shots with eggs in them"—she put in a request to spend extra time watching over him as he recovered. An officer turned her down. "I was done playing their games," she said.

She found herself working in a pawnshop. It was part of a chain; the hunched buildings with banners reading "Quick Cash Loans" bloomed here and there on weedy lots across Florida. She manned various sections. There was the jewelry that people had left as collateral and never reclaimed. There were the cameras, the televisions, the guitars. There were the lawn mowers that people brought over, telling themselves it wouldn't be long before they put their lives in order and began cutting the grass and dandelions in their miniature yards again.

"We had a very big gun selection, which was my favorite area to work. Sometimes you had to set up the displays. I didn't have firearms in my home. But I loved the way those guns felt in my hands. I enjoyed it in the military, and I enjoyed it in that store. I enjoyed the power."

℞

She had a new man, someone from the military. Male attention was never an issue for her. With Cecil having scurried away, with Cecil making no appearances and very few phone calls and fewer contributions, Barry took Adrian and Ryan to car shows, to video game shows. He gave Ryan a book about fighter jets, talked with him about F-14 Tomcats and F-15 Eagles. He took in Valerie and the boys to live with him in base housing. He asked her to marry him. "He was really the only father Ryan ever had. And he was nice to me." She said yes, and she and her sons moved with him when the military stationed him in southeastern Virginia.

But "something happened" during a tour he spent overseas; when he returned, the marriage grew violent. As Valerie spoke, we drove through that region of Virginia, past Yorktown, where the British had surrendered to Washington's army, past strip malls along a semirural highway, past narrow fields of soy and cotton behind prefabricated houses. She could not reconstruct the shift that she said had occurred in him, could not recollect the first spark. "Something changed when he came back. He was different. Things were different. It got dangerous." Any explanation remained out of reach of her mind, as though the trauma that followed eradicated the memory of what had led up to it.

As for the violence itself, Valerie's story was that Barry was the perpetrator, but her sons suggested that the culpability ran both ways. "Their relationship was toxic," Ryan said. The marriage lasted till he was around nine. "My mom was not a small lady. She was a huge part of the violence at home. She hit him. She hit me. My mom would get physical with me—and when you're a kid, how do you stop someone?"

Adrian said the same about Valerie's rage toward Barry and himself, and about his fear of his mother even as he began to pack on muscle, when he was twelve and thirteen. "Her violence wasn't normal, it was a whole different type of thing." He described her as something out of a movie where humans could transform into gargantuan, catastrophic beings. "With me, it wasn't just a mom whupping her child. I'm not going to lie, when I got out of hand I got out of hand. But she was coming in to destroy."

Valerie worked for a while at a Virginia shipyard, as a dispatcher for a security company that oversaw the docks. Freighters and cranes and stacked containers and mountains of coal loomed high around her, the coal doused relentlessly to keep the dust from blackening the air. She floated from job to job. She peddled insurance—"but Barry sabotaged that career. I started making good money, more than he was in the military. And he didn't like that. He was always taking the car we had that drove, and leaving me with the piece of junk. It was always breaking down."

One day a fight erupted just inside their front door. "I know Ryan was there. Adrian wasn't. Adrian didn't see it, but Ryan did. Barry punched me square in the face. I had to go to the emergency room. Having come from one failed marriage, I tried to hang in there. I didn't want to lose another. And I didn't want to mess up his career."

℘

"It was two floors," Ryan said. "We'd be up in our bedroom, my brother and I. Between our mom and Barry, there couldn't be a good week without a horrible one coming. We would hear our mom screaming downstairs. They would break stuff. Adrian would hold me. I was always crying. 'Why are they doing this?' I was the crybaby. He'd tell me, 'It's all right, man.' Or if I wanted to run down there, he'd tell me not to."

Adrian was an artist. Valerie had bought him a Godzilla doll during her time in Korea, and in Virginia it became his muse. Its haunches were ponderous with muscle, its lower legs had multiple bulges, its clawed feet were gigantic. Growths that resembled stalagmites rose jaggedly along its tail. In the bedroom he and Ryan shared, he drew the beast more and more precisely. Inspiration and instruction came from one of his favorite TV shows, a program for adults on PBS. It featured a bizarre white man with a floppy Afro the size of a small shrub. Wearing a powder-blue dress shirt unbuttoned to his chest, the man stood in front of an easel.

He held a circular palette of colors in one lightly freckled hand and a brush in the slender fingers of the other, and he taught his viewers how to paint. "Right up here we'll make a happy little cloud," he said, and demonstrated. "Let's use the fan brush. Look at all the paint in those bristles." His voice was soothing, and the quantity, the generosity, of the oil paint on his brush was like a balm. He proceeded to teach the painting of evergreen trees. "Leave some limbs out there," he said, to be sure his pupils didn't clump the boughs too tightly. "You need places for the little birds to sit."

Adrian didn't have a canvas or paint, only paper and colored pencils, and he wasn't portraying anything like the painter's trees and clouds, but show by show he gleaned techniques and soaked up confidence from the man's assumption that anyone could do this. "There we go," the teacher kept repeating in his soft way, and Adrian captured the scales, rough as barnacles, that covered much of Godzilla's body. He added the shingle-like layers of hide that protected parts of the monster, and built up the stalagmites into a profusion of irregular spikes that ran from its upper tail to its lower neck. Godzilla's jaw was open, and each tooth had its own individualized menace.

Then, as the voices and violence downstairs crested and fell away, and seemed to have subsided safely before they swelled again, and as Ryan watched his brother work with awe, Adrian shifted his focus from Godzilla to dinosaurs. While his mother and stepfather shrieked and bellowed and tore at each other, he followed Godzilla down a path into the Triassic and Jurassic periods, and from there he discovered Dinotopia. Ryan followed his brother.

Dinotopia was an island beyond school maps and surrounded by dangerous reefs, where all the inhabitants—the shipwrecked humans who'd been rescued and carried there by dolphins, and the dinosaurs who'd been there for millions of years, protected from the disasters that brought their extinction elsewhere—lived in serenity. Human families played at the feet of the massive, unflappable beasts. Children rode on endlessly long, swaying dinosaur necks. Adrian sketched and shaded and erased and redrew, trying to bring out every detail of the creatures, down to their beady, affectionate eyes, and Ryan gazed, enveloped.

The dinosaurs had an alphabet, intricate scratches they made with their feet. They had a language with words like *"cumspiritik,"* which could mean "breathing together" or "close friendship" or "marriage." A set of legal principles, the Code of Dinotopia, ensured order and tranquility. The source for all of this was the series of illustrated Dinotopia books that Adrian pored over, but in Ryan's eyes his brother's versions of the illustrations and copies of the alphabet and explanations of Dinotopian law were more magical than the originals. Adrian seemed to invent Dinotopia; drawing by drawing, he conjured the island.

℞

"He knocked me unconscious," Valerie said, remembering another incident. "I was glad my boys didn't have to see that one. Other than the time by the front door when Barry punched me, which Ryan was forced to witness, I never allowed them to see what was going on."

℞

Ryan had a different tally of what he'd seen. "Once, he literally knocked her out. I ran to her, I didn't know what was going on. She was on the floor. She was unconscious. I was crying, and Adrian was there, leaning over her and yelling at him."

℞

"I'd really like you to be there," he said after the semis. Ryan was on the phone with Cecil, the man who had let his and Adrian's birthdays go by, year after year, without a call or a gift. Christmases had gone by, too. There were long-distance conversations, sporadically, half a year sometimes stretching between them. Yet the calls sustained hope. "Did the box come for me?" the boys' aunt Esther, Valerie's sister, remembered Ryan asking. That was during a period when Valerie left the boys to live with Esther as a refuge from her marriage to Barry.

"Where is the box coming from?" she questioned.

"My father said he was sending a box."

Now Ryan told his father, "It'll be a concert in the biggest opera house in the United States."

℘

Ryan couldn't tell Adrian about making the finals because at that point he didn't know how to reach him. His brother had been released from prison not long ago. He was living on the streets or, at best, on couches—somewhere in California, probably. He had a seven-year-old son he hadn't seen in several years, not only because he'd spent two of those years locked away, but because his ex-wife had a restraining order against him.

Ryan and Adrian had exchanged vows when they were kids, vows spoken after Ryan burrowed into his brother's chest while the chaos of their mother's second marriage consumed the flimsy walls and floors, traveling through the house to swallow them, vows "that we would never be like that," Ryan said, "and that when we grew up we would never hit a woman." At birthdays and Christmases they made another set of pledges to each other. "We swore we wouldn't forget about our children."

They had made a habit, as kids, of teaming up to steal action figurines from a discount store. One of them stood watch in the aisle while the other took from the shelves. They collected the pliable superheroes, hypermuscled and heavily armed with rocket launchers and mega machine guns. They took Schwarzenegger more than once, took him in several of his roles, carried his spectacular body and bravery home, knowing that their father had once shaken his hand, knowing that their father loved him; they stole him again and again like stealing their father back into their lives, and kept him in their bedroom.

They had made their vows, yet the strength of family history could sneer at good intentions, Ryan felt. It could seize you from behind and shape you at its whim. It could turn you into a man, like Adrian, who couldn't legally go near the mother of his child, a man whose face his son would no longer recognize.

Best to keep thoughts of the past at bay, Ryan believed, to give history less chance of overtaking you, claiming you. Memories were forces to be fled from, muzzled, sung over. His voice could drown out what needed to be silenced and pull him forward, away from whatever might clutch at him from behind. He just had to keep singing and singing, refusing to let history come up on him as if he were prey. Warnings were everywhere. It wasn't only Adrian. His stepbrother, the boy who'd shared his and Adrian's bedroom while Valerie was in Korea, the son of the woman Cecil had then married, the sibling who was Ryan's age, was a Crip, wore Crip blue, had covered his body in tattoos of rappers, was currently incarcerated. The boys had slept side by side.

℔

Ryan and I had an arrangement, a rhythm. He would permit himself to linger in the past, then would shut down the conversation, his espresso-colored irises going instantly from liquid to solid, from remembrance to resistance. "I don't want to think about this anymore," he would say, and his lips would tighten. The rest of his features, usually so vibrant, would go lifeless.

He was self-aware and straightforward about his fears, his philosophy. The best way to move forward was to focus forward. The benefit of looking away from the past was that you were less likely to repeat it, less likely to be tricked—and trapped—by it. Of course, he knew the common wisdom that warned exactly the opposite, and he trusted in this to a degree, yet there were plenty of moments when he seemed to say, *I don't want to take this risk. I can't afford to.*

℘

But when it came to the prospect of his father arriving in Manhattan, and taking his seat at the Met, and listening to him sing, Ryan's apprehension about the force of the past was overridden by anticipation: that his father would see him on that stage performing for thousands. An entirely different sort of history would be at play; Ryan would be standing where some of the greatest singers of all time had stood. His father would watch him there, hear him there, hear how his voice carried, for he wouldn't falter, hear how masterfully he produced this music, hear him from the depths of his range to Banquo's soaring, resounding final note. Personal history would no longer matter; it would be

43

purged. His relationship with his father would begin from those minutes onstage.

He would be singing, too, as always, for his mother. Despite her violence against him and Adrian, Ryan felt he needed to win her forgiveness, prove himself worthy. He felt he had betrayed her. "My mom has had so much happen to her. She never caught a break. And then I became the not-catching-a-break. She's had an awful life."

He didn't know all of that awfulness, as I learned during one of the drives Valerie and I took through the region where he'd grown up. It was an area where American history hung densely in the air, some of it mythic, glorified, some of it hard to dwell on. Just to the northwest was Jamestown, where, four centuries ago, British settlers built their first surviving community on the continent and planted their first commercial tobacco. Farther up the James River—close to where Valerie's mother's relatives, a generation or two older than Valerie, were buried along a country road in a desolate church field, with bent and rusted metal signs the size of license plates driven into the ground as the only grave markers their families could afford—Gabriel Prosser, a literate slave, a blacksmith owned by a tobacco farmer, had plotted a rebellion in 1800. Alerted to the conspiracy, Virginia's governor, James Monroe, called up the state militia, hunted Prosser downriver, and executed the rebel and his fellow escapees. Seventeen years later, Monroe, whose slaves tended his plantations of tobacco and wheat, became the nation's president, like the slaveholding Virginians who'd been president before him. Just to the south of where we drove, Nat Turner, viewing himself as a prophet and reading a solar eclipse as a heavenly signal—as a black man's hand stretching across the sun—led an uprising that killed sixty whites with hatchets and knives before Turner was hung.

"It was suffering, depression, that kind of stuff," Valerie said about her second marriage as we passed a small, scrappy field of cotton, the clumps of white waiting to be picked and sold. "I was holding all that stuff in, not letting anyone know what actually was going on. Not even my sister. It was—" Her voice, already quiet, wafted away. She wasn't fully weeping; it was short of that. She said she tried to leave the marriage, was drawn back. "It took me to a point. I tried to commit suicide. There was something I tied a rope up to. I was going to hang myself, I guess." She laughed, the sound minimal and containing an undertone of shame.

Sometimes it was difficult for me to see the ferocity the boys had grown up with. It had died down in the last several years, it seemed. Her body, too, tall though it remained, no longer held the explosiveness it once had. She moved slowly.

"I checked myself into the hospital. I was there for a day and a half, maybe two days, before I got this call. Child services. I think Barry did something, called them, I can't remember what, to cause them to get involved. Talking about taking my boys away from me. I had to get myself out of the hospital and get home."

The suicide attempt was not something she had ever told Ryan about. Perhaps he had felt it on some level, perhaps not. "She's had an awful life. To survive, she built a wall surrounding herself. It got built steadily. She built it for everyone and everything except her children. And then she had to build a wall for me. Between her and me. A child can only do so much before that wall gets built. I know that. No mom is going to forget: my child threatened my life and probably would have done it if given the chance.

"My goal is to wear the wall down. By singing, living up to my potential—by showing her. It's something you have to wear down slowly."

℀

Ryan's unruliness had begun before elementary school: in the state records that would later be kept, there was a form that Valerie had filled out noting that Ryan "was kicked out of four preschool day care centers for violent/disruptive behavior." No one could recall the details, but the principal of one of his elementary schools remembered him clearly from when he was nine. The school was in Yorktown. After Valerie finally left Barry for good, she and the boys were living there, in a low-income complex of two-story clapboard buildings. The development had a name that spoke grandiloquently of quaint English countryside. Hip-hop throbbed in the parking lot, people sipped their forties, drivers drifted through to buy drugs, the woman upstairs was running a prostitution business. Blocks of low-slung bungalows sprawled beyond the development, the houses settling and sinking into the mud of their yards.

"Ryan was unusual enough, troubled enough, that I re-call him very well," the elementary school principal said. "Hitting. Throwing things. Knocking things over. He was one of the ten or so most troubled children I've had in my forty-two-year career. I recall his teacher actually taking all the other children out of the room in order to protect them"—and in order to contain him within the classroom till help arrived.

In the local middle school, meanwhile, Adrian was in special ed classes, "because," he recounted, "I couldn't be around a lot of students. Because of my anger. My rage. One of my teachers, she was pregnant, and one time I was doodling on my paper. I was doing a badass drawing I really liked, and she snatched it away from me. I flipped a wig. I threw a chair at her. I threw a table. They called the cops. They cuffed me. There weren't any charges or anything because I was already in special ed. But there was a lot inside me. I don't know, but I would say the rage came from my mom. When she got mad, she got *mad*."

Frequently the brothers turned on each other. Dependent though Ryan was on Adrian's comfort as their mother's life continued to reel, and reverent though he was of Adrian's art, the two of them battled. Adrian had a memory of Ryan throwing knives, missing. Adrian beat him. Once, during a visit that they'd made to their father in San Bernardino— one of the three times, in total, that Ryan would see his father between the ages of four and eighteen—Adrian lifted his brother and dropped him onto a hot grill. Ryan still had the scars on the backs of his legs.

♌

For the most problematic elementary schoolers in the entire district, the school superintendent created a special class. It was six or seven students, all boys, grouped together regardless of their ages. Ryan was going on ten when he was placed in this classroom. All day, every day, this was his room for the next two years. Yet it was one part of his past he had no qualms about revisiting.

The room was run by Mrs. Hughes, a short, round-faced Italian Irish woman with four inches of blond-tinted hairdo piled atop her head. She had wanted to be a teacher since she was a third grader in a Catholic school, imagining herself a Chinese nun in charge of her own students. Her father had been a ditchdigger, her mother a laborer in a lampshade factory, and how the wish to be Chinese got into her head she no longer had any idea, but in her bedroom in the family's cramped apartment in New Jersey, she used Scotch tape to pull and narrow her eyes, employed her mother's cotton housecoat as a kimono, and arranged a towel on her head to approximate a nun's habit. On her bed she lined up her dolls and stuffed animals; she sat opposite them behind a small desk and led them through their lessons. Her standards for them were high, her lessons carefully planned. She wedged pencils into their hands or propped them against their hooves, and taught them cursive. She taught them to write stories, which she produced for each member of the class, and she dealt them cards to excite them about math. The animals flipped their cards over. "Now, who has the highest number?" Another flip. "Now add your numbers up." At the end of the term, she sent everyone a report card with marks in each subject.

When the superintendent asked her to take on his newly created class, she refused. She'd been teaching regular classes happily for three decades; she'd just been named the district's teacher of the year. But eventually she relented. On his first day in the classroom, Ryan seized his desk and hurled it, sending his books flying and the desk crashing. "I'm not learning from no white woman," he said. The two of them stood amid the wreckage. She'd already been worried—Valerie had intimidated her, during an initial meeting, with her height and the bulk that had accumulated on her body. "Is that 'Green' with an *e*?" Mrs. Hughes had asked her.

"No. That's just for rich folks."

The teacher glanced at Ryan's desk and books scattered on the carpet. In all of her career, she'd never sent a student out of her room. "Never, never, never," she told me. "Because if I send them out, they're thinking, *She can't handle me.*" Later she corrected herself. Not long before Ryan came into her group, she had taken on a boy named Trevor. The superintendent had placed her class at the end of a corridor, next to a back exit door, so the havoc he counted on would be remote from most of the school and these kids couldn't destroy the chances of the rest. Two desultory tennis courts sat out back, and Mrs. Hughes bought rackets for her boys. They flailed at balls first thing in the morning, before she brought the students inside. But for Trevor, her attempt to exhaust some of his energy was irrelevant; he heard things, saw things. Besieged by voices and visions, Trevor sometimes cowered, sometimes railed, sometimes wandered about as though intoxicated, sometimes slept while class went on around him, his head in Mrs. Hughes's lap. Once, child services took him off to the dentist, where he grew so terrified he fled the hygienist's chair, zoomed out the door, and crouched behind shrubbery until Mrs. Hughes was called to talk him out of hiding. But one morning he grabbed a tennis racket inside the classroom and wielded the metal frame wildly against imagined enemies, and she had to send word to the principal to phone the police, who dragged him away.

Flatly, as though it was a logical solution, she suggested to Ryan that, if he wished, he could learn from the floor, since his desk and books were down there. She returned to teaching, and at the end of the day—by which point he had turned his desk upright—she walked over to the wall where, beside a sign that asserted "Self-Learners Are Happy Learners" and a chart titled "Climb to the Stars," she had put up a portrait of Martin Luther King Jr. along with lines from his "I Have a Dream" speech printed out in marker. She had posted the lines partially because it mortified her to recall the church minstrel shows she'd been featured in as a girl, tap-dancing proudly with the men around her in blackface; partially because just about all the students channeled to her by the superintendent were black, and she wasn't; and partially because of the phrase "content of their character"—she wanted these kids to focus on those words. She needed them to consider who they wished to be. They had to feel that they could construct themselves from this juncture forward, that they had the ability to do this, that whatever had been said about them in the past, whatever judgments they had absorbed, along with the stigma of being exiled to this room, did not matter.

She did not read their school records. She avoided hearing about their evaluations, their catalog of incidents; when her colleagues tried to help by telling her, she all but covered her ears. She understood that not all of them would end up reinventing themselves, that most wouldn't be able to, yet she was a woman who filled her home with porcelain figurines, with Santas during the weeks leading up to Christmas and snowmen through the rest of the winter and hear-no-evil monkeys year-round, a woman who adorned her dining room walls with folk art bearing messages like "Love Much Laugh Often." "Read this, please," she said to her class, pointing: "I have a dream that my four little children will one day live in a nation where they will not be judged by the color of their skin but by the content of their character."

"Now please begin memorizing these words."

℘

In the mornings, after they swatted tennis balls into the fences and trees, Mrs. Hughes's students set their chairs in a circle on the gray speckled carpet of her room.

"Does anyone have anything they'd like to talk about?"

Often she answered her own question. She said she had something, a problem on her mind. She and Mr. Hughes had squabbled last night. Or she was concerned about her daughter. Somehow the kids seemed to perceive a kind of equivalence—this bubbly woman with the hairdo had her troubles—along with the distinctions. Within the circle they shared things that had happened inside their apartments or outside their doors. They lived in places like the low-income complex where Valerie had settled with her boys. "Well, you don't have to worry about that here," Mrs. Hughes said. She kept the sessions brief. "Shake hands with each other," she instructed. "Let's wish each other a good day." They pulled their chairs back to their desks and school commenced.

Who are the people of the Amazon rain forest and how do they live?

What is the purpose of the human skeleton and what is its structure?

She spent her weekends designing separate lessons to match the divergent skills of the boys who'd been tossed her way, and Sunday nights she was nauseous: had she tailored the tasks correctly? To tug the slow forward? To challenge the ones who showed spark? She made a game called Cause and Effect by cutting out gingerbread men and writing a sentence on each one. "The gingerbread men are looking for their right partners, and you can help them. There is a cause or an effect printed on each man. Match the cookies together by reading the sentences."

There were other games: Fact or Opinion? Predictions. She built vocabulary puzzles. She didn't shy away from immediate rewards; rung by rung the boys rose on the "Climb to the Stars" chart, and she doled out candy, which Ryan, whose appetite was bottomless, craved. The fury, the menacing, the moments like the flinging of his desk were replaced, to some extent, by other flashes.

"Mrs. Hughes," he asked one day, as he wobbled on a low wooden balance beam at the school's playground, "have you ever been to Africa?"

"Yes. As a matter of fact, Ryan, Mr. Hughes and I went there last summer."

"Me too!" He told her the highlights of his trip, talked about the many lions he'd seen.

Still, he struggled. He wrote her letters.

Dear Mrs. Hughes, I have been a totle jerk. I did not control myself at math. I blue it with that attitude. You have done so many things for me but I have mean to you. I am really mad not mad at you but me. I know I hate you outside but inside I know its my fault. I just am lonely inside. I know you won't give up on me but I never improve. I just do it again. I will probly never get out of this class. I know sorry won't do it. I am asking for you to be more strict because I need to learn to control my attitude. I hope and wish by the end of the year I will be the most respected and trusted in this hole class.

Sincerely your friend,
Ryan

Dear Mrs. Hughes, I made a great fool of myself. I admit I did yell at him. I haven't been starting the day write. Even thow I am sitting in this seat I am lessening. I will try to start over. I see how better every one would be when I'm not here. People say life would be better without Ryan. And now I know they are telling the truth. You may think I am mean hearted but I'm not. I don't want to heart any one. I've always said I could work on it but it just happens again. Thank you for not giving up on me because it shows me I can do it if I try!

Your student,
Ryan

In the library, where she guided him from bookcase to bookcase, he discovered something. "I was capable of reading things other than Dr. Seuss," he said. He wrote a research paper about lemurs, the minuscule primates that evolved on Madagascar millions of years ago, after floating to the island on rafts made of tangled branches and reeds.

He wrote, as well, a haiku.

A new beginning
Shall I be a deffrent person
I shall change writeaway.

She led him along the shelves to the Chronicles of Narnia, to Peter and Susan, Edmund and Lucy. They stepped into a supernatural land and defeated the witch who had imposed a perpetual winter devoid of Christmas. He plucked sequel after sequel from the bookcase. "I would turn the light back on and try to read another chapter. Just another three pages. Just another page."

He wrote more haikus.

Sorry for bad times
Life can chang with a heart love
You can make it better.

Winter so beautiful
Makes my heart grow like a snow bird
After it ends I'm sad.

But what stayed with him more than anything else from his two years with Mrs. Hughes was the memorization of King's lines. The four words, "I have a dream," resonated in his mind years later, layered in personal meaning, during the week leading up to the finals at the Met. He sensed King speaking directly to him.

"To Mrs. Hughes," Ryan had written. Choppily he had cut a piece of white paper in the shape of a heart. In crimped, quavery, erratic letters, fitting his words within the heart's borders, he printed, "You have bin a very good teacher to me. You have change my life. I know you have by looking at my report cards and seeing the differens. This gift is for the sweetish of your love for us!"

FIVE

ARE YOU UNDERSTANDING?" the conductor asked.

Ryan stood before him in jeans and a bright blue dress shirt, the shirt taut across his colossal shoulders and biceps and untucked over the bulge of his belly, the bulge minor relative to his muscle. The shade of blue emphasized the softness of his face and the size of his eyes; he looked unguarded.

The conductor, Patrick Summers, was half Ryan's size. He was the musical director of Houston Grand Opera; the Met had flown him in for the week to prepare the eight finalists and then to lead next Sunday's concert. He didn't hold a baton now as he interrupted Ryan's singing and as the rehearsal pianist went silent. Instead, he held his reading glasses. He'd removed them as he lifted his eyes from the score and gazed at Ryan's open, eager face. On the page was Mozart—unimaginable inspiration and infinite complexity, the crescent of each fermata and the mark of each appoggiatura leaping from the composer's sacred, unfathomable mind across two and a quarter centuries—and in front of Summers was Ryan's willing expression, so empty of edges and facets.

Summers pinched his glasses. His mouth hardened, and below his receding hairline his forehead formed an expanse of dismay. Not only did Ryan appear incapable of reading music with rudimentary fluency, let alone with any appreciation for Mozart's nuances; in addition, he didn't know the basics of Italian, one of opera's most essential tongues. Summers pinched harder.

"Do you understand that the stress in *'Ispagna'* is on the second syllable?"

℘

"You have, with opera, these extraordinary works of art, and for the rare person who is gifted to sing in this way, truly gifted—and it is a very few people, and the gift only *begins* with the ability to perform in a mammoth room without a microphone—for that person, the voice is a life force, nothing less," Summers told me. "Perhaps the force is even more fundamental than erotic desire. Some would say that there's nothing more fundamental than that, but when a truly gifted singer attains the right technique, his whole body vibrates with the creation of this profound music.

"And the creation is occurring literally out of nothing. It's just air. Living, vibrating air. And maybe, as I think about it, it is tightly connected to erotic desire, not just because so much of opera is *about* desire but because of the way a singer can feel himself, or herself, bodily, physically, and because great singing—the voice without mechanical amplification; the naked, overwhelming voice—ties bodies together. The vibrating air leaves the singer and passes into you, the listener. It enters you."

Summers was a librettist as well as a conductor; lately he'd finished an opera based on the novel *Siddhartha*. It was the story of an ancient ascetic and seeker much like the Buddha, and the main character's quest for purity and enlightenment matched Summers's ideas about music: that unerring precision and piercing comprehension were critical to operatic singing—comprehension of what was printed on the page and what lay underneath. And meanwhile he lived in fear for his art form, sensing that it might be dying and—worse—deteriorating. America's regional houses were cutting their seasons or closing altogether, and New York's second company, where Sills and Carreras had launched their careers, was about to shut down. Europe's grand houses were flourishing, but not without government support. The Met wasn't quite selling out. But worse, for Summers, than worries about distant extinction was the threat of erosion, the danger that quality would crumble away, almost imperceptibly at first and then unmistakably, technique weakening and artistry diminishing and the voices of opera gradually less able to invade the body with the special, inarticulable meaning that great music could communicate.

He felt insidious factors at work, believed that the culture's ever-mounting emphasis on youth and beauty was applying an ever-heightening pressure. More than they once did, he said, looks mattered in operatic casting. He knew that they had always been relevant, yet appearance was, these days, much more valued in casting than a century or two ago—and beauty in Verdi's time had been defined differently. Its contours had been more full, and full contours tended to contribute to vocal strength, and sheer power was part of great operatic singing, especially in the most emotionally wrenching roles.

Heft might be involved, too, in more delicate aspects of the art. Was body fat linked somehow to the musical shadings the larynx and pharynx could produce? Summers couldn't be sure—and nor could any singer or scientist—but while listening to him I thought about one of the semifinalists. Her frame was oversized and well padded, and her arias, in the semis, rang out with promise. A voice teacher I knew, a man I chatted with in the interval between the singing and the announcement of the final eight, predicted that she would be chosen. He felt that she deserved to be, based on her talent. "As a child," she had said to me, "I always felt big, enormous. I could never be the fairy princess. With opera, there's something magical for me about getting to play dress-up and pretend, getting to be something you're not. And there's something about experiencing music from another century. I don't know if I could function as a person if I didn't sing. When I sing, my face feels hot and my mind shuts off; I don't know what I'm doing onstage. On high notes my vision shakes—it bounces. Without singing, I don't know if I could survive."

What made me think of her as Summers spoke was a story she had told, the story of Deborah Voigt, the illustrious soprano who'd won this contest in the eighties. Two decades later, despite her voice, she was fired from a lead role in London because her girth clashed with the director's ideas about an outfit her character should wear. Soon after

the firing, she resorted to surgery: she had her stomach sta-
pled. She was a hundred pounds lighter now, and lots of
her fans mourned a loss of vocal shades and warmth that
they blamed on the shedding of fat. Others disputed the
loss, and still others heard the loss but doubted the reason.
The semifinalist didn't doubt. She said she had considered
surgery to get her career going, but she was holding out,
guarding the mysterious instrument she'd been given.

She wasn't picked for the finals. Nor were the other
women of large proportions. The bodies of the three female
finalists were all fetching, one shapely and two svelte, and
all three faces were pretty. It was impossible to say that this
was why they'd been selected over some of the others. Cer-
tainly Summers wasn't saying it. Yet it fit with his fears,
anxieties that focused more on female voices but encompassed male singing as well. The Met's new live video
broadcasts drew millions into movie theaters all over the
country and the world, but they also compounded the
threats he perceived. The broadcasts were full of close-ups.
And they were full of amplified sound. They added to the
value of surfaces and negated the rapture of the naked
voice.

"Singing is the embodiment of inner beauty. There's a
completely individual imprint that comes from within each
singer." Summers's task, for the week, was to help the finalists to reveal who they were as artists, to help them "unlock
the scores, to express their individual connection with these
glorious combinations of words and music, with Handel,
with Mozart, with Verdi."

With Philippe, Summers worked at a high level, pointing
out gently that the particular ornamentations, the impro-

vised notes, that Philippe was choosing for one of his arias might not be quite optimal. With Deanna, he spoke about the rhythms of one passage and then about the distinctive harmony the Met orchestra would provide as she sang a specific measure—for it would be a full orchestra, not a mere piano, accompanying the finalists at the concert. With Michelle, he praised her lush tone and proceeded to the interpretation of character.

But he didn't see Ryan as ready for artistic analysis. "'Ispa*gna*'"—he demonstrated the pronunciation.

"'Isp-a-*gna*,'" Ryan tried, a glimmer of sweat emerging on his freshly shaved scalp.

"'Ispa*gna*,'" the conductor enunciated again. Pronunciation was prized as crucial to opera, even if half of any American audience wouldn't know the difference. To garble the language, which librettists and composers labored over like poets, was to make a mockery of the art.

Dutifully, avidly, Ryan turned to a table behind him and penciled a reminder into his score, for when he practiced later.

The pianist recommenced. Ryan reverted to his mistake, weighting the first syllable, and Summers, setting his reading glasses aside on the piano, recorrected.

The gleam of perspiration became a trickle.

The conductor took a breath. "Are you aware," he said, switching to another issue, "that you're actually adding notes?" He didn't mean the type of adding, of artistically legitimate embellishing, that Philippe had done. He meant notes that simply didn't belong, that hopped from Ryan's throat to spoil Mozart's music.

Ryan met his gaze uncertainly, smile collapsing.

Summers suggested that they move on to another aria. One purpose of these initial sessions was to decide which two pieces each singer would perform in the finals; unlike in the semis, there would be no requests from the judges. Now Ryan began "La calunnia," one of the arias he'd listed as possibilities. Summers put up his hand. The pianist stopped, his silence like a sudden abandonment. The conductor elaborated on a pair of failings, and Ryan concentrated with a seemingly limitless capacity for absorbing criticism. The piano fluttered to life once more, and fell quiet again at Summers's direction, the quiet resounding like a crash. "It's *'come un colpo'* "—Summers moved his mouth slowly, modeling the Italian. "It's *'temporale.'*"

Mired at this level of learning, nowhere near the levels of interpretation, Ryan started to panic. Foreign languages, he felt, were more than foreign to him; they were alien.

"It's *'tumulto.'* " Summers stressed the twin *u*'s. Ryan rushed to make another note in his score, then attempted to master the ill movements of his lips.

"You *must* work on that word."

Multiple rivulets of sweat forked around Ryan's temples.

"Let's try the Floyd"—the conductor named an English-language piece from Ryan's list.

Ryan sang it through.

"Do you even *like* this aria?"

Ryan did—he loved it. "Not really," he said. He couldn't bear to acknowledge his attachment to the piece and hear Summers tell him every way that he'd ruined it.

"What would your first two choices be for Sunday?"

"I'd love to do 'Come dal ciel' and 'Madamina.' " These were the two he'd performed in the semis; the first was the

Banquo aria, the second the Mozart that he'd just mangled with Summers.

The conductor pondered wordlessly, considering what he'd heard in the semis and today. "On the Banquo, well, we will have corrections. You will have to work. On 'Madamina,' no. No. You have a lot of learned errors. Too many. And I am constitutionally unable to rehearse it full of mistakes. I think we can choose 'La calunnia'—with me telling you what's wrong when we meet again." He paused. "As you plan out your pedagogy for the next years of your life, Italian needs to play a bigger part." He turned toward Gayletha Nichols, who was sitting in on the session. "Can he have an Italian coaching before the end of the day?" He turned back to Ryan. "So the next time we work together, you are better prepared."

SIX

Valerie wrapped Christmas lights around the shrubbery. She did what her father had done every Christmas when she was a little girl, when he'd adorned the front of their tower in the Brooklyn projects. The bushes—faint gestures of landscaping—stood in front of each low building in a rough complex in Newport News, where she'd found a job helping with upkeep. On the weekends, she took Ryan and occasionally Adrian to work. Ryan was eleven, twelve; Adrian was thirteen, fourteen. They helped her to scrub the kitchens, the toilets, when tenants were evicted; they helped her to clean the stairs, sweeping outside apartment doors where squatters had broken the locks. Sometimes a resident handed them a dollar or two for their efforts, and when the holidays came, everyone seemed to appreciate the way the shrubs flashed with blue and white and red light.

Valerie had found God. A believer had taken her under his wing and brought her gifts of psalms. "You will not fear the terror of the night, nor the arrow that flies by day, nor the pestilence that stalks in the darkness....If you say, 'The Lord is my refuge,' and you make the Most High your dwelling...you will tread on the lion and the cobra—you will trample the lion and the serpent."

She took God at His Word. And she thought of her periods of depression and her suicide attempt in religious terms. "There are powers and principalities aiming to work against us," she said. "The Devil gets in your head and gives you a false report, tricking you when you're weakest, telling you you're no good."

From studying the stories of the Old Testament, she drew one paramount lesson: "God doesn't play." When Aaron's sons, Moses's nephews, erred in their sacrifice to the Lord, lighting their own fire rather than waiting for God's flame, "He incinerated them right then and there." When Uzzah, transporting the Ark of the Covenant to Jerusalem, worried that the Ark would tumble from his cart and reached up to steady it, breaking His law against touching the shrine, the Lord slaughtered him instantly. "He was gone right like that." And when Moses, seeking water for the Israelites in the desert, struck the rock with his staff, instead of speaking to it as God commanded, the Lord barred him from ever reaching the Promised Land, despite all the faith Moses had shown. "That gives you an idea—God is serious about what He wants from us."

As though compensating for the anarchy that had dominated her life with her sons, Valerie now took her cue from these biblical lessons. She forbade Adrian and Ryan to play a popular card game pitting wizard against wizard, then discovered that they had disobeyed her. They had concealed a deck in their bedroom, with illustrated cards labeled "Lord of Riots" and "Fiend Blooded" and "God of the Dead." That afternoon, when Adrian and Ryan returned home from school, she informed them that she had set fire to their collection, burned it to cinders.

But her vigilance took more positive forms as well. During Black History Month, she demanded that the boys write essays. The African American past, she felt, was barely taught in the Virginia schools: slavery was treated as something to be forgotten, and more recent history as nothing worthy of study. She made Ryan and Adrian choose prominent African Americans, learn about their lives, describe their accomplishments. She made them read the essays aloud. "I'd check: did it have a beginning and a body and all that? And I'd ask them questions. I had to know: were they doing enough research? They had to be *telling* me something."

A semblance of order crept into their lives. They were able to move from the Yorktown complex with the junkies and johns to a tight two-bedroom in a better cluster of clapboard buildings, backing on an access road and a strip mall. After his two-year banishment to Mrs. Hughes's room of unmanageables, Ryan was in regular classrooms. Month by month, he navigated sixth grade without disaster. But the boys fought constantly now within the close walls of the apartment, their bodies large, Adrian taking after his father, short but thick and sculpted, adding inches in width when his height stalled, bench-pressing almost three hundred pounds, and Ryan, at twelve, standing five seven, just beginning to spike toward the six five he would eventually reach, his size, for his age, at the top of the graphs when he was measured and weighed. Heat, aggression, venom rose between them compulsively.

Still, the boys usually submitted to Valerie's punishments for their fighting. Sometimes she sentenced them to afternoons and evenings, a long stretch of them, in their room. Rage tended to subside, replaced by Ryan's admiration. Adrian's art continued to cast a spell. With Adrian schooling him, they created a comic book together: Tarzan rescuing the animals of the jungle, who were facing an onslaught of aliens.

Ryan watched his brother make scrolls. Adrian had announced his intention to become a paleontologist, and he would draw a dinosaur species, then fill the page with a host of information, from genus to diet, then roll the sheet of paper and tie it with a string. He fashioned dozens of these documents, a trove. Their cylindrical shape held an aura of antiquity. The idea came to Adrian from time spent in a library years earlier, when he had read Greek myths and stumbled upon Greek philosophers. He had caught a glimpse of their lives. "Aristotle, Sophortes, all those guys," he told me when I tracked him down at the edge of a town in the California desert. "I wanted to be—what's the word? Wise. I wanted to be wise."

The scrolls were his attempt. They accumulated in the room, repositories of his learning. And their antiquated look bore both boys away, toward a remote century.

Yet Valerie was only intermittently in control, of her sons, of herself. She took courses at a community college but lost her job doing upkeep at the complex in Newport News. She told Ryan that he had ruined her life, that she hated him. She yelled about his allergic reaction to the vaccine long ago, telling him that she'd had to quit the Air Force so she could care for him while he recovered. He had robbed her of the best job she'd ever had. He had robbed her of her Air Force career. She told him, as she struck him, that she wished he had never been born.

During her flare-ups, she whipped him with a belt, hit him in the stomach with closed fists, knocked him down, and kicked him, according to state records—though years later, with me, he said that he did not remember the kicking; the rest, yes, but not that; it was too painful to believe that she would assault him in this particular way, so animalistic, so blind.

Between the flare-ups, he lay, at night, under a winter blanket no matter how hot the evening. He insisted on falling asleep like this. He insisted on pulling the blanket up to his neck. It didn't help. Screaming and sweating, he woke often in the middle of the night, terrified by dreams he could never describe.

℘

Then, one May afternoon, at the end of his sixth grade year, when he was twelve, something occurred, some catalyst. Another fight with his brother? Over something they'd found along the access road behind their apartment or in a patch of woods nearby? A piece of broken equipment they each claimed? Or was the catalyst something else entirely, some infraction involving only Ryan? Everyone's memories were vague about this, blurred by what followed.

Valerie hit Ryan and dispatched him alone to the boys' bedroom. The door stayed shut. When he emerged quietly, without her permission, and when she glanced up and saw him, he held a weapon, a knife, she recalled.

He recounted: "I grabbed a weapon, whatever it was, a knife, I have no idea, I don't think it was a knife, and I was approaching my mom with it. I stared her down. I wanted to make her pay, hurt her for making me feel the way I felt. The worst you could possibly feel. I wanted her to fear me as much as I feared her, as much as I felt her wrath. I hated my life. And she was looking afraid. She asked me, 'What are you going to do with that?' I don't know if I actually wanted to kill her. Can a child really want to kill someone? I was past the breaking point. I was boiling over. I was incoherent. I wanted her to disappear. Disappear. She threw me against the wall and disarmed me. I didn't give up. I was fighting, and she grabbed me by the neck."

℞

She subdued him for long enough to notice what he'd set on the floor, in the open doorway of the bedroom. It was a drawing. In a frenzy, he'd been working on it before he stepped out of the room, outlining the bodies and faces, adding detail, deepening colors, putting to use everything his brother had taught him, hovering over the paper, his mind and hands racing, making the picture come to life. The family in the drawing was easy to identify: the mother, the two boys. "My killing plan," he would call the picture in the coming days, to those who questioned him. One of the boys held a knife; there was blood streaked everywhere; two heads were severed. Right after struggling with him, pinning him to the wall, and grabbing the weapon he held, Valerie saw the drawing and phoned the police.

"Clawing, yelling, crying, screaming. They had me on the couch, and they were trying to get handcuffs on me, and I was fighting, fighting the cops. Kicking. They were men, but I was jabbing out with my legs. 'No, no, no, no.' Till one of them got a hold on me. I couldn't kick. They got the cuffs on me behind my back. They lifted me into the air, my feet were off the floor. Lifted me out the door. I was still fighting, trying to get back inside. They carried me down the flights of stairs to the car. They put me in the back. Then one of them must have been taking my mom's statement upstairs. I was in the back of that car, thinking, *This is real*. I was begging, yelling, thinking if I apologized they wouldn't take me. 'I'm sorry, I'm sorry, I'm sorry, I'm sorry.'"

They drove away with him, along a river, up a hill. They took him inside a building, took him to an area with no windows. From a low ceiling, a few fluorescent bulbs cast the only light. The cell—seven feet by five—was a structure of black corner poles and crisscrossing black metal, like a heavy version of cyclone fencing. He was locked in alone. He was a kid who slept with his blanket tugged up around his chin. Now he was a kid spending the night in a cage.

SEVEN

HE TUNNELED THROUGH one of the subterranean levels
of the Met. Beams dropped low from the ceiling of the
corridor. Foam pads covered the beams haphazardly, protection for those who forgot to duck. Ryan bent under,
straightened, made his way forward, bent again. Busts of
Wagner and some other figure sat on pedestals in a dim corner along the passageway. Maybe they'd once decorated a
public part of the theater, or been bought for that purpose,
but now, with their stern features, they lurked in the gloom
like specters.

He found the room number he'd been given. The chamber just fit a baby grand and a desk, and he squeezed in,
shutting the door behind him. This was where he'd been
sent after his session with Summers. Nichols, the motherly,
rotund director of the contest, had called one of the Met
coaches. "We have a situation," she'd said.

In his mind, he'd been directed to this room to deal
with a problem, a handicap, a disability—his egregious
Italian—that was mixed up with bigger troubles. It was

71

entangled not only with his struggle to pronounce any of opera's foreign languages; and not only with a fact he kept to himself, that he hadn't completely translated and comprehended his arias word for word, as he knew every singer was supposed to do; but also with the scars that had come with deciding to speak grammatical English. That choice and its consequences were not so far in the past as to be unfelt, not at all. They were still present. "When you come from a certain demographic," he said, "it's frowned upon to talk properly. People around me called me an Oreo. They said these ridiculous things." The word "ridiculous" lingered as he related this, an effort to make light of the ridicule.

The coach who awaited him wore a gray sweater and a thin, airy scarf. Carrie-Ann Matheson, who was in her thirties, spent most of her working hours in this studio, three floors underground; if she used her lunch hour to practice the piano on her own, she didn't see natural light all day. It was a monk's existence—which she felt fortunate to be living. With each opera the Met put on, stars descended to ready themselves with a coach like her in a closet like this. "I've had the greatest singers in the world in here working. How lucky is that? To be sitting on this bench and to have Bryn Terfel come and sit next to me? Singers have more energy than just about any other kind of artist. And to connect to them musically, to hook into that energy, you have to understand what's deep inside them. To have Anna Netrebko sitting here? To have Jonas Kaufmann standing here? To have that incredible energy in this room?"

Matheson, like many of the Met coaches, was a pianist and had never been a singer. Instead, she was trained as a guide to singers on everything from cadence to characterization. Often, though, in the course of her day, she did have to sing. Untrained and ungifted, she ran through duets with the most renowned tenors and sopranos, so they could shade their interpretations and settle into their roles; she sang with rising mezzos and baritones in order to demonstrate a better way to phrase a passage; and, when she was assigned to be the rehearsal pianist for an upcoming Met performance, and when the lead soprano felt a worrisome tingle in her throat, Matheson sang the part on the Met stage, sang *out,* from behind her piano, so the cast could go on with its preparations. "You have to get over any sense of shame about the voice. You have to get over that hesitation that people have. It's a bonus if you have a not-horrendous vocal quality, but there are coaches who have horrible voices. Jonas Kaufmann knows I'm not Renée Fleming. And I'm not secretly wishing for Jonas to say, 'You should really have been.' When I have to sing, I'll sing in a range that's okay for me and then drop down an octave when things get too high. If I tried to produce that high note, it would be very unpleasant."

With Ryan, she listened to him attempt the two arias that Summers had declared at least potentially acceptable, and she tried to figure out where to begin. "A few simple ideas will have a big effect with you," she said as she sat at the piano with Ryan towering over her. But her thoughts weren't few, and to him, they didn't feel simple. "You have a wonderful rich voice, but can you move the sound toward the front of your face? You want the energy going out and up." And all the while, as she gave instruction on the mysterious physiology of vocal technique, she tried to adjust his pronunciation, measure after measure.

"*'Tenebre.'*" She spoke the word, meaning darkness, in Banquo's song. "Think about the vowel. Think about *e, e, e.*" The studio became an echo chamber. "Can you lengthen each vowel? And on *'petto,'* there is a silence before the double *t*. Can you hear it? It's *'pe-tto.'*" The hush lasted a sliver of an instant; it was hardly audible; yet, she said, it was vital. "It's the same with *'sospetto.'*"

She asked him to try it.

He did, and she asked him again. And again.

She shifted two measures forward. "*'Come.'* It's almost all vowel. The consonant, the *m*—your lips barely touch on it before you're gone." The *m* she manufactured seemed to defy physics. Her lips didn't seem to contact each other at all. It was something like the sight of a hummingbird suspended on invisible wings.

He mimicked her, his version like a stork's flapping.

With their hour running out, she turned to "La calunnia." The aria was partly about the evil potency of language, so it was all the more important that he get the language right.

"Not *'callllunia.'* *'Calunnia.'* A lot less *l*, a little more *n*."

She went on. "*'Un'auretta.'* Just listen to that pause before the pair of *t*'s."

"*Leggermente.* Listen. Relax. We don't want to tie you up in knots."

"*Sotto voce.*"

Her bits of advice, cheerfully given, piled up in his head, collided, crowded one another out.

"You're singing *'fiori,'* which is flowers, but it's *'fuori'*—

'dalla bocca fuori'—which means coming out of the mouth."

"Yes, Miss Carrie-Ann," he said. But behind his smile he was hardening, closing off, going blank.

"What I'd like you to do tonight is recite these arias in reverse. Start with the last word, the last syllable, and go syllabically backward. One syllable, two, three. Add a syllable each time."

This would be the best way, she said, to cleanse his brain, to fix the failures of his lips and tongue.

℞

Out of the cage. Into another police car. Into a courtroom with an American eagle and a Virginia flag. There, a mental health counselor testified. She'd met with Ryan before the court hearing, interviewing him and filling out forms. In court, she gave her evaluation to the judge. "Presenting problems include homicidal ideation." She introduced the picture he'd made. Valerie was there in the courtroom. She didn't protest when the judge sent him away.

With his wrists in cuffs and legs in shackles, cops took him on another drive. Trees enclosed the road. The drive was long, its end unknown, and the longer it lasted the more the world changed, the low-lying landscape of his home replaced by the hills and thick forest the police car carried him into. Branches formed an archway; it was near sunset, and the car sped through a tunnel of dark green.

Then the car slowed drastically and crept up a knoll. There was a slanted field. A sign warned outsiders away. They wound higher, turning into a circular driveway. From there, in his cuffs and shackles, he was led between brick pillars and inside.

℞

Ryan had been delivered to a facility of forty-eight cells and several chambers for solitary confinement: the DeJarnette Center, named for Dr. Joseph DeJarnette, a crusader in the American eugenics movement of the first half of the twentieth century, a proponent of Virginia's Racial Integrity Act, an open admirer of Nazi accomplishments, and the director, for four decades into the nineteen forties, of the state's main insane asylum. He had also been a poet.

Oh, why do we allow these people
    To breed back to the monkey's nest,
To increase our country's burdens
    When we should only breed the best?

Oh, you wise men take up the burden,
    And make this your loudest creed,
Sterilize the misfits promptly—
    All not fit to breed!
Then our race will be strengthened and bettered,
    And our men and our women be blest,
Not apish, repulsive and foolish,
    For the best will breed the best.

At the time that Ryan was escorted inside, the center had recently been rebuilt: a modern structure at the knoll's crest. The old facility stood boarded up on another hill close by, across a thoroughfare that ran through the town in the Shenandoah Valley, near the West Virginia border. But the center had retained DeJarnette's name. It seemed he was still deemed worthy of honor in the late nineteen nineties, much as he had been celebrated in the years leading up to World War II, and much as he had been venerated in the mid–nineteen seventies, when the original facility had been baptized the DeJarnette Center for Human Development. The state was attached to this man and his legacy.

DeJarnette, who died in 1957, had a square jaw and a bald, squarish skull. He liked to describe himself as "a country boy" who'd begun his professional life "carrying all he had in one hand in a dollar suitcase." But he grew to be one of the most influential men in Virginia, and in 1924 he pushed the legislature to pass two historic laws.

The Sterilization Act authorized the forced sterilization of "mental defectives," as the bill put it—the psychologically ill, the habitually criminal, the intellectually weak, the epileptic, the sexually promiscuous, those prone to pauperism—in order to "prevent the propagation of their kind" and eliminate the inevitable hereditary "menace" and public financial burden posed by their offspring. But beyond the social benefits of safety and fiscal prudence, there was a greater goal: to purge the white race of its unwanted genetic strains and, in this way, to ensure white supremacy. This legislation of DeJarnette's was part of the complicated history of the eugenics movement, a history not limited to Virginia or the South. The movement had gained early momentum in Britain, with Winston Churchill among its supporters, and by 1910, north of New York City, it had established an American research center whose data was soon influential when Congress, with few dissenters, all but barred immigrants who didn't have Nordic blood.

DeJarnette's Sterilization Act wasn't aimed directly at blacks. The majority of the thousands of Virginians who had sterilization inflicted on them were white—like the indigent hillbilly families rounded up by sheriffs and brought to DeJarnette's asylum, where he oversaw the surgeries of children as well as adults. He most likely believed, as plenty of American social Darwinists did in his time, that the Negro race was biologically so inferior—inherently given to such self-destructive behavior and so susceptible to disease—that it would run gradually toward extinction in the United States, where it couldn't possibly compete for survival with whites. In the meantime, though, the Sterilization Act was a method of improving on white superiority.

"I started it first," DeJarnette said about his campaign for the law. He spoke these proud words when, on the eve of World War II, less than two months before Germany's invasion of Poland, he addressed a crowd of dignitaries, among them Virginia's governor, who had gathered on the grounds of his asylum to pay tribute to his achievements. DeJarnette's statute had set a national precedent: it had been tested and found constitutional by the United States Supreme Court in 1927. The approving justices were led by former president William Howard Taft, who served as chief justice after his presidency, and, following the enthusiastic decision written by Oliver Wendell Holmes Jr., around half of the states in the country enacted similar laws—and carried them out.

But pleased as he was with his accomplishment, in 1934

DeJarnette lamented, in a major Virginia newspaper, "The Germans are beating us at our own game." And he stated, a few years later, "Germany in six years has sterilized about 80,000 of her unfit while the United States, with approximately twice the population, has only sterilized about 27,869." He added that, to make the score worse, the United States had been at it longer.

The second law that DeJarnette helped persuade the Virginia legislature to adopt back in 1924 was the Racial Integrity Act. The Sterilization Act and the Racial Integrity Act were twin statutes, passed on the same day. The Racial Integrity Act classified all Virginians as either white or colored, and pioneered what was called "the one-drop rule." Until then, a person with one-eighth black ancestry was considered white. Now even a drop of black blood put a person in the "colored" category. The only mixture to be tolerated was a minor fraction of Indian heritage—up to one-sixteenth. This was termed "the Pocahontas exception," necessary because a number of elite Virginians traced their families back to the legendary union of the Indian princess with the British tobacco planter John Rolfe in the first years of the Jamestown settlement. The law prohibited marriage or sex between white and colored, with a punishment of up to five years in prison; the statute was meant to protect the biological strength of the white race from being diluted.

With Hitler six weeks from marching into Poland, with Hitler preparing to exterminate six million Jews and millions more undesirables, DeJarnette, at the ceremony in his honor, extolled the area of Virginia where he stood. Here, he said, "the setting sun" leaves "a trail of gorgeous colors," and here the "people are homogeneous." The governor praised DeJarnette's "splendid character" and announced, "I want to record the appreciation of all the people of Virginia." One of the state's former governors, who'd gone on to the U.S. Senate, sent a telegram from Washington, DC, hailing DeJarnette's "outstanding service" and "high patriotism."

Three decades later, in a case brought by a Virginia couple, Mildred and Richard Loving, a black wife and a white husband who avoided prison by exiling themselves from the state, the Supreme Court overturned the Racial Integrity Act. And the Sterilization Act was repealed in 1979, forced sterilizations having been performed less and less since the late fifties. Yet DeJarnette's name blessed the newly constructed facility where Ryan, in 1998, taking his shackled steps, was deposited inside the front doors.

℞

Begin at the end and relearn the aria in reverse.

"*Ror... terror... di terror,*" he pronounced, alone in his hotel room, obeying Matheson's instruction that he start with the final syllable, then add a segment of a word, and add again.

The room was fancy but compressed, the furniture too bulky for the space. Even the boxy lampshade on the bed table claimed too much of the scarce air between the walls, and the dimensions of the bed demanded that Ryan shrink himself to maneuver around it.

"Constitutionally unable," Summers had told him. "I am constitutionally unable to rehearse it full of mistakes." The words, loud in Ryan's head, contained a severe distaste; their tone was all aversion. And though he reminded himself that the sentence was aimed at only one of his arias, it seemed to cover all his singing. It seemed to apply to Ryan himself. *I am unrehearsable. I am offensive. I am unfixable.*

"No di terror...brano di terror...gombrano di terror...ingombrano di terror."

He made his own rule: *If you mess up, you begin all over.* He listened for his own failures and kept his recorder on as well, the machine vigilant, unforgiving when he touched the play button. "*Ve...larve...di larve...no di larve... brano di larve...*"

My thoughts are overwhelmed by ghosts...

Repeatedly the recording sent him back to the last syllable; repeatedly he began climbing again from the base of the mountain—the exercise was like scaling a peak, reaching one-quarter of the way, one-third of the way, before being tossed down. He decided to allow himself a quick nap; he'd heard that sleep helped with the transfer from short-term memory to long-term. He shut his eyes. A few minutes later he was upright, squeezing his body toward the mirror.

He stood with his face close to the glass, taking a break from pronunciation and focusing on his voice. Matheson had suggested watching himself sing as a way to help tinker with the sources of his sound in the areas just behind and farther back from his facial bones. He stared at his lips, at his nose, at the surfaces surrounding them. But the anatomy of resonance was bewildering and mostly hidden, and how to control the anatomy was a riddle. And he wasn't sure, at this late point in the contest, that he should be tinkering with anything so vital as the color of his notes or how they carried. Hadn't she said "You have a wonderful rich voice"?

He sang and scrutinized his reflection and had no clue about which of his shortcomings to attack. Summers's "constitutionally unable" chased him back to his woeful pronunciation. *"Par…crepar…a crepar…va a crepar…"* He slogged backward from the closing syllable of his second aria, "La calunnia," slogged aloud and then inaudibly, merely moving his lips, afraid because if he didn't make sound he couldn't hear his mistakes but more afraid that all the restarts from the ends of the arias, all the spoken vowels and consonants, in addition to all the day's singing, had worn away at his voice, stressing and inflaming the two delicate flaps of mucous membrane that were his vocal cords.

"I'm concerned with how hoarse you sound," Summers said when they met the next day. "Let's be careful about singing over the hoarseness. Shall we work just a bit on the Scottish opera? You know we never say the name of that opera inside a theater. It's considered bad luck." The conductor seemed kinder today; his tone wasn't so brittle.

Ryan sang the first few passages before Summers interrupted. "Exactly," the conductor praised, then corrected, "It's important to be both really legato and really defined." Each syllable and each note needed to be both fluidly connected and keenly distinct, the musical lines unbroken yet the clarity of language uncompromised. Summers had said "exactly," but Ryan heard the message: he hadn't gotten things exactly at all.

At least his pronunciation was improved. They progressed to "La calunnia," and it seemed that Ryan had solved his problems with Italian well enough to escape the conductor's distaste, that Summers judged him ready to concentrate on more sophisticated things, on artistry.

Then Summers cut him off. "Really roll the *r*'s." And once the pronunciation pointers began, they became a barrage. "The last syllable on *'cannone'* is *eh,* not *e*…It's *'temp*-o-*rale,'* not *'temp*-a-*rale'*…It's *'tum*-u-*lto.'*"

"*'Tumolto.'*"

"*'Tumulto.'*"

"*'Tumulto.'*"

"*'Tumulto.'*"

"*'Tumulto.'*"

"There you go. Good. *'Tumulto.'*"

"*'Tumolto.'*"

"No. You had it a second ago. Once more…I know you'll get it. You've come a long way since yesterday. No more singing for today. You've worn yourself out trying to be good. Now take it easy. Find yourself a humidifier and a glass of wine."

☙

Ryan's father appeared at the security booth, at the waist-high gate of scratched wood through which the greatest singers in the world had passed on their way to their dressing rooms. Over the years of Ryan's growing up, the two decades since Cecil and Valerie split apart, the two decades during which Ryan had seen him a handful of times, he had put on a substantial belly. He had ballooned. His face was all flesh. Yet standing there at the gate, he seemed somehow ghostly.

He had divorced his second wife and was with a woman in Bakersfield. She worked at a car dealership and had treated him to his hotel room in New York. When he came to the gate, and when Ryan emerged from within the Met and asked the security guard to let his father in, they'd already had a reunion moment. They'd shared a meal at a diner upon Cecil's arrival in New York, a meal perhaps stunted in its conversation. When I asked Ryan how it had gone, he couldn't recall much that was said, just that his father told him he was proud and told him that his relatives sent good wishes.

Now they met for a tour of the opera house that Ryan wanted to give. Cecil's full name was Cecil Speedo Green, and off and on since childhood, sometimes over his mother's vehement protests, Ryan had asked people to call him by the middle name that his father had bestowed. There was a family story about Cecil slipping out through his mother's birth canal with shocking velocity. In turn, Cecil had given Ryan the middle name, for two reasons: as a second-best alternative to naming him Cecil, which Valerie wouldn't permit, and because, as a bodybuilder at the time, he liked to flex in the brand's minimal swimsuits. Ryan had often asked people to use the name, as though, if he honored his father by doing this, Cecil would reciprocate and become a constant in his life, as though the name would conjure him, make him materialize, make him remain.

Now, at the Met, Cecil carried a coat over his arm and wore a sauce-stained sweatshirt. He'd realized a long-held dream to some degree. He'd found work as a cook in a chain restaurant, and then, some years ago, he'd taken over the barbecuing at a Bakersfield ribs joint, a few tables in a strip mall storefront, with his smoker, his grill, sitting in the mall parking lot. But despite the mound of his belly and the stains, there was something incorporeal about him. The sight of him seemed to make clear that he would swiftly be out of sight again.

"Hi, Daddy," Ryan said, his voice saturated with hope and restrained by trepidation.

He led Cecil into one of the Met's private corridors but turned into the public spaces, wanting his father to see and be swept away by what was most grand. They stepped along the scarlet carpeting and beneath the chandeliers; they passed the gold-framed portraits of opera's historic basses and sopranos. None of it seemed to make much of an impression. The Met seemed to strike his father as baffling, or maybe just dull; in his slightly high-pitched, raspy voice, he remarked mostly, simply, on its size.

"It was," Ryan said afterward, "like showing all this to a child."

℞

In some ways, Verdi surpasses Shakespeare. As the composer refashioned *Macbeth,* he wrote music that swells, at certain points, beyond what the playwright could achieve through his poetry, and Banquo's aria, the foreboding he feels and protectiveness he communicates to his child, is one of those moments. From the opening measures, even before Banquo's first line, "Watch your step, oh my son," the orchestra's introduction, the low quivering that builds and builds, evokes an inarticulable danger, something more than the specific villainy lurking nearby, something elemental and amorphous, covert and universal.

In the play, Banquo describes the moonless and ominous night.

There's husbandry in heaven;
Their candles are all out....
A heavy summons lies like lead upon me

But in the opera, the libretto's words—stripped down, simpler—are only a fraction of the emotional equation. Adding the languages of music, adding the interactions of sung and played notes, Verdi, who worshipped Shakespeare, infused unutterable meaning into the word "darkness." The score creates a medium capable of bypassing the intellect and burrowing deeper than the rational, a medium of immediacy rather than interpretation, a piece of art made to evince a palpable, unnameable anarchy and peril.

With the concert forty-eight hours away, the finalists assembled in a Met rehearsal space to practice their pieces with the orchestra. The singers sat in a row while the musicians drifted in and tuned up. Fragments of old sets leaned against the walls: a door topped with a ruffle of thatch, a painting whose canvas was torn. To Ryan's left, Deanna readied herself, stretching her voice high; to his right, a bass-baritone bellowed. Ryan made hooting sounds, like a demented owl.

Philippe was beckoned first to run through his arias. Without a discernible flicker of uneasiness, he stood before the orchestra. When Summers interrupted and asked not Philippe but some of the musicians to adjust their cadence, when Summers led a section of the orchestra through a series of recalibrations, the singer didn't remain still. While the musicians pulled themselves into line with the conductor's baton, Philippe danced, spinning, giving a quick performance blending Astaire and Baryshnikov. As soon as the orchestra had learned the corrections, he resumed singing so well that, when he had finished and taken his seat a few chairs down from Ryan, a Met coach asked him to write out the embellishments he'd sung above Handel's score. Then Michelle sang about the frailty of passion with such beauty and pain that a clarinetist rapped on the back of an empty chair in front of him, applauding.

Ryan wasn't prepared for Verdi. He wasn't prepared for the danger Verdi could generate through an orchestra, especially one as sizable and skilled as the Met's. He'd never been to a performance of *Macbeth,* only listened to his aria on YouTube. He'd only sung it with a piano. Right away, the low quivering crescendo of strings, of violins and violas and cellos and basses, caught him by surprise. He felt a dense forest close around him. He began:

Studia il passo

Summers wagged his baton in Ryan's direction. "No," the conductor said. "You're coming in a little too soon." The wag was brief, but the reproof of the baton was plain and public. No one else had been stopped in this way.

"Breathe with me," Summers said. He took an exaggerated breath just before Ryan was supposed to enter, so that

Ryan could watch him, inhale with him, slow himself, and join the orchestra on the proper beat. It was a crutch no true singer would need.

⅋

Along the halls, the linoleum floors were so clean that they glared. The cops had left, and now others led Ryan through a series of heavy doors that unlocked with the swipe of a card and opened with a piercing beep that sounded like an alarm. They took him deeper and deeper into the facility. They deposited him in a cell. The cinder block walls were tight, and the tall ceiling made the room—they called it a room—feel like the bottom of a narrow pit.

There was a bed: a plywood platform with a mattress that was too small for the platform, leaving a border of bare wood exposed. The mattress was thin; its plastic crinkled. A hulking unit of empty shelves and cubbies towered at the foot of the bed. It looked too high and too heavy, as though it might pitch away from the cinder block at any moment, all its weight falling, slamming. There was a window, but it was covered with a plate of plexiglass bolted to the wall. The window blind was locked behind the plexiglass. The blind was down and couldn't be raised.

Outside his cell door were the cells of other boys, then a common area, then the cells of the girls—twelve kids to a pod in all, four pods in the facility. The kids floated through the communal area, some in street clothes, in jeans and sneakers, others in gray sweatpants and socks. The long windows of the staff office, panes of plexiglass that looked out on the unit's communal zone, rattled. During his first hours, Ryan heard the shuddering again and again from his cell; it sounded as if the windows of the office were about to splinter and give way. Whoever it was kept at his pounding.

The shrieking began during his first evening. It rose from one of two special cells off the communal section. He tried to tell himself that he would never wind up there. He was not that bad, not that crazy, not that evil.

But his mother, his own mother, had put him here, he thought; she had decided that abandoning him to this was the only thing she could do. She had done nothing in court to stop the judge from locking him up here. His mother, the cops, the law, everyone believed this was where he belonged.

$\mathcal{L}$

The facility, in its new building when Ryan arrived, faced its old location on the opposite hill. Over there, the pair of defunct buildings, elaborate and crumbling, stood in an overgrown field behind a Walmart. The two pillars framing the entrance of the new building were short, their red masonry a vague effort to be upbeat. The eight Georgian columns of the old complex were overbearingly tall; the buildings sprawled across the hillside, dormered windows looming. The columns were cracked and a second-story balcony was collapsing.

That was where Ryan would have been sent until recently. "Huge corridors with archways leading from one section to another. Bars on the windows," a woman told me. She'd been taken to the old center, in cuffs and shackles, a few years before Ryan's time. She'd been a teenager then, and now she was one of the fortunate ones: those who'd gone on to adulthoods lived not in halfway houses or prison cells or psychiatric wards. The threshold for "fortunate" wasn't high. You had to have fallen low to be locked in the center. Either the state's psychiatric system had decided that it couldn't handle you anywhere else, or the juvenile criminal system had decided more or less the same thing and sent you there from detention or incarceration. Though Ryan hadn't been involved with either system before, his attempted attack on his mother and his "killing plan," so graphically depicted, had alarmed the authorities enough to put him in this facility of last resort.

The standard for "fortunate" was functioning, which this woman was doing in a fragile way. She lived in the town, though she'd grown up elsewhere; she hadn't made it far since getting out. We met at a coffee shop along the road that ran between the two hills, below the old and the new centers. Everything about her—her constrained voice, her deliberate gestures—spoke of tenuousness.

"Sometimes it was quiet. Sometimes there was someone running naked, yelling. Sometimes someone was smearing feces on the walls. The first day I came in it was screaming, banging—someone in seclusion. I see a girl around town lately. She's in a community program. She would hurt herself with a hairbrush. Gruesomely. In her vagina, tearing herself up. Then she would put that on the walls.

"There was a guy who vowed either he was going to murder or rape me. I had taken a liking to this lady at the nurses' station. The door at the station had a top part and a bottom part, and one day she didn't have the bottom part locked while she dispensed medication. This guy barged in. I saw him bash her head against the floor. So later on, I said something to him about it. When I said that, it flipped a switch. Now I was his target. He was in four-point restraints. Ankles, plus his wrists hooked to a belt. But it didn't matter what he had on. He was chasing me down the corridor, yelling what he was going to do."

In Ryan's time, the setting was different, but the kinds of kids were the same. It was a place, I was told by staff whose years at the facility spanned back to when Ryan was locked up, where no staff member could ever really feel certain about what to do. Every crisis was confusing, and the crises were relentless, routine without their constancy leading to clarity about how to respond. A few days of inexplicable calm might go by on a unit, but almost as inexplicably it would be shattered.

"Banging with everything, their fists, their heads. Spitting at staff. So many of them are hostile. They externalize the turmoil they feel on the inside," one employee said. "It can easily become a group contagion, three or four kids at once. Sometimes eight or twelve. Throwing chairs across the dayroom, slamming doors with tremendous force. Slamming meal trays. People who work in youth facilities like this are more prone to be victims of violence than people who work with adults. My kneecap was broken. A woman I worked with, her hair was yanked so hard her nerves were permanently damaged. She lost sensation in her face."

A state investigation of the facility—spurred by the escape of a teenager who'd earlier been charged with walking into a bank armed and ready to commit a robbery—was made several months after I visited. The report described an unmanageable mix of purely psychiatric and criminal kids. "Staff stated that higher-functioning adolescents from correctional settings often preyed on the more vulnerable...and often brought a gang mentality to the setting, which in some cases resulted in gang-related rivalries being acted out in the facility." There were no security guards at the site; the funds weren't available. In dire emergencies, the staff called the security team from an adult psychiatric facility down the road, or they called the police.

The unit where Ryan was placed, for kids around the age of puberty, might well pose the most risk, a former staff psychologist said to me. The pubertal ones were big enough to do harm and even less easy to reason with, to talk down, than the older adolescents. But reason ran scarce on all of the institution's four pods, and deception compounded the staffers' helplessness: "Some use the center only to escape the correctional facility," the psychologist said. She talked about a gang member who was cutting himself. Was he inventing his distress? Was it as real as the agony of the others who slashed their bodies?

And the techniques for aiding anyone, for transforming anyone, were limited. In the late nineties—and to a fair extent still—the prevailing method was operant conditioning. The staff bestowed points for positive behaviors. Brushing your teeth or taking a shower—some resisted even these basic acts, and a few were too depressed to carry them out, so even the simplest steps were rewarded. Making your bed. Attending Anger Busters. Demonstrating cooperation. Gradually, point by point and day by day, you could climb a series of levels, claiming privileges like watching a movie or playing a video game. But a slip into defiance could mean not only stalling in your rise but tumbling to the bottom, all your points revoked by the staffer who witnessed your refusal, your rage, your failure. You would have to begin again.

"If you're you or me," an administrator said, "you work with the system. But most of our kids, they get wiped back to zero, they feel like they can't possibly get anywhere. They feel like, *That's it, screw it.* Or they're on level four and feel they can't conceivably get to five—you feel you're going to blow it, you know you're going to, so you say to yourself, I'm going to blow it on my own terms."

The explosions, whether catalyzed by the impossibility of rewards or by surges of other despair, took all sorts of forms. "It's fine until it isn't," the administrator said about the rhythms of the place. Above his words a hoarse cry came through the cement walls from one of the pods, units whose communal walls were decorated with displays featuring curious animal facts: a rhinoceros's horn is made of compacted hair; a crocodile is incapable of sticking out its tongue. The cry resembled the protest of a giant bird. "Our kids are, it's true, kids, but they have problems of a magnitude that is so much greater. Otherwise they would never get here. When they lose it, they lose it huge, in incredibly self-destructive or other-destructive ways. Sometimes it's a period of psychosis—they're not connecting with the reality the rest of us are connecting with. And sometimes it's a level of anxiety or depression so much more intense than what the rest of us experience that it causes a fundamental breakdown of self-control.

"Pounding my head against the cinder block and then

cutting myself until my arms are just flayed open. Or 'I want ramen noodles. You better find me some ramen noodles or I'm going to beat the shit out of you.' Or I'm ripping out clumps of my hair. There are patches missing. And I'm ripping out the hair of staff, because there's this porous boundary between myself and you, and I want to meld. If you're working on that unit with the hair-ripping kid, you're coming to work in a hoodie. Or I'm tearing stuff off the walls and hurling whatever I can and flipping over tables that are too heavy to throw and yelling that I'm going to fucking kill you if you come anywhere near me."

Ideally, the blowup abated before staff had to close in. "We don't want the physical confrontation. It's dangerous for the kid and even more for staff—it's almost always the staff that gets injured in a situation of trying to physically restrain. And it's traumatizing for the kid. And the kid has been traumatized his whole life."

The decision to close in wasn't always rational. "When you're threatened? Working in this environment?" the staffer whose kneecap had been broken said. "I've been hit upside the head with as much force as you can imagine. I said something I thought was helpful, but the kid misperceived. That happens with kids who've been mistreated. And we all have a fight-or-flight response. Sometimes it's easy to apply more force than necessary to contain a kid's aggressive impulse. The job is to figure out how to minimize, how to respond therapeutically, but—" Sometimes, too, confrontation was triggered by more than a kid's aggression. "People drawn to mental health work are often damaged themselves."

"Staff might be dealing with trauma issues of their own," the administrator agreed.

When they closed in, it was frequently in pairs or groups. Groups could be more gentle. "We would literally lay down on them. I would lay my upper body across the kid's lower legs," a former employee remembered, "and someone else would lay on their upper legs, and someone else was on the upper body, and someone was up at the head, trying to make sure the kid didn't hurt himself, banging his face against the floor."

In pairs or alone, they used a system of holds, maneuvers designed to immobilize, to pin the arms, to render the hands useless, to contort the body. No physical injury was inflicted. The physical pain was brief. But to be overwhelmed in this way, to be a kid and to find yourself suddenly and completely helpless, paralyzed, taken in one instant from a state of frenzied autonomy to a position of absolute futility, was a journey of infinite emotional violence.

On the platform of each kid's bed, along the rim, was a set of slits. If need be, staff bound a kid to the bed. More often they shut the kid in one of the seclusion chambers: empty of everything, just the floor, just the walls. "It can be intolerable," the administrator said. He was trying, years after Ryan's time, to persuade the staff to rely less on punishment, less on seclusion especially. The persuasion wasn't easy.

"Every minute alone in there can be discombobulating. Unbearable for different reasons, depending. Take a common cognitive error that a depressed person makes: *My life was always this bad, it is always like this, it will always be like this.*" Time in the cell felt eternal. "Or take the kid with PTSD. She copes by pushing away whatever it is. But alone, she can't push it away. Or the kid with a horrible sense of self: *I'm a horrible human being.* There's no escape from that in seclusion."

But now and then, no matter what they would have liked to do, staff couldn't intervene at all to quell a situation. The psychologist recalled a huge teen who, one night, seemed too dangerous to subdue. "Everything on the unit—down, demolished. It was like a tornado." Other kids on the pod locked themselves in their rooms, using the button locks on their door handles that only staff could open. Taking flight, staff members bolted themselves into a miniature courtyard adjoining the pod. The courtyard, with high brick walls, was where a kid could be given thirty minutes of fresh air if he couldn't be allowed outside. From there, staring in at the teen, the staff phoned for rescue.

℞

"Ryan was observed without incident on this shift." This is the way Ryan's record from the facility begins. The log runs shift by shift, hour by hour. "He interacted well with peers and staff." This was his first afternoon and evening. "He was cooperative and polite." He woke in his room in the middle of the night, the immense structure of shelves and cubbies leaning over his bed, each empty section a gaping hole.

He discovered a game during his initial days. A TV and a set of Nintendo controls sat on a black metal stand in the common area, and the staff permitted him to play for short periods, though he hadn't yet accumulated much in the way of points. The screen filled with a radiant blue sky and a bank of puffy white clouds. His plane, an old-fashioned propeller rig with wings stacked one over the other, was painted bright red. Cheery electronic music played softly, the notes like a high-tech version of a carousel's singsong. He piloted into the blue. Clutching and tapping his controls, he steered above a desert and aimed for a landing strip up ahead. Three bursts of triumphal music sounded when he touched down. "Great Landing" flashed on the screen. He planned, he told the staff, to earn tons of behavior points. He made his bed, brushed his teeth.

Yet over his initial days he deteriorated. Familiarity with the center seemed to remove fear and restraint. "Cooperative and polite" gave way to "borderline rude." He was "a bit argumentative." He made "inappropriate" comments with "sexual undertones." He was "loud and overactive."

On the fifth day he heard his mother's voice. This was not a reward for however many points he'd earned. The facility's policy was to try to keep the kids in contact with their families. His mother couldn't make the long trip to visit. She didn't have money for gas, she'd told the social worker who phoned her. She couldn't afford the bus; she didn't have anywhere to stay. But this wasn't the only issue. Ryan didn't want her to visit. He refused to have anything to do with her. He told the staff that he would not talk with her on the phone. He agreed finally to a call—if a staff member was there, not just on the line but standing next to him while they spoke.

When the conversation with his mother was over, he declared, nearly yelling, "I don't want to see her. I don't want to look at her." He talked about her abuse. All he wished for, he said, was to forget everything.

If my father was like Arnold Schwarzenegger, he thought, *if he cared as much as Arnold, I would not be here. If he was like the man who defeated the T-1000, if he was like the man who triumphed over evil, if he was that big, if he had that heart.*

In his Anger Busters group after the phone call, the kids were given a list of triggers and told to write the letter *A* beside whatever made them angry. Ryan wrote *"AA!!"* beside "someone breaks a promise." He printed *"AA!!"* next to "someone is nice to someone else." He pressed his marker doubly hard—*"AA!!"*—alongside "someone reminds me of my past."

The staff parceled out what compliance points they could during the days following the phone call, when his deterioration accelerated. He played as much of the Nintendo game as he was allowed. He piloted the propeller plane, controlled a skydiver, manipulated a man strapped into body rockets. He soared over the desert, over a green peninsula, over wide water. He swooped toward runway after runway, toward circular landing pad after circular landing pad. Sometimes the screen flashed "Landing Failure." More regularly it beamed "Great Landing." Told to relinquish the controls, that his time was up, he ignored the voices. Ordered to obey as he tried to go on flying, he railed at the staff. "Jackasses!" he shouted.

He hovered over the other kids while they played the game that he coveted, watching them hungrily, coaching them belligerently, deriding them for their blunders. A staffer with tawny skin commanded him to settle down in his room. "White Hawaiian bitch!" he screamed. "Racist Hawaiian bitch!" He extended his middle finger. "Suck it! Suck it, bitch!"

The facility was prescribing him a mild sedative. Policy was to try to avoid powerful, involuntary medications. The drug didn't seem to dull his sentiments, his reactions.

The staff erased all the points he'd been awarded. He was at the bottom level. Somehow Mrs. Hughes found out where he'd been sent; she called, and he went to the phone. Her words were reassuring, but he cried afterward, disconsolate for hours, alternately sobbing and silently distraught, awash in shame that this woman who had led him to the Narnia books, led him to Martin Luther King, led him from being someone terrible to being someone almost normal, a kid in normal classrooms, had now discovered him in this locked unit in this locked place.

The center offered to pay for a motel room to make it easier for Valerie to visit, and she borrowed money for gas. The staff coaxed Ryan to say that he would see her. In the days before her scheduled arrival, he became fixated on a black girl within the pod. She was tall, with very dark skin and an asymmetrical shrub of hair that he detested. It was uncombed, knotty. Her lips were cracked. She never seemed to change her pajama-style pants. He believed that she was tracking him, moving wherever he moved within the tight, windowless common zone, sitting wherever he sat. He warned her to keep her distance: "I'm going to kick your ass." He announced it to everyone: "I'm going to kick her ass." He told her, "I'm going to kill you if you're not careful."

After talking with him, a psychotherapist noted down

his "preoccupation with thoughts re: killing or injuring this peer. He is angered by her affection for him and her habit of following him around and invading his personal space." He feels, the therapist wrote, that she is "the source of all his difficulties." There are strong signs of "obsessive-compulsive symptomology. He reports that he had similar feelings toward his mother" when he threatened her life.

His mother, at the same time, was irate over a letter she'd received from the facility. It referred to her son as Speedo. The day before her visit, she phoned the facility and insisted on speaking with the administrator who had signed at the bottom of the page. She never wanted her son called Speedo on paper, she told him. He replied that the center usually honored a child's choice of name. She repeated herself: *never* on paper, *never* in a document. "Why would you do that?" she berated. "Why would you put that in a letter? That's not his name. I don't want to see that."

Would she like him, the administrator asked, to resend the letter with the name changed?

She said she would.

The next afternoon, Ryan and his mother met. The meeting didn't last long; staff cut it off. In Ryan's memory, years later, it hadn't occurred at all. He believed he'd refused to leave his pod to spend time with her. He believed she'd driven for hours, and driven away, without laying eyes on him. He recalled changing his mind, but too late—the staff told him that she was already gone. He remembered the ache of his own regret. He blamed himself for not seeing her, for rejecting her.

But that wasn't how it happened. The visit was so

painful that he purged it from his memory. His mother did the same.

"Met with mother today alone, and then with mother and Ryan," the notes recounted. "She presents as a very angry woman who also experiences depression. She is currently medicated with Zoloft. She acknowledges that she harbors a great deal of anger and attributes it to years of physical abuse in her second marriage. But she has little insight into the ways that her anger affects her interactions with Ryan. During the visit, she was very negative toward him. She criticized. She was very confrontational and punitive toward him. He vented his anger at her. He was taken back to the unit."

"I don't give a fuck anymore!" he shouted when he was back within the pod. He chastised another boy because the bathroom floor was wet. The staff tried to quiet him. "I don't give a fuck!" he proclaimed again. They reminded him to use his "self-calming techniques," to breathe steadily. The girl with the horrid Afro appeared. "I'm going to kill you! I'm going to rip your fucking face off!"

He warned that he would do the same to the staff. "You're doing this to me! You're the fucking reason!" he told them. They pinned his arms behind his back. They shut him in one of the seclusion cells.

There was nothing. The cinder block walls were off-white. The linoleum floor was a watery blue. The cell throbbed—fast, loud pulses of sound from an air vent above. The rhythmic noise encased him, invaded him, vibrated inside his skull.

Why do they think you're so evil? Why are you so evil?
I'm crazy, I'm crazy, I'm crazy.

He gazed through a slit of glass in the door. It gave him only glimpses. Staff were smiling, a kid was smiling. He couldn't hear them but knew they were laughing. He lay on his belly on the tiles. "Get me out of here!" he howled into the gap at the base of the door. "Get me out of here!"

He stood, pounded on the door, pounding, pounding. "I'm going to put my foot up your ass!" he shrieked at the girl who haunted him. "I'm going to kill you, white bitch!" he told a nurse. "Racists!" he accused. "Hawaiian bitch! I am perfectly fucking calm! I want the fuck out! I promise I will kill each and every one of you!"

His voice left him. He sat on the floor, mute. He leaned his back against the wall, but the rough feel of the concrete on the backs of his arms was unbearable. He slid over and collapsed against the door.

℞

A half hour before the finals—after ardent days of trying to drill into himself everything Matheson had taught him and root out everything Summers found repellent, days of wishing to believe that the way Nichols had saved him for last when she'd named the eight finalists on Sunday, "and last but *not* least," meant that he was somehow a favorite of hers and possibly had a chance to win, days of looking in the direction of Lincoln Center every time he exited the hotel, even if he was going the opposite way, to a deli to get something to eat, as if paying this tribute to the opera house, no matter how badly he needed to put it out of his mind, might bring it into his future, days of avoiding any touring around the city for fear that inhaling the wrong bit of airborne dirt or dampness would leave him infected, worsening the scratchiness in his throat and killing any prospect he had of victory—Ryan and three of the other singers gathered in the lounge between the dressing rooms.

There were soft chairs, a stretch of red carpet. Philippe was shoeless in his tux. The whimsy of his argyle socks pronounced that he hadn't a care, that he would be among the victors. An unspecified number of the finalists would be picked as winners; maybe the judges would anoint five of them for their quality and promise, maybe they would name only three, but the number made no difference to Philippe. He twirled balletically, arms wide, then squatted and hopped like a Slavic dancer, then struck a set of martial arts poses, extending his arms with his palms turned outward. He mimicked a hero fighting in a futuristic movie, killer rays shooting from his hands.

Following his mishap in the *sitzprobe,* the orchestra rehearsal, and the sting of Summers's baton, Ryan had gone to Philippe for solace and advice, and Philippe had reassured him. But now Ryan stared at his show of invincibility and understood that his new friend could give him nothing. They were too far apart. The other finalists in the lounge stared, too. One ate a banana, potassium being known to prevent trembling. Another, shifting his eyes away from Philippe's animation, gazed down at the ungainly bulging and buckling of his own shirt above his cummerbund. Ryan paced. He touched his toes and did jumping jacks but felt the feebleness of his movements. He grabbed a banana.

A finalist sped past them into a hall beyond, the cuffs of his shirt flapping. He mumbled that he was locked out of his dressing room. But he seemed reluctant to call out for help, like a man suffering the first moments of a heart attack on the street who feels as much embarrassment as fear.

On the carpet in one of the dressing rooms, Deanna lay on her back and just tried to take full breaths. She stood between the Yamaha upright and the crimson sofa, putting herself through mental exercises she'd been taught, tricks that would somehow enhance her high-flying voice: imagining an "openness in the area behind my eyes," or imagining a fountain of water spurting from the top of her scalp and a Ping-Pong ball kept aloft by the vertical stream.

Philippe interrupted his tai chi and burst into Sinatra.

Come fly with me, let's float down to Peru
In llama land there's a one-man band, and he'll toot
    his flute for you

Finishing his banana, Ryan attempted equal insouciance. "I'm a Chiquita banana"—he sang a line from the advertising jingle. The line fell flat. Philippe spilled into a chair. Things got quiet.

"Now we wait," a finalist said, sitting next to Philippe and asking him, "Do you think it'll be any different with everyone out there?"

The singers all knew that the house was packed. Getting no reply, the finalist answered himself: "With the stage lights, we won't even be able to see them."

"Yeah," Philippe said, "but we'll feel them. It'll be a buzz."

"Do you have any weird little things you do before you sing?"

"No," Philippe said.

The finalist bent forward in his chair, almost doubling over. He tapped his heels against each other at a frantic pace. "I brush my teeth with mouthwash," he shared. "Listerine. Afterward, I'm like, *Aaaah! Aaaah!*" He let out two operatic notes.

Philippe said, "I wish I could find someone to play badminton."

To Ryan, everyone's words—even the fact that they were speaking at all—seemed incomprehensible. He had a premonition. If he opened his mouth to say anything, his voice would flee. It would be gone, his larynx useless. Everyone's chatter was making him dizzy. He left the lounge and took refuge in his room.

The concert's master of ceremonies, Joyce DiDonato, one of the Met's star mezzo-sopranos, wafted from her dressing room, blond hair sculpted and blue gown gleaming. Lately, between singing bel canto arias, she'd been performing the role of Sister Helen Prejean, ministering to a rapist and murderer on death row, in an opera of *Dead Man Walking*. Backstage, DiDonato seemed irrepressible; she fluttered past some of the singers, encouraging, ebullient. She strode to the podium, joked with the crowd about never having made it to even the semifinals of this contest, and announced the first singer.

Summers and the Met had selected Philippe to open the performance. The eight would sing their first arias, followed by an intermission, after which the lineup would return, in the same order, with their second arias. Philippe crossed to center stage. The stage floor had been laid with sumptuous reds and blues. Philippe was, in his aria, a king whose army was under siege. He awaited the orchestra's regal phrases and sang a sequence of defiant runs.

Deanna was slated next. Her lovestruck character inhabited her body, and her culminating note soared above the orchestra's strings. "Brava! Brava!" the audience cried.

Ryan's turn came in the middle. The Met had positioned him neither early nor late. They had given him the responsibility neither to seize the crowd's attention nor to stir raptures at the end of the show.

He walked from his dressing room through the yellow-striped doors that cautioned "Do Not Enter." He walked past a crate marked "Dry Ice," past a stretch of gray metal wall, through the stage technician's nook with its video screens. Above him: scaffolding, cables, piping, all of it rising a hundred feet into blackness. He stepped out from the wings and into the lights; he stood on the red and blue flooring. The orchestra's tremulous harmonies rose from the pit, louder and louder. He came in on the right note.

Studia il passo, o mio figlio!

He surrendered some of the ambition that had constrained him in the semis, some of the insistence on purity that had stiffened his performance. A Met coach had suggested that he unlock his feet from the floor. Now he took a step or two in either direction, and the motion was just enough to hint—though there was no set—at the menacing forest surrounding the castle, the peril surrounding him. He relinquished some of the nobility that had hardened his face and dominated his singing. His expression became doleful as well as steadfast; his voice became lost as well as resolved. Unmoving in their seats, the audience seemed to reach out protectively.

Next, the finalist with the lowest voice sang his liquid depths. He engulfed the crowd, and they rewarded him with applause that surpassed Philippe's or Deanna's. Michelle sang after him. Her phrases were sometimes feathery, sometimes on fire. Someone near me murmured, "She's got it," well before she was through. Thrilled with her sustained final note, the audience erupted into approval while her voice still carried. It was intermission.

℘

They let him out of the cell. They led him to a lesser form of isolation in his room. When he "contracted" with staff—the facility's term for making a pledge to show self-control—he rejoined the eleven other kids on the pod. This was the cycle that defined his days: release from isolation; relative calm; freedom within the unit; isolation.

They had to remove him from Anger Busters: he was too hostile. When they escorted him to his room and shut him in, he whipped the door with his belt, lashing and lashing with the buckle. "You are pushing my anger button!" he yelled under the door. "You are pushing my anger button!" He contracted. He came out. The girl he'd targeted came near. He reminded her what would soon happen to her. He informed the nurse who intervened that she would get the same treatment. "White bitch!" he screamed, and faced the nurse with his belt in his hand. Two staff wrenched his arms and ripped the belt away and put him in the seclusion chamber.

The throbbing permeated his brain. "I am uncalmable! I can't manage my fucking anger! It won't work with me!"

He contracted.

He tried to bite a staffer.

Punished. Reentered pod. Traded punches with another boy.

"White Hawaiian bitch!" he yelled at the worker with the yellow-beige skin and inky hair. He could see everyone laughing through the slit. "I know all! I know fucking all!" He beat at the door. "What I'm fucking going to do is not a threat, it's a promise!"

Always, when he folded to the floor, he avoided the texture of the wall, making sure that he didn't lean against that surface, that the backs of his arms below his T-shirt sleeves didn't touch it. He revived, threatened, asserted his omniscience until eventually there was nothing left.

He contracted.

The white Hawaiian bitch was named Priscilla Jenkins. She was Cuban. "He had these gorgeous eyes," she remembered despite the years and despite having left the facility for another career. "But he had nothing except anger. He led with it. Talking to him was like walking on eggshells, because you never knew what would set him off. Punch you, cuss you, kick you. I can picture them both, him and the girl. The wild-haired girl. Big girl for her age. They came at around the same time, both from really broken homes. Her goal was a ride in my Cadillac. I had a white-on-white Fleetwood. A lot of the kids knew about the car.

You share some of your life with them, because you want to connect.

"The two of them would set each other off. When they wound up in the two seclusion rooms at the same time, they would battle it out, screaming. The whole unit echoed. I would think they were done, and they would fire up again. I hated those seclusion rooms.

"After the center, I don't think things went very well for her. But she did get her ride. I told her, 'You give me one good week, and you and I will take a spin.' She had to work so hard to make that happen. The drive was just down the hill. Down the avenue and back.

"I used to tell both of them, 'You're just a mini me.' I couldn't tell them exactly why; that wouldn't have been right. But I'm sure I told them something. I wanted them to know I understood. I wanted him to know I understood his anger. My family came over to Miami when Castro got in power, and my mother, in Miami, this was before she had me, she got on the wrong path. She became a drug addict and a prostitute. My grandmother would get calls when I was a baby. She would find me with a dirty diaper and Coca-Cola in my bottle. My father was gone around the time I was two. I got dumped on my grandmother when I was eight. Off and on my mother would come in, come into my life, high, needles on the glass table. She would cuss me out. She told me, 'You're never going to be nothing but a whore, just like I am.' She said, 'I'm going to wind up taking your child from you, just like Grandma took you from me.'

"A lot of the kids, their relationship with their maternal or paternal figure has been awful. I wanted to introduce them to a healthy relationship, and me being a Cuban woman, I'm big on giving hugs. But this wasn't always going to work. On the unit, you have to be careful. I had a girl, she called me out from the fishbowl, where the staff have their office behind the glass. I was four months pregnant. I went around. I must have ticked her off somehow, because right away she started kicking me in the gut. I couldn't try and stop her—that's what she wants, so we can struggle. I just turned my back, let her kick me in my back, till another staff pulled her away.

"I had a boy tell me—it was during that same time—'I'm going to kill your baby.' That one apologized. But Ryan was from a little earlier. He had those big eyes, so you could see, even with that anger, even with how much he needed you to feel as angry and hurt as he was feeling, there was more to him. You could see his soul. You could see how smart he was. He would challenge you on everything. He was wise with his words. He could pierce your heart. It didn't matter to me. I knew I was just the one in front of him. Sometimes I gave him points when he didn't deserve it. Maybe he was one or two points shy of being on the next level. I would tell him, 'This is a down payment. I know you'll get this—I know you'll get this by the end of the night.' So he could play that Nintendo."

&

Someone on the staff gave him something else: a small radio. He lay still on his crinkly mattress and listened. He landed on a pop station and stayed there. Usher sang, "All

I seem to think about is you." Backstreet Boys sang, "Back-street's back, all right, all right."

He listened and began to sing along softly. He wrote down the lyrics, song after song, as the radio played. He memorized, and joined his voice to Usher's and Nick Carter's and dozens of others, joined his voice to the outside world. What came from his throat, he was sure, wasn't anything anyone would want to hear. If he sensed someone right outside his room or about to open his door, he cut himself off.

He lost the privilege of the radio if he lost control. No set of incentives, not the radio itself, not the Nintendo game, not Jenkins's approval, was able to prevent that: the loss of control. He shed the rewards and was given them back and failed to retain them, as though self-discipline wasn't within his capacity at all.

"Her face will be part of the floor!" he screamed from seclusion, screamed about the wild-haired girl. "They better be ready! They better be ready when I beat her into the floor! They better take me away!"

Isolation ended. He lunged at a boy who would not give up his seat in front of the television. Isolation was reimposed. He focused again on the girl — "I will get her tomorrow morning!" — then switched to his mother, spewing from solitary, "If I ever get sent home, there will be blood and death."

Subdued days went by, comparatively quiet days when the log entries read:

"Watched peers play Nintendo. Prompted numerous times for being disrespectful toward peer, hard time using self-calming."

"No problems observed."

"Prompted for cursing and disrespectful peer interaction."

"Did use self-calming during altercation with peer."

"Observed without incident."

"Some demanding behavior but basically did very well."

"Watched movie with peers. Prompted about talking very loud but lowered voice."

Then, on the day before a scheduled conference call with Valerie, he tried to goad a boy into helping him attack the staff. He told a woman on duty that he would smash her head. He elbowed another worker. Between periods of isolation, he stormed through the unit: "I want fucking popcorn! Bitch, I want some popcorn!"

He grew furious with his mother on the phone the next afternoon and, with a staff member on the line, restated that she had abused him. Not for the first time, he made it clear that he did not want to be sent home. On the unit, he spiraled. There was more seclusion. When he emerged, he was, in the words of the log entries, "hyper...unfocused at times...arguing...loud...very demanding." He seemed, meanwhile, to be skidding backward through years, playing with a remote control car someone had donated to the institution, playing with Legos.

The facility, for reasons unclear in the record, chose to persuade Ryan to agree to live at home again. The state social worker assigned to Valerie had failed to convince her to accept any kind of counseling or guidance within her home if Ryan returned. For Valerie, a few hours of home visits per week was a few hours too many. It was too much intrusion. But she had begun to see a therapist, and perhaps the facility judged that this was enough. The center was under budgetary pressure to move kids through, to avoid the expense of keeping kids for long stretches. The facility might have placed Ryan in foster care, but, by whatever logic, unnoted in the record, the administration decided against this, though Priscilla Jenkins recalled thinking that a foster family would have been the better choice.

Ryan eventually relented, giving his agreement. In the week leading up to his discharge date, after about two months at the facility, he degenerated yet further; he would not brush his teeth, shower, or comb his hair without the staff prodding him through these steps. One afternoon, at a table in the communal area, he sat with a group making bracelets. They slid colored beads onto string. But he couldn't keep his body still. He was so jittery he couldn't get the beads onto the string. He mocked the others at the table, scorned their jewelry, meddled and taunted to keep them from finishing. He went into isolation; he contracted; he railed that he would kick a boy in the head until his skull caved in. Staff members wrestled him into a seclusion cell.

He pledged not to hurt anyone. Soon after he got out, he slapped the face of a woman on staff. "I hit Beth!" he bragged. "I'm going to kill all of them! Look at how many people they need to control me! I'm glad I hit her! Do you see how many fucking people they need?"

Three days before his release date, he let everyone know that a man on duty was about to have his head cracked to bits. He let the girl with wild hair know how pathetic she was.

At breakfast two days before the date, he challenged a boy by pouring milk down his back.

One day before, he told the pod, "I am never wrong!" That same day, a therapist evaluated him. "Met with Ryan. Behavioral and emotional functioning seem well stabilized.... Will be discharged to his mother tomorrow."

EIGHT

At intermission, relief floated through the lounge between the dressing rooms. Exhales and giddy exuberance filled the air. Everyone had sung an aria to a packed Met house. Everyone had won applause. For a minute, the finalists put aside private comparisons and reveled in having completed, together, the first half of a successful concert. DiDonato, the MC whose mezzo voice commanded major roles all over the world, was caught up in the rush and dealt out high fives.

Ryan, his relief sweaty and outsize, nearly let himself wrap her in a hug. His voice hadn't fled. He'd committed no offenses of timing or pitch. He steadied himself, keeping himself from throwing his arms around her bare shoulders and crumpling her gown. But he was light-headed. Inspired by all the grand dresses and tuxedos in the room, he asked her, "Will you be my prom date?"

She pulled him aside. "After you're done with your aria," she said, "stay out there. You were in such a hurry to get off the stage. Let them applaud."

"Will you take a picture with me? A cheesy prom shot?"

He got one of the other singers to snap a photo on his phone. He stood behind DiDonato, smiling wildly.

The relief ebbed from the lounge. Philippe watched Ryan's playfulness, deserted by his own whimsy. He sat in despair, worried that he'd looked frightened as he sang. "I want this to be over," he said almost inaudibly. "It's been too much craziness."

"La calunnia," Ryan's second aria, was a comic tribute to sleaziness and manipulation. In spirit, it was close to "Madamina," his second piece in the semis, and now, as he took the stage after his banter with DiDonato, he embraced the humor and perversity of the role without reservation. He took his hamming to new heights, fingers caressing the air with deceitful, ruinous charm, wide eyes widening with malign obsession, voice seducing with sly excess. On one of his climactic phrases, *"colpo di cannone,"* he advertised his own destructive talents in a voice so rich and explosive that it seemed everyone in the crowd was riveted.

He clenched both fists on his final note, heeded DiDonato's advice, and soaked up the ovation. But his pronunciation had been abysmal. He'd botched the first line. He'd mangled the second. *Leggermente…sotto… tumulto*—all the backward practicing in his room had accomplished next to nothing.

Again the eight gathered in the lounge. The judges were debating, tallying. The audience waited in their seats, trading predictions. The singers told one another that they'd won just by being here, just by getting to the finals. They said this over and over, like a mantra. Ryan tried to believe it.

Through speakers in the ceiling, a voice directed, "Finalists, please come stage right." They proceeded behind the stage to the wings. Two walked arm in arm; the rest surrendered to their separateness, their hunger. They clustered behind the curtains. "Come on," a singer whispered as DiDonato, at the mic, praised this year's group and the tradition of the contest.

"We have five winners today," she announced, and began to read out the names.

"Mr. Philippe Sly."

"Yes!" He expelled the lone word from his body with such energy, and with such constriction in his throat, that it was less than a word; it was a growl—primal, animal. He sprang into the lights and applause.

"Miss Michelle Johnson."

She glided toward center stage.

"Mr. Ryan Speedo Green."

Behind the curtains, before walking out onstage, he danced. He slid sideways, heels and toes twisting in unison. His brain went blank. His soles zigzagged and skated; he slithered and churned. His joy held the force of a mild concussion: a half hour later, he didn't remember a thing about his dancing.

NINE

W E SAID TO him, 'Opera? Where'd you get that from?' "
His aunt Esther—who'd taken in Ryan and Adrian for
a time back while Valerie was with Barry—remembered
when she and her husband first heard about Ryan's new interest, when he was in high school. "We asked him, 'Isn't
that a white thing?' "

It was, from perspectives both African American and
white—and to some degree wasn't. Race in opera was
like race in so many areas a half century after the trans-
formations of the nineteen fifties and sixties: complicated,
fraught, permeated by intractable problems of perception
and preconception.

The history ran like this:

Elizabeth Greenfield, born a slave in Natchez but
adopted by a Quaker from Philadelphia, sang arias for
whites-only audiences in Manhattan a decade before the
Civil War, and Sissieretta Jones, an African American soprano, performed operatic selections at Carnegie Hall in
the eighteen nineties. But these were *concerts*. Greenfield

and Jones and their black descendants in classical singing, no matter how glowing their reviews, weren't welcome in the glamorous realm of opera itself, not in America and only rarely in Europe. Across the Atlantic, a few African Americans sang scattered roles on opera stages during the first half of the twentieth century; in the United States, even when there were black characters to be cast, in Verdi's *Aida* or *Otello*, opera was a white domain.

In the nineteen thirties, when the Met produced an opera of Eugene O'Neill's play *The Emperor Jones*, about a railroad porter, a black man, who becomes a tyrannical ruler on a West Indian island, Paul Robeson was considered for the title role. Robeson, whose father had escaped slavery on a North Carolina plantation and become a Presbyterian minister in New Jersey, was a football all-American, Phi Beta Kappa scholar, and class valedictorian at Rutgers; a Columbia Law School graduate; and, by the nineteen twenties and early thirties, a theater star, celebrated in London and on Broadway for his portrayal of Othello and for two black roles in works by O'Neill, including *The Emperor Jones*. And Robeson's bass-baritone voice was so heralded that he'd been beckoned by British royalty to sing at Buckingham Palace. But the Met passed him over—and gave the part to a white singer, who performed in blackface.

It wasn't until 1955 that Marian Anderson broke the unofficial color barrier at the Met. She had, by then, been celebrated as a recitalist in both America and Europe; the Italian conductor Arturo Toscanini had declared that she had a voice "heard once in a hundred years." In 1939, because of Anderson's race, the Daughters of the American Revolution barred her from giving a concert at Washington, DC's Constitution Hall, but Eleanor Roosevelt arranged for her to perform at the Lincoln Memorial instead, and there, for a crowd of seventy-five thousand, Anderson sang a Donizetti aria and "My Country 'Tis of Thee." That another sixteen years went by before she played an operatic role at the Met was not a simple story. It was not a tale solely of bigotry. Anderson herself felt that she was better off sticking with concerts. Still, those years did go by without the Met courting her or casting any other black vocalist, and when she finally appeared at the Met it was front-page news.

"An impossible childhood dream came true for Marian Anderson last night," the *New York Times* wrote. "It was the culmination of a brilliant international career as a concert performer, and for other Negro singers it was the opening of a big new door to opportunity.... The excitement had been building up ever since Miss Anderson's engagement was announced two months ago.... People from all over the country had ordered tickets, and some in the opera house last night had traveled from as far west as California to be present at this debut. Customers for standing room began to assemble in front of the Metropolitan at 5:30 a.m.... Some of these were Negroes, a rare sight in the standees' queue.... It was a safe guess that no previous Metropolitan Opera performance had so many Negroes in the audience as last night's show. Reporters from the Negro press in the Far West, the Midwest, and the East were in the theater.

"In the center box sat Mrs. Anna Anderson, the contralto's frail, old mother.... In less glamorous locations of the theater were men and women for whom Miss Anderson had been not only a singer but the voice of a people. Two Negro porters at the Metropolitan bought tickets for this performance and proudly took places as members of the audience.... Many in the audience knew that Miss Anderson—like Joshua, but more quietly—had fought the battle of Jericho and at last the walls had come tumbling down."

Anderson was then fifty-eight years old. Her voice was past its prime, and as it turned out, other African Americans did not pour through the "big new door to opportunity." Among black women, Leontyne Price earned an ovation that lasted half an hour after a Met performance in 1961, and she was followed by a thin line of black female voices—Jessye Norman, Kathleen Battle, Denyce Graves—a line that had attenuated by the time Ryan entered the Met contest. Among black men, the history, within or outside the Met, was even more tenuous. Robeson sang in the 1959 Hollywood movie of Gershwin's composition about black life in a South Carolina slum, *Porgy and Bess*—a work that most critics refused to recognize as opera at all until the nineteen seventies, well after Robeson's career was over. William Warfield, one of the richest male voices of the twentieth century, was relegated to a *Porgy and Bess* tour in Europe in the early fifties. Robert McFerrin performed at the Met as the Ethiopian king in *Aida* following Anderson's breakthrough, and in 1956, he starred as the hunchbacked Italian jester in Verdi's *Rigoletto*. But in all the decades of opera after that, in America and Europe, only a handful of black men had made anything of a significant mark.

Eric Owens, who was in his mid-forties, was perhaps poised to become one of those black men. He'd made his career playing a pair of warped creatures—the monster in *Grendel* and, at the Met, Alberich, the fierce and lonely dwarf of Wagner's *Ring* cycle—and I talked with him about the forces at work in keeping African American opera singers so scarce. Partly it was the sentiment that Ryan's aunt had expressed—that opera was "a white thing," that its very sounds were at odds with black identity—and partly it was a matter of education and exposure, of opera being thoroughly unfamiliar, foreign. But Owens, whose upbringing wasn't anything like Ryan's, and who had studied piano and oboe before attending one of the country's most elite conservatories for voice, spoke about other obstacles.

"It's quite a nuanced situation," he said. "We're dealing with art, with the subjective, the incredibly subjective—with the immeasurable. But do I believe that black singers have a harder time—that they're at a disadvantage before they even open their mouths, as they step into a room with the casting director sitting there? Yes. Things are a hell of a lot better than they were sixty years ago. But yes. And some of it is just marketing; it's what your ticket buyers are going to feel comfortable with, unconsciously. There's a song from the musical *Avenue Q*, 'Everyone's a Little Bit Racist,' and that phrase doesn't mean that everyone's closed-minded. But there's a tribalism, a social thing and an evolutionary thing; there's the comfort we feel with the kind of people we've been around since we were born, and, going back to the beginning, there's the whole survival aspect: those other people over there are competing for our food, and we've got to get out and hunt before they do, and be on guard because they're coming to steal our stuff. This mind-set might not be of any use in this day and age, but it's in the backs of our brains. Underneath, it's there. And it bleeds into every facet of our lives. So if I'm a casting director, a white guy, there are a lot of things playing around in my head, things I'm aware of and things I'm not, when a black singer walks in the door.

"It's true that some people are championing the idea of putting singers of color in roles that aren't characters of color, that aren't Othello or Aida or the cast of *Porgy and Bess*. But for the black artist, more often than not—hello and welcome to earth!—there is a double standard. That's the planet we live on. Some of it is a laziness of imagination. You can't ever assume, though, that the color of your skin is why you didn't get a role. Because that can breed your own laziness. The antidote to color, to all the crap going through the minds of the people behind that casting table, is to sing so well that people go, *Oh shit*. You have to overcome the visual. You have to make the visual irrelevant. You have to overcome aurally. I knocked it out of the park in certain roles, and people suddenly thought, *Where's this guy been?* Well, I've been right here, incognegro."

℆

"After the center, I knew where the lowest of the low was," Ryan said. "And I never wanted to end up there again. I was so scared of being put back in that place. I was so scared of being in seclusion. I was going to do whatever I had to never ever to go back, whatever it took mentally. I was not going to be the person I was."

Valerie and her boys moved from the apartment complex, where the police had carried Ryan down the stairs, to a trailer park in Isle of Wight County, halfway to the North Carolina border. This was where he found himself after he was let out. The skinny aluminum boxes floated on a lake of grass, some of it mowed, some of it mangy. Both blacks and whites lived in the trailer park, the blacks mostly on the lesser rows. Ryan's row was all black. Across the road was a treeless cul-de-sac, an all-black low-income housing development. The trailer park and the cul-de-sac lay at the edge of a town whose main intersection, marked by one of the town's two traffic lights, had a Dairy Queen and a couple of gas stations. Up the road, past acres of cotton and corn, the shacks of a black hamlet crowded the pavement, porches spilling forward and outhouses standing behind the shacks.

Ryan and his mother didn't see their new home the same way, not then, not a decade later, in memory. Even the phrase they used to categorize it was different. Ryan called it a trailer park, but as Valerie and I turned at the light and drove toward it, she wanted something understood. "There's a difference between a trailer and a mobile home. I call this a mobile home park. A mobile home is more like a modular home. Anyway, people hear 'mobile home' and they think drear and whatnot. Good gracious! Shoot! I kept it really pretty inside."

The life they lived there, at any rate, was not pretty. The violence persisted, between the brothers, between Valerie and the boys. "I remember one time Ryan said something to someone, running his mouth, talking smack, and these dudes started hitting him," Adrian said. "He was on the ground. Dude kicking him. I was there, and I just stood and watched. I was like, that's what you get for talking smack, you're going to *get* smacked. Then my mom found out about it. She beat my butt, because I didn't try to protect my brother. So I turned around and beat him up all over again."

Not long after he left the facility, the police locked Ryan up again briefly. Neither he nor Valerie could recall what he'd done that time; the past was just not a safe place to travel. And the record on this incident, unlike everything having to do with the center, had been expunged. "Maybe stole something," he said. "Maybe threatened someone at school."

The facility he'd left, the trailer park he'd come to, the family he was imprisoned within, the person he'd always been, the person, he said, who was "the worst of the worst"—he needed to escape everything, escape himself. He had scarcely any notion about how to achieve this. But his desperation was extreme; it exceeded his cluelessness; and he had one advantage. He held within him the lessons Mrs. Hughes had taught, the lesson she had taught with the phrase "content of their character" and the lesson contained in the fact that, until he wound up being driven across the state in shackles, he'd made it from her classroom out into the normal world.

Haphazardly, he took paths of escape. He glimpsed routes away from himself and raced down them. He got inspired by a TV show. *ER* had a character named Dr. Greene—this seemed to Ryan a magnificent coincidence. There was also Dr. Ross, who'd been abandoned by his father long ago and who was now a renegade pediatric surgeon doing anything he could, within and beyond the emergency room, to rescue children. Ryan decided that what he had to be, what he was going to be, was a pediatric surgeon.

And he started to imitate the pronunciation of the doctors. He listened keenly to their patterns of speech. He did the same with the anchors on the TV news. "I wanted people to think I was smarter than I was. To think I didn't live where I lived. I wanted to be different from the kinds of kids I'd always been around. I didn't want to use slang and say the *n* word and sag my pants and spend my time up to no good."

Fear and need and sheer will led him to make the least predictable choices. A year after getting out of the facility, he joined the Latin Club at school. "I was going to hang out with the nerdy kids—not just the nerdy kids, the nerdiest kids. And the teacher who ran the club, and who taught Latin class, he was unbelievably nerdy. We read *The Cat in the Hat* in Latin. We watched a newscast about Pompeii in Latin. I was so bad at it. I was probably the worst kid in there. The other students were the only reason I could do the work at all. They helped me. With the club, we did quiz bowls. You had to slap the table in a specific way. 'Who were the Greek and Roman goddesses of wisdom?' 'Who stabbed and killed Julius Caesar?'"

"It's true," his Latin teacher told me, "that he was not a great contestant. But he was an avid contestant."

Ryan made another decision. His school was integrated, about half white, but divided. "All the black kids hung out with the black kids, all the white kids with the whites. And I tried to hang around with the white kids—the white nerds. They were the ones who were the most different from what I knew. I was going to get as far as I could from what I was accustomed to. I wanted to be part of their world, the white world. I attached myself."

❧

Jared Poulter was scrawny and taciturn, a hermit, and Ryan befriended him in the way that the garrulous can befriend the nearly silent, leaving the reclusive little room to retreat. One afternoon, Ryan invited himself over to Jared's house, in a white neighborhood about two miles from the school and, it seemed to Ryan, in a different universe from the trailer park. "They came in the kitchen door," Jared's mother said. "In walks this black kid in a neighborhood where you don't see any black kids. Jared kind of pointed over his shoulder with his thumb and mumbled, 'This is Speedo.'" Ryan was much taller than his new friend; in the kitchen doorway, his face rose behind Jared's head. "And Ryan stepped up and said, 'How do you do, Mrs. Poulter.' He always addressed us that way—Mr. and Mrs. Poulter. Jared was shy, and here's his new friend, forthcoming and making eye contact."

The Poulters were from Ohio, the father an engineer in the Coast Guard, and the mother a nurse at a hospital. "Get on the back roads here," the father said, "and there's a lot of Confederate flags. They'll tell you it's heritage, not race. But I don't know. Back in Ohio there was surely racism, but it was covert. Here it's public; if you're white you assume any other white shares your opinion. 'Too many niggers there,' they'll say about a certain town. Or

'The wind's blowing the wrong way,' if it's coming from a direction where black people live."

"I was frightened for him," the mother remembered. "Because at that time the sheriff and the deputies here were all white. I was worried that when he was out walking on one of these roads around here, they might take him off to jail. Or he'd say the wrong thing and they might give him a beating."

But Ryan wasn't concerned about the dangers: "I was too excited to be going to Jared's house." The risks were outweighed by the wish for white friendships—and for a connection to what was, for him, affluence. The Poulters became a second family. He loved their house and everything outside and within it. "There was a huge yard with a fire pit. They had a garage and a huge living room, and the kitchen was beautiful—it was so big."

Jared's father liked to have a home improvement project under way at all times. Ryan tagged along on trips to buy supplies; he helped to build a new fence. Amazed that a person could do such things, he looked on and took what roles he was given as the father put up a wall, installed a cabinet, laid a tile floor, mounted a sconce.

"We would cut and chop in the kitchen for Jared's mom," he said. "She made seafood ravioli. She made lamb. She cooked these things I'd never had before." She cooked on appliances that seemed to gleam miraculously.

In the yard, behind the screened-in back porch the family had built, a truck dumped a delivery of firewood, and the father taught Ryan to swing an ax. They split the thick logs and carried the quarters inside and set them aflame in the fireplace that was surrounded by a special type of textured white brick. The family gathered there, Jared and his younger brother and sister, the parents, Ryan. "They were tight-knit," he said. "I have this memory of Jared telling me, 'I think you like my family more than I do.' And it was probably true. There came a time when he was more in his room on his computer, and I was with the rest of them. I was like the misfit stepson. We would watch television together, history shows. They were always educating themselves, always reading books. They were very intelligent. I idolized that. They would pick programs about World War I or World War II, or National Geographic shows, and discuss them. But we joked a lot, too. Later on, when I started dating, a girlfriend of mine visited me at their house, and after that Mr. Poulter would ask me, 'How's that new girl going?' He'd ask me, 'When are you going to find a girlfriend for Jared?'"

Ryan enlisted Jared's little brother to type his papers— his own typing was excruciatingly slow. He joined the family at the edge of the sloped yard, where they ignited more of the wood Ryan had chopped; they fed great quantities into the fire pit, watching the blaze leap and bend as they sat on an old tire and a few lawn chairs. He slept over. Regularly his feet dangled off the top bunk of Jared's bunk bed.

"My mom would get so upset. 'You don't like what I have? What I'm doing for you isn't good enough?'"

The Poulters bought a four-wheeler, and not only did they let Ryan drive it, they forgave him when, halfway around on his first lap, he crashed into the side of the house. And the Poulters rigged up potato guns. He'd never seen anything like it. Beside the fire pit, he stuffed a potato down into the barrel and, wary of this strange weapon, blasted the potato into the sky. It soared over the field of corn that lay behind the Poulters' yard. Exultant, he watched the others stuff and fire, waiting his turn, giddy over their shots and ecstatic over his own: the explosions, the velocity of the potatoes through the air, the distance they traveled above the stalks. They descended only when they were almost gone from view.

"Roman Candles. Bottle Rockets. Screaming Eagles. Helicopters. I don't think he had ever set off fireworks," the father recalled. "When we did that together, he lit up. There was pure joy. He would get the fuse going and step back, and it was ten shots right in a row. Two hundred feet high. Straight over the corn."

Valerie phoned the Poulters' house and ordered Ryan home when he stayed away for days on end—away from the trailer park, away from his mother, who seemed to cast a spell over him. Outside her presence, he was changing, he could feel it. The evil in him was decreasing. The craziness was creeping backward, shrinking. He could banish the memories of his own voice: "I am uncalmable.... I'm going to kill you if you're not careful.... I don't give a fuck anymore.... Look at how many people they need to control me.... I'm going to rip your fucking face off.... I'm going to—" He could come close to trusting himself.

But near her, within the narrow rectangle of the trailer home, he felt the evil resurging, the craziness crouching and ready to take control of him. He struggled against the force she exerted, the way she unchanged him.

He couldn't understand the power she had to weaken him, to leave him helpless against the past. It wasn't that she wanted him to disintegrate, to lose hold. He knew that.

She was proud of the person he was piecing together. She was hawkeyed about his schoolwork, warned him when he slipped. She posted his grades on the refrigerator door. Yet her presence was some sort of poison. She had found work with a real estate agency, pushing rental units, and she was back in community college, close to graduating. But she always seemed to be flailing, and the bitterness she exuded, the discipline she began to delegate to a new boyfriend, the listless air of the trailer park, the semivagrancy of the people there—all of it infected him in a way he felt he could not defeat.

He returned home from the Poulters at her demand. But as quickly as he could, he took his place again at their dinner table. He watched a military history program in the nook with the window bench and the matching green recliners, and fell asleep on Jared's top bunk. His mother told him not to come home. She told him she meant what she said. Since he didn't appreciate what she had to offer, he'd better not set foot inside her door.

"He was on the kitchen phone with his mom every night," the father said, "begging her to take him back."

"We tried to give him his privacy, but we could hear," the mother added. "He was pleading with her, working to get in her good graces. 'Please, Mommy, let me come home.' He was in tears."

Valerie relented after two weeks. He was more cautious after that. But he left a particular remnant of himself in the Poulters' house after every visit, as if to hold his spot there. "Whenever he had a snack—and Ryan loved to eat—he took napkins and twisted them up," the father said. "White paper napkins, in a shape like a ghost. Half the time he seemed to have a napkin in his hands. We'd be sitting there talking, and he'd be winding them up. Or we'd be out, and we'd come home after Ryan had been over with Jared, and lots of food would be gone and the napkins would be all over the house."

"We never knew why," the mother said. "I don't think he was aware of it."

"I never mentioned it to him," the father said. "I was always picking them up. On the chairs. Everywhere. Twisted-up little ghosts."

℘

Ryan and Adrian were together less and less, though Ryan followed his brother into organized football. Adrian played out of desire; Ryan played in emulation and with less talent. They both had size, Ryan's in height and nascent heft, Adrian squat and chiseled, his body not only a salute to his father but a reaction to the asthma he had developed: he refused to be sick.

On the field, Adrian turned himself into a weapon. He played linebacker and was on the special teams; his positions gave him a kind of extra license. "I always wanted to be like the Hulk," he said, talking about the superhero whose herculean strength doubled and quadrupled as his anger rose. "Stronger, faster, hit like a brick. It was too easy. Having armor on my body—it made me feel indestructible, like I could take out kids like no tomorrow. So I became more violent. I sent kids to the hospital."

"He was smelling himself, as we say," Valerie remembered about Adrian during the time they lived in the trailer park. "Acting up and smelling himself and trying to be my senior. One evening I told him to do the dishes. He said something nasty to me, and I threw my slipper at him. He was mouthing off really bad. He told me, 'From now on, I'm not your son. From now on, in this house, I'm the devil.' We tussled. I picked up a pool cue and started swinging at him."

She struck him across the back. He shoved her into a wall and threw two punches. His fists landed a few inches from her face. They crushed two holes into the wall.

He hurried from the trailer park but was soon in a police car, and soon in a group home, where one of the teens ran a drug ring, with the other kids as his salespeople and some of the staff as partners. After a few months, Cecil arrived to take custody. Valerie wasn't having Adrian back.

Ryan hadn't been home when Adrian put his fists through the wall. He was left with the ragged holes and his brother's absence; he didn't get to say good-bye. Gradually his mother explained what had happened. She told him that his father had flown in from California and proceeded straight to the group home. So Ryan understood. He understood that his father had traveled across the country and made no effort to see him, that he'd claimed Adrian and gone.

TEN

At school, Ryan's football coach steered him toward chorus class for an easy credit, and the chorus teacher prodded all her students to audition for the Governor's School for the Arts, a selective program that took kids for the second half of each school day and trained·them in one of various disciplines—classical voice, orchestra, theater, visual arts. Ryan was an eighth grader with little interest in singing. Valerie made Sunday church mandatory, but joining the kids' choir never crossed his mind. Though he had sung—quietly, privately—pop hits at the center, as a way to float beyond his cell, at fourteen he didn't feel drawn to singing of any kind, and he harbored no thoughts that his voice held any talent whatsoever.

He knew nothing about classical music, let alone about opera; but if he didn't audition, he believed, he might not get credit for chorus. He already knew most of the words to "The Star-Spangled Banner"—he guessed this would serve well enough. He just needed one other piece. The chorus teacher handed him a CD and made him memorize the lyrics of a short eighteenth-century love song, "Caro mio ben."

The Governor's School, in Norfolk, took students from all over the southeastern section of the state, and it was required to accept a baseline number from each area. Some districts were easier to get in from, all the more so in classical music.

"We went to the various areas to audition the kids," Alan Fischer said, thinking back to hearing Ryan. Fischer, the chairman of the vocal music department at Governor's, had a trim white beard and prominent dark eyebrows and a rim of gray hair. He'd had some minor success as an operatic tenor, singing secondary roles with regional companies and giving recitals on cruise ships, before coming to Governor's. For the auditions, he brought along Robert Brown, a pianist and voice teacher with a thunderous bass and a dramatic presence. Brown was six four, with an additional inch of box-cut Afro. When they stood beside each other, Fischer's pale scalp was on a level with Brown's chin. Brown accompanied the kids and helped with the judging.

"And at some point before we heard Ryan," Fischer recounted, "Leon came in and told Robert and me, 'There's a young man who's going to be singing for you. Bette taught him. He's a nice kid.'"

Bette was Mrs. Hughes. Leon was her husband, an administrator in the Virginia school system who'd lately been assigned to be the principal at Governor's, though he had no artistic talent of his own. He sported a hairdo that outdid his wife's tight blond curls. His ringlets were dyed a brilliant gold, his nose was large, and his smile was larger.

His body was spritely. He looked like a fairy-tale figure who flitted here and there, blessing those in need. Ryan had known him during his years in Mrs. Hughes's class, because the class had gone on outings to the Hugheses' house and even once to the Hugheses' beach house in North Carolina, with a side trip to the Wright Brothers National Memorial and the hill where the brothers flew their double-winged aircraft.

Mrs. Hughes recalled, "Leon came home that evening and said, 'You'll never guess who auditioned for Governor's today.' And I said, 'Who?' And he told me. I laughed. I said, 'In art?' Because Ryan could draw. But Leon said, 'No, in opera.' I just about fainted. It was impossible to picture."

Alan Fischer said, "Leon must have seen Ryan's name on the list. So he poked his head in and told us, 'Give this kid a chance. Just give him a listen.' He didn't say more than that. But as soon as he left us, I glanced over at Robert and said, 'You know we're going to have to take this kid.'"

Ryan stepped into the audition room and, a cappella, made his way through "The Star-Spangled Banner." Fischer asked what else he had.

"'Caro mio ben,'" Ryan answered, and, unaccompanied, launched in.

Fischer interrupted, commanded him to stop. He told Ryan that he needed to sing with accompaniment. From the piano, Brown asked if he knew when to come in.

He didn't.

Brown asked if he knew how to read music.

He didn't.

Brown motioned for him to stand at his shoulder and

told him he would point to the note when he was supposed to start singing.

As the moment arrived, Brown's finger jabbed the page. Ryan stayed on the melody, but his voice—it was a tenor at the time, before it changed—sounded indifferent to Fischer's ears.

"It was an extreme case of serendipity," Fischer explained about Ryan's getting in. "If you want to talk about luck or the forces of the cosmos lining up, it couldn't have been more so than in his case. He was fortunate to come from where he came from. That gave him a chance. Had he been from another area he probably wouldn't have made it. And he was a boy, and we needed boys in the opera program. And there was Leon to consider. But there was nothing remarkable about Ryan's voice when he auditioned. He could carry a tune—that was it. That may be hard to conceive after hearing him win the Met competition. But there was nothing."

$\mathscr{C}$

When Mr. Hughes phoned to say that he'd been accepted, Ryan was dumbfounded. He understood that it was an honor, and right away his disinterest about auditioning turned into anticipation about going. He had hardly any sense of what he would be learning; he was eager for whatever demands the teachers would make. Then September came, and with it an onslaught. The clefs and accidentals, the measures and signatures and dynamics of a score were totally strange and inscrutable to him; they might as well have been Chinese calligraphy. Ear training was like an exercise in trying to hear a dog whistle—he could no more identify a note played by his teacher on the piano than a human could register the special sounds that dogs obeyed. Was that a G? An F? An A? An E-natural? And what did it mean for a note to be natural? And what was a tonic? And a musical interval? And a chord progression? And timbre?

Valerie's mother, who liked to wear her long gray hair in a style vaguely resembling Thomas Jefferson's wig, had moved into the mobile home because her health was deteriorating. Ryan went to his regular school in the mornings, then rode a bus for forty-five minutes to Norfolk, attempted to learn music throughout the afternoons, and, if he didn't head straight for the Poulters' house, returned home at the end of the day. There his grandmother awaited him. She had dementia.

He loved that she still called him Boo-Bear. Some of his fondest memories were of being at her house in Florida, when he was four or five. He and Adrian had watched pro wrestling with her on TV. Now, though, whenever he walked in the door, he didn't know if she would see him as a stranger or call him Adrian. Usually as he crossed into her sight line she grasped that he was her grandson and which grandson he was. But at random times she identified him as someone—it wasn't clear who; maybe it was Ryan himself—who had come to attack her.

Not everything changed with her illness; it didn't seem to impair her recognition of her favorite wrestlers. Her mind cleared for the epic battles of the WWF. As the strobes pulsed, as the announcers bellowed, as the wrestlers strutted and preened and sprang off the ropes to pummel and lariat and pin each other, she sat transfixed in front of the TV, cheering for her titans. "You got 'im! You got 'im!" Her silvery hair caught the TV's glow.

At his regular school, Ryan made the honor roll. "Some of the white kids would tell me, 'You know, you're the whitest guy we know.' They thought they were being nice, but it definitely hurt. Because I am black. They thought they were complimenting my intelligence, but I would think, *Do you mean that black people are dumb?* It made me—I doubt there's a word for that exact type of anger. And meanwhile, in the honors classes I took, I was one of two African Americans. How messed up is that?

"Black and white kids, both, called me Oreo. The white kids said it thinking they were being funny, thinking *I* thought it was funny. The black kids said it differently. 'Why are you such an Oreo?' 'I can't understand you.' 'I don't speak *proper.*' 'I don't speak white.'

"I wasn't turning my back on them. Or maybe, at that time, I was. In the places where I grew up, there was such a feeling of separation. Black people used to call middle-class blacks, any black who succeeded, bougie. It was a field slaves, house slaves kind of deal. The black kids who told me I was too white, they weren't educated, and they weren't going to get educated. It wasn't even what they wanted. The stereotypes were just fine with them.

"Being African American is so convoluted. It's two hundred and fifty years of slavery. Two hundred and fifty years of endless days, endless servitude. No race since the Jews in the Bible can attest to that longevity of persecution. It was being three-fifths of a human being. And then it was being recognized as one hundred percent of a human being, and still, for another hundred years—no, for longer than that—having to prove yourself to *be* human, to be equal, mentally, physically, socially equal. Even though you picked their crops, even though you built their houses. Even though you built this country. Being African American is overcoming. It's willpower.

"Every other race came here by choice, starting with the Native Americans walking across from Asia. We are the only race who didn't. I was put here. My forebears were brought here in the galleys of ships. There is nothing prouder to me than being African American. There's no race more special in the United States. We persevered. With everything I do, every success that I'm hoping for, there's some spirit out there, the spirit of a person in rags who dreamt of being able to read a book. Or go to a movie. Or run for office. Being African American is the greatest gift God could have given me."

At Governor's, musical terms rushed past him in a torrent, or bobbed meaninglessly in his brain. The only things he understood were the basic facts: that in the classical voice program, in his year, the few other blacks came from backgrounds that had nothing to do with his own; that everyone besides him seemed perfectly familiar with signatures and dynamics; that he had nothing to add when kids talked in the halls about favorite composers; that he had no money and so stayed in the lobby when everyone else went outside for snacks; that his clothes came from Walmart; and that he could not sing.

"I was hopeless. It didn't help that I auditioned as a tenor, and that I grew that summer and walked in with a voice that was who knows what. Low sometimes and squeaky others." Not only was his voice erratic, but he had no concept of how to study a score and work on singing a piece of music. "My voice teacher, my first year, she was a nice woman, but she'd never dealt with someone like me, who didn't know what he was doing at all. She would give me pieces, she would say 'Go learn this section of music,' and I would go home and just stare. Make some sounds. Quit. She didn't understand that I knew absolutely nothing. It was like taking someone who's never once played football and showing them play formations and saying, 'Learn this tonight and come back tomorrow and do it on the field.' She was flabbergasted. She didn't think I belonged in the program, and she let that be known."

He was counseled. He was warned. "I was failing tests right and left."

Fischer remembered, "There was a lot of negative stuff. His attitude—he frustrated easily. He talked back; he muttered. He stormed out of situations. I don't know what his home life was like, but it was like he'd had a lot of negative reinforcement. He was anxious. He had a very, very volatile energy."

On the brink of being told that he could not return after freshman year, Ryan was given a tiny part in the spring production of *The Ballad of Baby Doe,* an American opera. He stepped out onstage and forgot his one line.

⅋

"I have told everyone," Mr. Brown informed him, "that *I* am going to get you where you need to be."

The two of them—Mr. Brown, dapperly dressed, stretching six five to the top of his impeccably trimmed box-cut and booming out every word, and Ryan, at fifteen, only a few inches shorter—seemed to occupy every inch of Brown's studio at Governor's. "So I am letting you know, I am going to beat you into shape. There's no playing around. You are going to do what I say, or it's going to be me who personally kicks you out of this school."

It was the beginning of Ryan's sophomore year. Mr. Brown directed him to lie on the floor below the piano.

℘

Brown had grown up, during the late fifties, the sixties, the early seventies, mostly in Virginia Beach, just outside Norfolk, in a subdivision newly built by an undertaker who wanted a community for his kind of people— blacks who went to his church or churches like it, blacks who shared his way of thinking, blacks of a certain accomplishment, a certain standing. The low, modestly spacious brick houses faced a line of pear trees whose fragile blossoms appeared in profusion every spring. A swath of well-tended lawn, shared by all the residents, sloped down to a small lake. The lake belonged to the community on the opposite shore, a community of similar houses and similar trees, a community for whites. The residents there put up a chain running tight to the waterline on the black side, a chain defending the purity of the water, a chain with signs that read "Keep Out."

Some of the signs bore the additional letters "KKK." The blacks gazed out their front windows at the ripples on the water, the warnings.

Three years after Brown was born, the governor of Virginia gave a speech that was televised and broadcast by radio across the state. "To those whose purpose and design is to blend and amalgamate the white and Negro and destroy the integrity of both races...to those working day and night to integrate the schools...to those who defend or close their eyes to the livid stench of sadism, sex, immorality, and juvenile pregnancy infesting the mixed schools of the District of Columbia and elsewhere, to those who would overthrow the customs, mores, and traditions of a way of life which has endured in honor and decency for centuries and embrace a new moral code prepared by nine men in Washington...to those who would substitute strife, bitterness, turmoil, and chaos for the tranquility and happiness of an orderly society...let me make it abundantly clear, as governor of this state, I will not yield....I call upon the people of Virginia to stand firmly with me in this struggle."

Virginia schools had yielded only slightly to integration by the time Robert Brown, living beside the lake, began attending them. But he was able to visit a local library with his father, who worked as a laborer with the Department of Defense, and with his mother, a teacher of home economics. And there, at the age of six, he picked out biographies of Bach and Beethoven. His parents had no idea why. It was a puzzle—how he got those musicians into his head. But he read their stories and said that he needed to learn the piano.

143

ℒ

"Now take a breath," Mr. Brown instructed as Ryan peered up from the floor. He lectured on relaxing the abdomen, on letting the belly puff, on putting the diaphragm to full use. He assigned Ryan fifteen minutes of breathing on his back each day at home. He admonished that he would know if Ryan failed to do this, and he made the pronouncement that every kid at Governor's knew: "Education without practical application is useless information." This was Mr. Brown's line, his invention and motto; he delivered it constantly to his students, and it echoed through the rehearsal spaces of the school.

Mr. Brown's bass voice, cascading down from his great height, dominated classrooms and corridors, dominated the program's theater as he conducted the chorus.

"I have had an epiphany," he would declaim, prefacing his ideas.

"Do not mess with a diva," he would warn students who were slow to heed him.

"The quarter note is *not* the center of the universe," he chastised singers who blundered in their timing, lingering on a syllable.

"You sound like a bad Baptist choir," he scolded his chorus.

"You are disgracing me. Give me more consonants!"

"This is not Robert Brown's sound! You are not giving me Robert Brown's sound! And yes, it *is* all about me. I'm the diva here. You are an expression of Robert Brown."

Everything he said was spoken at high volume; everything he did was done with animation; every mood that

144

crossed his face was pure—fury, joy—and was accompanied by dictatorial certainty. To the teenagers, he was a
legend, fearsome, loving. And for Ryan, to be singled out
by him, to be made his personal project, to absorb all his
attention during their sessions in the studio, was to feel that
good fortune had scooped him up.

That first day, after the breathing exercise, Mr. Brown
told him to stand. "Now you are going to drop the chain.
Singing is like a sport. Singing is physical. You played
football—you wouldn't just go out and start hitting
people." He showed Ryan how to stretch, how to "let the
chain go," link by link, slackening the body in increments
at a pace that seemed, at first, unbearably slow, from his
scalp to the base of his spine, from the backs of his knees
to the bottoms of his heels.

There was exercise after exercise like this, addressing
Ryan's anatomy. Somehow Mr. Brown unlocked his rib
cage; it felt like Mr. Brown stretched his very bones. He led
Ryan through scales and through octave leaps so he would
begin to intuit how that span sounded. They couldn't easily
find time for lessons. The only chance for a regular slot
was in the early evenings; Mr. Brown said that he would
stay late. "I don't know what I'm going to do with you,"
he lamented during their initial hours. One meeting per
week, he said, would never suffice, though their goal was
that Ryan learn just enough so he could remain at Governor's. Ryan required two meetings, minimum. Mr. Brown
offered to tutor him, unpaid, as much as he needed. And
because Ryan had no way to get home once the last school
bus was gone, Mr. Brown drove him the forty-five minutes
to the trailer park in his car with the license plate that

read "Batovn." The law didn't allow enough letters to spell "Beethoven."

⚬

As Ryan entered the trailer, Mr. Brown's aura tended to fade. He felt foolish breathing on the floor. But if he went for his next lesson having skipped any of the exercises he was assigned, exercises that became more complex as the months went by—minor scales, scales with melismas at the end—Mr. Brown would cut him off. "That's it. We're not going to be singing any music today." He seemed, to Ryan as a teenager, semitelepathic in his ability to detect when Ryan had failed to practice, though, more likely, mistakes on the scales and melismas gave him away. As punishment, he would torture Ryan with an hour of theory.

Partly through his powers of understanding and partly because Ryan confided in him during breaks in the studio and along the nighttime highway heading home, Mr. Brown knew that Adrian was gone, that Ryan's father had been gone basically forever, that his grandmother had recently died, that his mother was struggling, that she was proud that her younger son was in Governor's but doubtful that this training in classical music could be of any use, that it could amount to anything of value.

There were things Ryan didn't say. One was this: his mother had taken him to Hooters on his birthday, snapping photos of him surrounded by breasty waitresses in low-cut tank tops and red short shorts. She had determined that without a father in the picture this was what a mother ought to do. Somehow she arrived at this conclusion despite her churchgoing and her Bible study and her decree that he couldn't date until he turned sixteen.

Her efforts at being both mother and father didn't make much difference in the way things went between them. At the door of the mobile home, Ryan found himself, one night during his sophomore year, picking up a metal stake from the horseshoes game his mother kept outside. He clutched it in his hand. Valerie was inside; she had locked him out for some infraction. He stood there, poised to smash his way in.

He put down the stake before following through on his impulse, but not before his mother phoned her current boyfriend and told him to deal with the situation. The man drove over and told Ryan to get into his car.

He steered them to a local baseball diamond, unlit and dusty. He directed Ryan to get out, stepped out himself, and made a show of locking the doors. Ryan got the message: he wasn't going to be able to scramble back into the car for refuge.

"You going to threaten your mom?"

Ryan said that he hadn't.

The man shoved him backward against the hood and doubled him over with the first of his punches.

℘

"How he came to love classical—that is a mystery," Yvette Wyatt, Mr. Brown's cousin, said. "Robert and I grew up like brother and sister, but how that came to be I do not know. All I know is that he always did. He ate it, he drank it. That was his passion. In the car, he kept his radio locked on the classical station and waited for opera to come on."

Wyatt led the chorus at Booker T. Washington, a high school across town from Governor's. Her singers were black. She, too, had been drawn to classical music as she'd grown up, but for her, the attraction had begun as a teen, not as a young child, and it had taken hold through a teacher, rather than arising without cause, as it seemed to have done in Brown's mind. And for her, it was only a fraction of the repertoire that moved her. For him, it was almost everything.

The two of them had collaborated during their college years: their voices, his piano. They gave small concerts, performing classical pieces and, too, spirituals like "Steal Away to Jesus," songs he cherished for the history they contained, the lyrics whose lineage ran back to slavery. He loved to perform them with classical formality. Listening to Leontyne Price, the African American opera star, sing "Ride On, King Jesus," in the same shimmering and vaulting tones that had won her ovations at the Met, put him in a place of bliss.

"But gospel," Wyatt said, shaking her head, "gospel he called trash." The distinction was in the style, in the purity and operatic flourishes and meticulous tempo of spirituals—at least when they were sung the way he felt they should be sung—and in gospel's graininess and raspiness, its howling and carrying on. Gospel was rough; it was clamorous. In the back and forth between lead singer and choir, in the competition between choir and band, in the convergence of lead singer and choir and congregation, gospel bordered on sheer noise.

Yet for all his devotion to the music he considered superior, and for all his disdain for the music he thought was barely music at all, the church sounds he grew up with were inside him. Shiloh Baptist, where his father was a deacon, dated back over a century. Its stone building east of downtown Norfolk had grand turrets surrounding its main steeple. Inside, behind the pulpit, the choir's pews rose sharply toward a scarlet curtain, and behind that lay the baptismal tank. The sanctuary, with its paneled wooden divider in front of the choir's section, and with its high-backed wooden altar chairs for church dignitaries, expressed a measure of reserve. But reserve gave way when Shiloh's choir got going.

I'm going to take a trip in that good old gospel ship
And go sailing through the air

There were howls and cries, hissings of cymbals and poundings of keyboards, abrupt pauses and abrupt accelerations, surges of voices and drums. The choir wasn't as unbound as some; at Shiloh, the lead singers didn't tear utterly free of melody and harmony, giving themselves over to hoarse and plaintive half shrieking as they left language behind. Still, there was no shortage of raw yearning.

When that ship comes in, I'll leave this world of sin
And go sailing through the air

That yearning was part of him, embedded in him, Wyatt said. She had grown up in an African Methodist Episcopal

149

church that favored relatively restrained music, but she sang gospel in her current church choir. She seemed to radiate the jubilance of her Sunday music. Big glittery earrings lent extra light to her toothy smile. Brown, she went on, was gay—more or less openly in some areas of his life, like at Governor's, and secretly in others. He'd told Wyatt back in high school, and she'd assured him that she'd already guessed it and that it wouldn't change a thing in their friendship.

In his thirties, Brown wandered away from Shiloh. Eventually he settled at the nearly all-white Unitarian Church of Norfolk, and took on the part-time job of directing the Unitarians' two-Sundays-a-month choir. This wasn't because he felt affinity with the Unitarians' almost secular, God-free ideas. And it wasn't because he enjoyed their constrained, uninspired, and feeble singing. It was because the church had openly gay members; it was because the church made its acceptance of homosexuality and all manner of diversity prominent in its principles. Shiloh, like the other traditional churches that he knew, and like the church Wyatt now attended, took Leviticus at its word: "If there is a man who lies with a male as those who lie with a woman, it is an abomination." Death would seek out such a man if he did not reform.

§

The classical singers of the Governor's School took a trip to New York, to the Met, during Ryan's sophomore year, and Mr. and Mrs. Hughes paid his way. The kids saw *Carmen*. They crossed the plaza with the white stone columns; they passed the fountain with the innumerable plumes; they approached the immense windows of the opera house with the murals—angels and their instruments—hanging behind the glass; they stepped under the chandeliers and stood at the top of the winding stairs with gold railings. "It was like being inside a palace. It was like being inside a royal wedding. It was so overwhelmingly beautiful."

The curtain rose, the opera began. "The singing, the sets, the outfits—I was transported," Ryan said. The toreador, his lapels lined with brocade, swaggered through the horde of bullfighting fans, touched their outstretched fingers, flung them his hat, took as his due the fawning of women wearing ruffled, plunging necklines. He sang about his own life, and everyone in the crowd onstage—men lifting their drinks in tribute and women lifting their hands to be kissed—sang in choral agreement.

Le cirque est plein du haut en bas
Les spectateurs perdant la tête...
Car c'est la fête du courage
C'est la fête des gen de coeur!...
L'amour, l'amour, l'amour,
Toréador, Toréador, l'amour t'attend!

The arena is packed from top to bottom
The spectators are losing their heads...
It is the celebration of those who have courage
It is the celebration of heart!...
Love, love, love,
Toreador, Toreador, love awaits you!

151

"*Carmen* is in French," Ryan said, "and up to that point I'd had no exposure to French, none, zero. One of my teachers had us do some research about the story, so I knew a little about what was going on. And at the Met, there are the translated words on the back of the chair in front of you. The whole opera, I was reading, looking up and down, up at the stage and down at the words, trying to follow. But then, during the toreador's aria, something happened. I stopped. I quit reading.

"The second he started to sing, everyone's attention—not just the cast and the chorus, not just Carmen, I mean the attention of the audience—it hit a new level. The energy. It was so intense. And I don't think I breathed for five minutes. My eyes were glued to the stage. It didn't matter that I didn't know the words. I knew exactly what he was singing—a song about power.

"There was a standing ovation when he was done, an ovation in the middle of the scene. I'd never heard applause like that, like thunder. There wasn't anyone in the house who wasn't up and clapping.

"I knew I wanted that feeling. Some of it was all the masculinity in the song, and some of it was the ovation, but it was also about the language, how he bridged that gap of language between me and him with the music. He made me understand."

That night, the mezzo playing Carmen was an African American, Denyce Graves. Her voice dipped seductively, elevated coyly, turned every man onstage into a supplicant. Mr. Brown was acquainted with Graves somehow, and after the performance he took the kids backstage. Ryan didn't know enough to realize how unusual it was to be there. But he was stunned when Graves, saying hello to the students, singled him out for a hug.

Minutes later, as the kids traversed the plaza, with the chandeliers at their backs and their evening ending, Ryan veered over to Mr. Brown.

"I'm going to sing at the Met," he said.

ELEVEN

G IVE ME YOUR T. rex mouth," Mr. Brown demanded
in the studio. Dissatisfied with Ryan's attempt, he demonstrated. He opened his own mouth wide. Even in normal
positions, Mr. Brown's was an oversized mouth. Now it
looked like the mouth of a monster in a children's book. He
twisted his jaw this way and that, baring his teeth, grimac-
ing, making Ryan laugh, making him feel childlike, even
as they grew more serious after the New York trip. Ryan
mimicked the gaping jaw, the teeth. It was all an effort to
heighten his awareness of the muscles in his lower face.

"That's it, that's it!" Mr. Brown's approval verged on a
roar.

But whenever they moved from exercises to singing,
Ryan sensed his teacher searching around inside him in
futility, trying to find a voice that might lurk somewhere
within. "Sing," Mr. Brown urged. *"Sing."*

He asked if Ryan was tired. He asked if he'd gotten a
snack before their session. He asked why not, and began

154

giving Ryan money for food. This didn't cause impressive tones to suddenly flow from Ryan's larynx, through his pharynx, and out his mouth, any more than Ryan's hopeful words about someday singing at the Met turned him into a fast-progressing student of music's technical aspects. Bewilderment didn't clear; mental stamina didn't arrive. He didn't begin doggedly cracking the codes of notation and identifying pitches and mastering musical theory. But Mr. Brown's gesture of keeping him fed before their lessons made Ryan feel that this man was absolutely determined to shape him into something worthwhile, even if the exact form of that something was unknown, even if it might have nothing to do with singing.

⅞

At a gathering of high school chorus singers from around the area, Ryan met a soprano, a girl whose straight red hair swayed in a ponytail, who popped up in front of him and said something nice about his voice. He stammered out praise for hers. Her mere awareness of him came as a shock, and that day they ate lunch together, took their breaks together. At the end of the weekend-long event, he knew that both her mother and father had died years ago. She gave him her phone number, and from that Sunday evening on, they talked by phone nearly every night.

She lived with her grandparents, and whenever he called and one of them picked up, he took care to chat with them politely. Then they handed the phone over to their granddaughter, and she and Ryan mapped out their future together. He had explained his mother's rule about not dating till he was sixteen. They both kept track of precisely how many days remained until his birthday.

The calls were their only contact. But she mentioned that she would be singing in her school's talent show a few weeks before his birthday, and he promised he would be there, that he would win his mother's permission, that he'd convince her not to count it as a date. Even if his mother refused, he said, he would see her performance one way or another; he would be in the audience no matter what. She told him not to do that. She insisted that they should wait; his birthday was so close.

He agreed. He said he would be patient—but told himself that she was uneasy about how well she would sing. What he should do, it dawned on him, was surprise her: go; sit in the back; make sure she didn't notice him; hear her sing; wait in the lobby, or wherever people waited at her school; walk over to congratulate her when the show was done and her insecurity was in the past. It made sense to him that she didn't want him there. She'd told him that she'd auditioned for Governor's and hadn't gotten in. Her insecurity was partly on account of that. But he knew she would sing wonderfully.

He needed a ride to the show. Valerie listened to his plan and decided that it was okay. She helped him pick out a necklace at a discount store, to give the girl after the performance. She paid for the haircut he begged for, a box-cut Afro. He dressed in the best clothes he owned, picked and patted and picked and patted his hair, and drove with his mother to the girl's school. Valerie and Ryan slipped into seats at the rear of the auditorium, where, watching his soon-to-be-girlfriend onstage, he felt tears creeping from the corners of his eyes, caused by how well she sang.

After the show, she burst into the lobby and hugged her grandparents. He sidled through the crowd of families and teachers. He told her how amazingly she'd sung, how amazing *she* was, how he'd hatched his plan of surprise, how he'd made it all happen. He reached out to shake her grandparents' hands, introducing himself. Yet he was hardly conscious of them; he was still gushing over her talent and his own stealth.

Valerie tugged at him from behind.

"I want to talk with you," his mother said, grabbing his hand and pulling him away. He was baffled, angry, but she wouldn't let go. She drew him across the lobby. He was too confused to resist. "I saw the way they looked at you," she said.

He refused to believe what she told him in the car: that he would never speak with the girl again, that her grandparents would forbid it, that they hadn't known he was black, that Valerie had seen the entire story on their faces.

On the day before his birthday, his mother picked up the phone. She asked who was calling, handed him the receiver. The girl was sputtering, crying, making clear in halting phrases that she was at a friend's house, that her grandparents had put the phone off limits, that if she ever saw him or spoke with him again she would be put out of their house.

He managed to ask why.

"Because they don't want me to become something I'm not."

157

ℒ

The twice-weekly sessions with Mr. Brown were supposed to last one hour but sometimes went twice as long. He had Ryan run scales while rocking back and forth and side to side, as if to shake free any potential he had, to loosen it from the lining of his lungs. He had Ryan sing with one arm starting across his torso and sweeping slowly outward, openward, degree by degree along a half circle, the painstakingly gradual motion meant to improve the way he utilized the most crucial part of his instrument: air.

There was, after a year of lessons, an increasing solidity to Ryan's sound. It was as though a dimension had been added; his tones were more spherical, less thin, more plush. Fleetingly, his singing could be entrancing. And confidence was nudging aside the terror that had made him forget his single line in his first opera. In a school recital, when he was sixteen, he sang a romantic ballad from the musical *Camelot*. The ballad had a classical formality; opera singers frequently performed it. Mr. Brown felt sure enough of Ryan's skill to suggest that he flood the last word with emotion by cresting higher than the written note.

No, not in springtime, summer, winter or fall
No, never could I leave you at all

In the audience, Valerie was weeping, as was Mrs. Hughes, who'd come to hear him. "There you go," Mr. Brown said afterward. "There you go." Then he and Ryan got back to work.

"Robert's own training was much more in piano than

voice," Yvette Wyatt, his cousin, said. "He did sing in the Virginia Opera for a good little while, though. And anyway, he could teach opera like nobody's business. He could fill those kids with that tremendous passion he had, and he knew how to bring out that operatic sound. But then the kids at Governor's, they're different from the kids I'm teaching. My school is what is considered an 'urban' school; we're ninety-five percent African American. The students are poor. Lots of them come from where Ryan comes from, those kinds of family situations, that kind of hardship. At Governor's, even the black kids, when they reach there, most of them, they've already been exposed somewhat to a mixture of music, because of the better environments they've grown up in. Robert used to tell me, 'I don't see how you do it. I couldn't teach at your school.'"

As a teenager, Wyatt had been enchanted by a wide array of genres: pop, classical, gospel, spiritual. They had all beckoned, and she sang them all, bewitched by the beauty of each. But she subscribed to a controversial theory; in the world of music, it was rejected as often as it was accepted. "The African American voice is located lower down. It's more about the throat area, less about the head tones. The difference is natural." She had needed training, during college, to sing classical pieces in the intended style. "I had a teacher who helped me to develop, I won't say a more European sound, but a more pure sound. More legato. Smoother and brighter and not so heavy and grainy. And more coming from the head, the face, the mask. So the sound comes out this way." She gestured, her hand at her cheekbones, her nose, her brow, and moving forward, away from her face. "And less from here." She moved her hand to her throat. "It was a challenge for me to learn. It was a struggle. But for my students it's even more diffi- cult; it's harder than it was for me. That's because for my kids, it's not just the naturally heavier timbre of our African American voices; it's that they've never had the exposure to that other music. And it's another thing. It's their *lives*. Cer- tain brighter styles of singing don't make sense to them. I have to do a lot of explaining.

"I have a small ensemble of girls, and I taught them, for competitions, 'In These Delightful Pleasant Groves.' It's a Henry Purcell piece. It has a lot of *ta ta ta ta-ta-ta-ta- ta*. And they said, 'I can't sing like that, my voice is not like that.' I said, 'Y'all going to have to become little white girls.'" She laughed. "They were like, 'All right, Miss Wy- att. I don't know how we're going to do *that*.'

"I taught them what was going on in history. This is who was king. This was where the singing was performed. I gave them visuals. I taught them, 'This is what you have to do: it's airy. It's not harsh and it's not heavy. You got to get away from that weight. It's got to be *dee dee dee*. And you have to have the proper dynamics. The pianissi- mos have to be pianissimos, and even when you're singing forte, you've got to keep it light; you can't oversing.' It took work. It took me almost six months for them to finally get it. But once they did, they loved it. In competitions, they scored superior. It gave them something.

"What I'm saying, though, it isn't always the case. I had a young lady, she had an operatic voice. It was her God- given voice. That was where her voice sat; that was where it lay. She tried to sing R & B. She loved Alicia Keys. She wanted to *be* Alicia Keys. But that's not what her voice was. I told her, 'You're not an Alicia Keys.' I had her listen to Denyce Graves. That was the sound she had. But I couldn't really get her to change. And meantime, she dropped out of school. That's the world I teach in. She didn't even get to graduation. She just let it go. She took that talent and isn't doing anything with it at all. She's working at McDonald's."

What Robert Brown had gleaned in Ryan's voice when he first offered to teach him privately for free, what, if any, sliver of special talent, Wyatt didn't know. Had he heard intimations of natural operatic tones? Or had other vocal qualities pulled him toward Ryan? Had he sensed a potential for uncanny volume, a voice that might one day carry throughout vast halls unamplified, a sheer strength essential to opera? Or had Brown been inspired, at first, by nothing about Ryan's singing? Had he simply responded, as a teacher, to a young man on the precipice of failing out of Governor's, and, all the more, as a black teacher to a young black man in danger of being tossed out of his mostly white school?

What Wyatt recalled, more specifically than how her cousin spoke, early on, about Ryan's sound, was how he spoke about Ryan's life. "He would talk about his situation. He would say, 'I've got to get him something to wear. We are going to Nordstrom's.' I would tell him, 'Robert, you don't necessarily have to take him to Nordstrom's. You can take him to J.C. Penney's.' But he would say, 'J.C. Penney's is not where I shop. That's not where we're going.'"

It wasn't only clothes. Mr. Brown gave him driving lessons. This followed their work in the studio. He let Ryan steer his car around an empty parking lot and then to a fast-food drive-through. Sometimes, after retaking the wheel and driving Ryan home, Mr. Brown went in if Ryan and his mother were spiraling.

"He was our middle guy. He would intervene," Ryan said. "I needed that."

"Ryan was trying to figure himself out, smelling himself, and whenever it got serious enough, it prompted me to telephone Mr. Brown," Valerie said. "He would get Ryan to behave himself. Straighten him out."

Or as those on the Governor's faculty who heard Mr. Brown's account of his role with Ryan and his mother told it, he would calm Valerie down, run interference for Ryan. "That woman!" he would say.

꧁

During this period, at his regular school, Ryan said, he felt at times like a foreigner. "In history, it was like I was a liaison, like I was a representative from all the chapters of oppression. I don't think there were any other black kids in my honors history. We didn't have any Jews, so even on the Holocaust it felt like the questions were aimed at me, like everyone was waiting for my opinion, like, *Your people were oppressed. What do you think about this?*

"We spent a good while on Hitler and World War II. Then we watched *Schindler's List*. And after the movie, I got upset. I asked why we didn't watch a movie about slavery. We'd studied slavery for maybe two or three days. Our teacher said something about not wanting atrocities like the Holocaust to happen again. And I said, 'Didn't the Holocaust happen in Germany, and didn't slavery happen

here? Weren't my ancestors enslaved by your ancestors?'
We ended up watching *Glory,* that movie about black soldiers in the Civil War. And after that, I was *really* the
representative. Everyone wanted to feel like now that we'd
discussed the movie, we'd done enough."

℘

Valerie's life was in yet another vortex. She had a car acci-
dent. "An old man ran me off the road," she said. It left her
dependent on painkillers and, for a while, unable to work.
And she was feuding with her family over medical bills that
remained after her mother's death. "I couldn't make my
payments, and I couldn't make the electric bill, and everything just got out of hand." Valerie and Ryan were forced
to move out of their home when he was seventeen, during
his junior year. She told him they were leaving because the
trailer park wasn't safe. A pair of kids from the low-income
apartments across the road had broken into their place.
They'd broken into twelve others. Valerie didn't say that
the real reason they were moving was because she could no
longer afford the mobile home.

She found something in a town closer to Norfolk, a tiny
green wooden house that looked to her like a shack. When
she first saw it, people were drinking on the back steps, and
there were empty bottles and used condoms along the strip
of side yard and on the tight square of dirt and grass behind
the house. But she had no better options; she signed the
lease. She and Ryan moved their belongings one afternoon,
driving across the concrete overpass at one end of their new
street. The overpass spanned railroad tracks. It rose and

descended steeply; it felt like a wall, separating the street from the rest of the town and making the street seem like a remote valley. The wider houses of the valley were fronted by porches with crumpling roofs; windows were covered by trash bags instead of glass; train horns resounded. "No Trespassing" signs marked most of the front doors. Valerie thought of the sign nailed to the clapboard of her place as a plea to any cop who might come by on patrol. It meant that if a cop noticed anyone on her low stoop, he should deal immediately with that person; he should assume that person was trouble; the cop shouldn't hesitate.

When she and Ryan had finished most of the move, when she had screwed a light bulb into the fixture above the stoop and flipped on the switch as an announcement that this was now a home, she drove him back to their old town, where he would spend the night with a friend while she cleared the last things from the mobile home and did some arranging in the new house. It was after dark when she returned. It took her a few moments to recognize what was wrong. The stoop light was out, the bulb smashed and the fixture pried from the wall, dangling by wires. Above the air conditioner, which she'd mounted in a side window earlier that day, the glass was shattered and gaping.

She got into her car and locked the doors, called the cops, and waited. They arrived and escorted her into the house. She saw the spots of blood where someone had cut himself trying to steal the air conditioner or trying to open the window and get himself inside. A shard of cement, hurled through the glass, lay on her floor. More than one squad car appeared, and the cops questioned neighbors who were now looking on from their porches, from their yards. The police came back to her; they said there had been no witnesses. They asked if she had another bulb.

As one of them worked on rigging the fixture back onto the wall, something overtook her; she sprang down the two steps and into the middle of the street. "Nobody saw nothing? Nobody got nothing to say? You maggots," she yelled up the block, in the direction of the railroad bridge. "You maggot butts. Nobody couldn't call the police?"

A cop moved close. The bulb blazed again, reaching across the pavement. He nodded toward the house opposite hers. "They don't want that light on," he told her.

The dilapidated house across the street, she and Ryan learned over the next days, was the headquarters of a drug trade that went well beyond the two-bit dealing they were used to living with. This was a thriving business, with a moneyman always stationed under a tree at their end of the block, taking cash from the cars that streamed through, and a dispenser posted under another tree at the far end, handing out whatever had been paid for. In plastic garden chairs, henchmen and hangers-on spent their hours under the branches. A supervisor strolled up and back, governing in red sneakers, red jacket, red cap. Car speakers reached annihilating volumes. Ryan's bedroom window, with blinds he kept down, faced the street.

Years before, Valerie, with Ryan in tow, had begun attending a fledgling church in this town, a twenty-minute drive from the trailer park. The church's flock was led by an elfin pastor, a Nigerian. He favored sharply pressed khakis and pin-striped shirts when he wasn't conducting services. In the pulpit, he wore only white. Pastor Ola considered himself a missionary, sent from Africa to rescue souls in America, and over the years that Valerie had known him, his congregation had grown. The church was about to move from rented rooms to a strip mall storefront next to a Domino's Pizza. Valerie told Pastor Ola her fears about her new neighborhood, her street, her house. "I don't know what might be in there," she said.

Ola mobilized his wife and several congregants, and the prayer team bunched into the kitchen and then clustered around the stoop. "We thank you for providing this place, Father; we thank you in the name of Jesus," Ola prayed loudly, wearing large eyeglasses above his thin mustache. "It's a new place, Father; it's a different place from the trailer where they were. The community, O Father, is not the best of communities. And we petition you, O Father. We petition you to send your ministering angel to this mother and her son, Father, to shield this house, Father, so if they shoot, Father, the bullets will go this way and that in Jesus's name and miss this house, Father. Send your security; make this house a house of refuge. Father, provide this mother what she needs to raise up her son. We pray in Jesus's name that destiny will come forth in this young man, Father. We pray that he will be all you have designed him to be. We pray, Father, that even as people listen to him speak and sing, Father, and hear him sounding different, Father, that it will be to his advantage, Father, and no weapon formed against him will prosper."

The neighborhood used their side yard as a cut-through. One afternoon, in the space alongside the clapboard wall, Valerie put her body in front of one of the dealers.

"May I help you?"

He indicated that he was headed to the next street.

She let him know about the difference between private and public property.

He asked if she was serious.

She said that she was, and the dealer retreated, to the laughter of his colleagues on their chairs. They taunted him; he tested her again. But after a second standoff and another spray of laughter, a new map was drawn in the minds of the community: the route to the parallel street involved walking to the corner. The lady who'd called the cops and screamed down the block on her first night was too crazy to educate.

But the map didn't always matter. Ryan was out one evening and Valerie was home with a niece of hers when gunfire erupted alongside the house and behind it, bullets striking just above Valerie's bedroom window while she and the girl pasted themselves to the floor. She phoned 911. The cops came, arrested no one. That was the way it went when she called, and she called frequently—to report the dealing, the thudding music, the cars idling constantly on her side of the street.

The dealers didn't appreciate the attention. They surrounded Ryan on the street. "You calling them? Your mamma calling?"

He had begun to think of the area not as a valley but as a crevasse, the people there having plunged to the base of an unclimbable chasm. No one in that chasm was going to come to his rescue as the group encircled him; no cop car was just going to happen by. "Half of them were in their twenties. The tallest one was six six, no shirt on, in my face about snitching. It was broad daylight, but people on the block were pretending nothing was happening. These guys were getting ready to beat the living shit out of me. You grow up in places like that, you know there's no one going to stop it when someone gets jumped."

But his mother, ever vigilant in their new neighborhood, charged out the front door and off the stoop. "Don't you know I come from New York? Don't you know I'll get half of New York on your maggot butts?"

Slowly, a kind of three-way equilibrium was established. Valerie persisted with the police, clinging to the trust that if she called enough times, eventually the law would shut the dealers down; the police drifted through, their sympathy on that first evening, when they had reattached her fixture and replaced her bulb, amounting to nothing; and the dealers did some policing of their own. One night someone knocked on her door. Alone in the house, she peered through a window: the man at her door wore only his underwear. He seemed to be a customer of theirs, an addict who'd lost his bearings. He banged at the door again and again, and railed, "I know you're in there." She yelled at him that she was calling the cops, and he warned her not to, and kicked and slammed and threatened, and went quiet. From the window, she watched the dealers drag him into the street and stomp him with their Timberlands until he lay still and bloody, and was loaded into an EMT truck.

The first half of Ryan's days were spent at a new school.

In the halls and on the bus that brought him there, the kids announced that he was a snitch, because of his mother's campaign. For the same reason, they declared that he hated black people. On the bus one morning, he studied a score.

"What's this shit?" Someone took the music from his lap.

"It's opera."

"Opera? Opera? You singing opera? You singing white people music?"

From the rear benches, an impromptu chorus emitted operatic trills.

"You trying to be white?"

The chorus sang out in screeches.

"Yeah, opera. We knew you was white."

&

He endured the mornings by daydreaming of the afternoons. Sometimes, at the piano, Mr. Brown stomped his polished shoes, ecstatic over the improvements Ryan was making after all their sessions together. "That's your voice!" he cried out. "That's your voice!"

It wasn't that layered tones were flowing endlessly from Ryan's body. It wasn't that he could create enchanting vocal hues throughout an aria or even just produce every note in a piece without tipping sharp or slipping flat. But there were measures, runs, passages when the notes were immaculate and the hues were lush. In his senior year, he won the lead male role in Mozart's *The Marriage of Figaro*, which the school did in English. His character, the count's valet, worried that his true love might be ravaged by the count. Pacing the stage and vowing to thwart his master, Ryan

169

was captivating, his voice fluctuating between a guileful lilt and vengeful, barrel-like depths.

That year, Mr. Brown and Mr. Fischer helped to make Ryan an audition video, so he could try to get into conservatories. "Hello, my name is Ryan Green," he said into the camera, "and I'll be singing 'Riding to Town.'" The song was an early twentieth-century poem by the black writer Paul Laurence Dunbar set to music by the black organist and composer Thomas Kerr. As Mr. Brown played the introductory chords on the piano and Mr. Fischer aimed the camera at Ryan, he blinked and blinked. His forehead creased into furrows. He exhaled visibly, licked his lips, looked to his side and down at the floor.

When labor is light
And the morning is fair

The song was composed to be cheerful, even rollicking; Ryan's expression was stoic. His arms hung immobile at his sides. He hit some notes with verve and sustained them with burnish; other notes brought strain to his voice and to his face. He finished and waited through Mr. Brown's final measures with a look of half-concealed dejection.

Yet the passages that he'd sung well were enough. Through the lobbying of Mr. Fischer and Mr. Brown, he was accepted at the University of Hartford's conservatory, up in Connecticut, and offered a scholarship. It wasn't a first-rank music school, but it was a place where the faculty might be willing to invest their time in him, to do at the next level at least something of what Mr. Brown had done for the past three years.

Fischer sent him off with trepidation. He feared that although Ryan had done excellently in *The Marriage of Figaro,* his handicaps were too severe. He feared that his voice sounded unshaped by conservatory standards, that his comprehension of the technicalities of music was much too crude, and that he lacked any realistic sense of just how much work would be required to lift his singing to even a low professional level, that, without Mr. Brown to drill and correct and scold and coddle him, he would founder.

Ryan packed his bags without much concern. Fear was what he felt walking the two blocks from his house to the corner store for a carton of milk. He assumed nothing about his chances of making it as a musician. He hadn't forgotten his words after *Carmen,* but in his mind he had adjusted their meaning. He had realized how rare it was for a singer to reach the Met stage, and he had relinquished the ambition of singing there in a role as big as the toreador; that was an idle dream, not a goal, not even a wish. Maybe, he thought, if all progressed perfectly year by year, through the conservatory and through the decade or two after that, he could somehow be chosen for the Met's chorus. Maybe. For now, he knew only that he was going to a university— the word itself sounded dazzling—and that he was making it out of the crevasse.

℘

"That's your voice!" Mr. Brown had cried. But while he had drawn out glimmers of what was unique in Ryan, he kept an essential part of himself buried. The ardent religion he'd grown up with, the quest for God's love that saturated the music at Shiloh, the urgent gospel singing that he criticized but had been filled by—he kept these interred within him in order to worship at a church that welcomed him as he was. The Unitarians did not expect him to deny half of himself, the sexual and romantic half, in order to pray in their sanctuary. They didn't take Leviticus as truth, not at all.

Yet death, as Leviticus foretold, did seem to search him out. HIV spread through him while Ryan was up in Hartford; then AIDS; sores crept over his body. His hands cramped and stiffened; his fingers slowed and faltered on the keys. His accompaniment couldn't buoy his students as it once had, couldn't keep them afloat, aloft. "Fischer," he told his boss, "I just can't."

For Wyatt, his cousin, he had a question. Back in high school, when he'd confided in her, she'd pledged that his being gay would make no difference in their friendship, and it hadn't. Now he needed to know—because she was so committed to the church where she worshipped, because she was such a woman of faith—what she thought God must think.

"Robert, why would you ask me that question?"

But he asked again.

"You grew up Christian," she answered him. "Your daddy's a deacon. Your momma was a Sunday school teacher. You grew up knowing God. I'm not going to browbeat you, but I'm not going to sugarcoat. Sin is sin." She cited the verses. "Robert, I want to see you go to heaven."

Shortly before he died, he went with her, one Sunday morning, to her church. The sanctuary was modern, streamlined, expansive. Atop a few steps, on a low platform, the pulpit was made of plexiglass. Black faces packed the white-painted room. Behind the preacher, the choir dominated the altar, the women in red blouses and the men in black suits; speakers were mounted on the walls and ceiling throughout the sanctuary, surrounding the parishioners; and lyrics were projected on the walls on both sides of the altar, emphasizing that here, music was almost everything.

In her long crimson tunic, the pastor spoke that morning on the Lord's love and the Lord's commands. God gives His love despite what His believers have done, she taught, but God demands far more of his faithful than what they are doing. The instant the sermon ended, it was underscored and overtaken by song. Gospel music engulfed the room, louder and louder as the choir and congregants responded to the pastor's rapture and encouragement: "Tear the roof off! Sing the songs of Zion!"

Hands were outstretched with palms upturned, beckoning God's love to settle in the soft flesh. Heads were tilted back in singing or bowed forward, soliciting forgiveness. Ushers hurried up and down the aisles, bearing yellow boxes of tissues for those in tears. "Based on our past performance, based on what we deserve," the pastor injected, "God has been so gracious, *so* good! And when people say God is too loving to send us to hell—they're right! We send ourselves to hell by refusing His word!"

The house held a special guest that morning, a backup singer to a rhythm and blues legend. She prayed at the church when she wasn't traveling, and that Sunday she climbed the carpeted steps to the altar's platform and turned to face the congregation with the choir behind her.

Her singing was nowhere near Robert Brown's ideal; it was anything but classical in style, anything but operatic. Her voice was throaty. She bellowed and half howled the names "God" and "Jesus" with a religious aching so deep it sounded as much animal as human. She hit high, raspy notes that turned the effort to beseech Jesus in heaven into something acutely real. Then, swooping down octaves, her singing became a thrum of overwhelming need.

Brown was weeping. When the singing was over, in the hush that poured through the sanctuary, the pastor made her call. "All of you who have strayed, all of you who want to redirect your life to the Lord, I want you to come to the altar."

Brown walked toward the steps. At the base of the platform, he let his neck fall, let his head fall, lifted his hands.

"You have strayed, but you are returning!"

A church elder set his palm gently on Brown's forehead.

TWELVE

AFTER RYAN'S VICTORY in the finals, Valerie and Cecil stood beside each other, quietly, near the plate glass windows that overlooked the fountain with its lavish display of shooting water, the breadth of the plaza around the pool, the city beyond. They didn't have anything to say to each other. Even after Cecil took Adrian to California, there hadn't been much contact between her and Cecil; their conversations had been, at best, barbed. Now they watched their son—vibrant, aglow with sweat, taller than anyone in the crowd, broader than anyone in the crowd, the height and mass of him magnetic—being swarmed by opera devotees, by gray-haired couples, a young woman in a black pencil skirt, people handing him their cards, a woman in leather pants holding out her Met program to be signed. Valerie and Cecil stood a short distance from him, separated by the well-wishers and by the other singers and their families. She wore a dark dress, he a black suit and purple tie. Their bodies were still, and their faces, except for the glitteriness of Cecil's eyes, were almost impassive, as if they were statues—statues who'd been hugged tightly by Ryan as soon as he'd stepped off the elevator that carried him up from the level of the stage, statues who'd been released from their stillness and silence by his hug, brought to life, to exuberant, beaming life, for a moment.

Now they seemed to be gazing at him across a sea, watching him on a far-off island.

₰

Not long after that, though, he was in a borrowed car, driving with his father next to him. They were headed up into the mountains of Colorado, toward a town of casinos called Central City, where Ryan would be performing. This trip with his father was one of the two best things that happened because of the contest.

The other was an invitation to audition for the Met's own development program for young singers. The Lindemann Program was a rarified incubator; a few artists were chosen each year for the two or three years of training. In total, there were around ten singers in the program at any given time. They received a comfortable stipend, free voice lessons and artistic coaching from the best teachers in the country, and minor roles in Met productions. Winning the contest did not lead automatically to the chance to audition. Winning the contest meant a check for fifteen thousand dollars, which, for Ryan, meant the opportunity to pay down a portion of the money he'd needed to borrow, beyond his scholarships, in order to finance his musical education after Governor's, at the University of Hartford and then in graduate school at Florida State, another second-

or third-rank conservatory. And winning the contest was a credential and an affirmation that might translate into invitations from lesser development programs with lesser companies than the Met; into exploratory, noncommittal meetings with managers; into medium-size roles at summer festivals or with regional companies; and into the thought that aiming for a sustained professional career at some modest level was no longer as irrational as it had been before the competition.

Winning seemed to say, as well, that fantasizing about the stardom reached by a small subset of past victors was not quite as fantastical as it had been a day earlier, though it was hard to forget the metaphor Gayletha Nichols had used during the previous week. Winning put them at the base of a new and extraordinarily arduous, unforgiving ladder, a ladder packed with talented singers vying for work in an art form whose regional American companies were shrinking their seasons—a ladder, she told me, that most winners would ultimately either fail to climb or tumble off. Being asked to audition for the Lindemann Program was like being told that you belonged a rung or two up from the bottom, nothing more. But Ryan was the only one of the finalists who received this invitation. It came in an email the day after the finals. The audition consisted of two parts: a series of coaching sessions with the Lindemann staff, and then arias sung for the staff and the Met's beloved conductor and Lindemann founder, James Levine.

Ryan got the invitation despite the limitations in his performance of Banquo's aria, limitations that had persisted from the semifinals to the finals, even as he'd been less rigid and allowed something more of himself to enter his singing, his face, his body. "Generic" was how one of the Lindemann faculty critiqued Ryan's singing of the piece. It had pleased the crowd well enough, at an event where the audience was feeling forgiving, but the same performance would have made no impression—except maybe for the mispronunciations—within a full Met opera.

But his delivery of "La calunnia" was another story. On this darkly comic aria, his flagrant gestures, his unhinged expressions, his voice that ventured to extremes had been, for moments and even extended passages, mesmerizing. It wasn't absurd to imagine that someday his singing and charisma would help to make an entire Met production riveting. Seven years in the future? Ten? Fifteen? Given the low range and arresting size of his voice, and given the length of time it took for such a heavy instrument to come under a singer's control and attain full resonance, there would be year after year, phase after phase, of uncertainty. The anatomical reasons for such slowness were unknown, Dr. Paul Kwak, who worked with singers as an accompanist and an ENT surgeon, told me, though he added that "learning to capture an explosive subglottal pressure, the pressure just under the vocal cords, and learning to organize the sound that results from that explosiveness" might be part of the long maturation.

There would be, for Ryan, phase after phase as he grew capable of more and more demanding roles, weightier and weightier roles, phase after phase *if* he progressed without faltering dismally, without revealing unalterable shortcomings or irremediable bad habits that would relegate him permanently to secondary parts in secondary houses, or that could cause him to injure his cords, to damage them beyond repair, leaving him unable to sing much of anything.

But there were immediate problems. "He couldn't read the recipe, let alone cook," Ken Noda remembered thinking about Ryan's ability to comprehend a score. Noda, one of the Met's most revered coaches, worked with Ryan as part of the audition process, to better understand what he lacked and how easy or laborious it would be to lead him past the deficiencies. To grant him a place among the Lindemann trainees would be like welcoming him as a novitiate in an exalted monastic order. The teachers needed to be as sure as they could about whether he was up to it. When Noda and other faculty ushered him into practice studios for solo sessions, it was to test whether their time and the Lindemann Program's funds were best offered to him or some other aspirant in this art form whose future they were perpetually guarding and constructing. But there was also something more. They needed to know whether he was likely to thrill them in the way that teachers can be electrified by their most inspiring students. "It can be agonizing if the singer is not giving back," Noda said. He was middle-aged, but his faintly brown Japanese skin was flawless. His black bangs were youthful, his clothes crisp, his body spare. "It's like having sex with an inert object. You use every position in the world to try and try to get the person to respond. But you get nothing back."

Noda had been a prodigy at the piano, a stunning musician at the age of seven, when he was accepted into Juilliard's precollege program, and an international soloist by his late teens. At twenty, he'd played duets with the violinist Itzhak Perlman at the White House. Noda's mother, a printmaker who'd emigrated with his father from Japan, pushed him as a young child, propelled him later. "But I didn't love the piano enough as an instrument. Some pianists have a sensual relationship with the piano; they adore the keys. I thought the instrument was utilitarian, unfriendly. It's so large; you sit behind it like a desk. And a piano's sound—the note is dying the instant you play it. A string player—or a singer—can control the vibration of his sound. It's intimate. He can extend the sound, make it live. But as a child, what I had was the piano. I was like a little prize horse, put on a track by my mother. I was being trained and trained."

His parents took him to the opera as something ancillary, inessential. But he was lured by the voice, drawn to the theatrical; early on, opera became a covert obsession. With his parents at home, he practiced his solo pieces. When his parents left the apartment, he propped opera scores on the music rack and mastered the accompaniment for arias. At nine, in the precollege program, he made use of Juilliard's library to read through more arias and overtures. At ten, he composed his first—and only—opera, the tale of a singing canary who is trapped inside a baseball, gets discovered by two boys who take it to a pet shop, and is then trapped inside both the baseball and a cage until the story arrives at a happy ending. The twenty-five-minute work was performed by New York City Opera throughout the city's schools. "But my parents thought opera was a musical side hobby. They didn't think I would ever work in it." His mother kept her prize horse, her prodigy pianist, racing around the track.

By the time he was in his twenties, he felt suffocated

by his burgeoning career, soloing with orchestras from Los Angeles to Vienna. "I kept thinking, *When are people going to find out that I don't even like this repertoire? This is not going to last. They are going to hear it; they are going to find out.*" With concerts booked five years ahead, he walked into his manager's office. He quit. "My mother was so angry. Devastated. But for me, it was exhilarating. It was an act of total self-destruction, but I was tearing down this false edifice she wanted me to keep building. And a year later, I was at the Met. She's still condescending about the work I do here. No matter how respected I am at the Metropolitan Opera, she will never fully accept it. To her, it is something *nice*. To her, the important question is whether I ever think about giving a solo concert again."

The interaction between music and libretto enthralled him; the suppleness, the living vibration of the voice galvanized him; the collaboration between coach and performer consumed him. He loved the way a blend of fealty to what was written and interpretation by the singer could bring about a performance that felt like a revelation. This was his focus, this combination of faithfulness and vocal interpretation. In the upper echelons of opera, a distinction was drawn between two types of instructors: voice teachers, who were specialists in the production of sound, in the mechanics of projecting and shading notes, and coaches, who specialized in sensibility, in helping the singer to understand the nuances in the score and to add the singer's own spirit. The line was blurry, but Noda worked on one side of it: he was a coach. He worked with Met divas as well as Lindemann trainees. He played for them, sang for them in a voice that appalled him but that provided rough demonstrations, led them deeper into the page and into themselves. Except for when he slept, he worked all but ceaselessly, studying scores when he wasn't in sessions or speaking with colleagues about how better to elicit, to guide. This, not a solo career, was now his existence. One had replaced the other. "I have to do what I'm doing in order to live. I would be dead if I didn't. I might be alive, but I would be just dead." Every year, the summer weeks when the Met went into hiatus were torment. He knew that he needed to rest, to restore himself for the next season. He walked through the city for hours at a stretch, kept a stack of books beside his bed—the novels of Thomas Mann, a biography of Verdi—and waited for his vacation to end.

Was Ryan the type of singer who could meet this level of teacherly intensity, receive what Noda and the others had to give, and reciprocate with enough that was already his own? The team had their doubts about whether he belonged in the program; they wondered if he could so much as survive it. "The recipe, the most fundamental ingredients—he really didn't even know how to read the rhythms correctly. He didn't know the difference between a teaspoon and a tablespoon of salt. And a musical score contains so many expressive markings from the composer. He didn't know what cloves were. He didn't know what ginger was."

It was almost unfathomable that he'd passed through his undergraduate conservatory, plus two years in graduate school, without gaining a fair grasp of these notations. Yet, Noda thought, instruction was seldom as exacting as it should be. And then there was something about Ryan that appeared at a loss, out of his element, no matter that he'd just won the contest. It was endearing. He carried no hint of the entitlement Noda sometimes felt in the Lindemann singers. During the audition sessions, Ryan's forehead was forever glazed with perspiration. Apologetic laughter leapt from his throat. The glaze and the smile that went with the laughter gave him a radiance but also showed a disorientation, as if he'd been abducted and dropped here rather than arriving step by step. And maybe at his undergrad and graduate schools the mental noise and clutter of nervousness and disorientation had gotten in the way of his truly taking in what he'd been taught.

So he was left confused when the recipe demanded cloves. "And he had very little linguistic skill. It wasn't only that he didn't know how to pronounce a good percentage of the words; it was that somehow he hadn't been trained to *translate* the words, all of them. He hadn't learned that this is the necessary beginning, and that then you have to delve into the psychology of a character. I was making suggestions, and he had this respectful, uncomprehending look, like I wasn't quite speaking English. It was alarming. We thought, how would he ever be able to catch up? The program is loads of pressure. This is the Met. The standards, the constant judgment. There's no grace period. You feel the pressure in the first month, and he needed so much remedial work."

After the coaching sessions, Ryan performed for James Levine, Noda, and two other Lindemann faculty members. Levine had been conducting the Metropolitan Opera for forty years; he was one of the most legendary maestros in the world. This part of the audition was held in a small theater within the opera house, and Levine rode into the room on an electric cart. Back injuries had left him barely able to walk. When Ryan auditioned, Levine could still get up from the cart and get himself into a regular seat, but he would soon be partially paralyzed and conducting operas from a customized wheelchair that rested on a motorized platform. The impediments only added to his artistic reputation.

Around the back areas of the Met, Levine wore rumpled polo shirts and gray sweatpants, with aviator-shaped eyeglasses on his cherubic face. Thinning frizzy hair bloomed from the orb of his head as Ryan sang the Banquo aria and "La calunnia." Levine and the Lindemann team thanked him, sent him out, and deliberated.

The decision was a weighing of the deficits against the possibilities contained in the raw voice, the comic flair, something more: he stirred a reaction. "It was to *him,* it was to the person," Noda said. "There's something about his emission of personal energy. You could tell. He was singing to live."

℥

Back when Ryan had entered the first round of the Met contest, he'd been singing in abridged operas, performing *Hansel and Gretel* as part of an operatic road show in Colorado. He'd also been given an upcoming role in a festival in the town of Central City. He still had to fulfill the commitment, though he was now one of the Lindemann trainees.

Central City was an old gold-mining settlement, known in the mid–eighteen hundreds as the richest square mile on earth and packed with ten thousand prospectors. These days it got by on some tourism, on the slot machines and roulette wheels in a few homey casinos. Cecil loved to play the slots; Ryan had recently learned this about his father. His father had told him about a trip or two that he'd made, driving from his home in California to gamble in Nevada. Since the finals, Ryan had hoarded information like this from their phone conversations. The talks hadn't included any heart-to-hearts, but he collected the gems and insights, which he stored carefully, as though his mind contained a built-in jewelry box designed for such items.

In his rented room in Central City one night after rehearsal, Ryan thought of the casinos around him. He phoned his father. He told him about the slots and about opening night, which was near, and said he would pay for his trip. At the airport, he picked Cecil up in a car lent to him by a patron of Opera Colorado, and he drove his father to the restaurant he'd chosen. Cecil was an avid football fan, and the restaurant was an upscale steak house owned by a fabled quarterback for Denver's football team.

The place was perfect: a dazzling mix of flat-screen TVs tuned to sports events, sumptuous upholstery, gleaming wood. They started with a round of Dark and Stormies, a cocktail of rum and ginger beer that Ryan had just discovered. He wanted his father to like it, and Cecil did, and they ordered another round. "I never thought the day would come when I would see one of my sons..." His father's voice faded.

Cecil's stepson had just been sent back to prison on gang-related charges. Adrian, after Cecil had whisked him away from the group home and taken him to California, had dropped out of high school. He'd put his strength and anger to use as a local-level extreme fighter, battling in cages where all manner of bodily assault was approved. But he'd brawled outside the ring, too, with Latin gang members. He'd punctured someone's lung, and there had been a shank that Adrian "deflected," he claimed, into one of the gang. This had all led, according to him, to a trumped-up statutory rape charge pressed against him by the gang members, for having sex with an underage Mexican teenager. He'd been put in prison for two years. Since getting out on parole, he'd been homeless and unemployed and barred, because of his violent temper, from seeing the son he'd had when he was twenty-one.

"...when I would see one of my sons do something like this. Fly me here. I have no words." He was tearing up; they switched to talk of sports. Cecil wore a football jersey from his favorite team and billowy pants imprinted with a pattern of tamales. The pants might have been embarrassing if Ryan hadn't been so happy and if his father, between their chatting about the recent basketball play-offs and their discussion of the approaching football season, hadn't said just that: "I'm so happy."

The waitress came over to deliver more drinks and get their food orders going.

"Do you know who my son is?" Cecil asked.

She said she didn't.

"Well, he's an opera singer. He's a professional opera singer."

She asked where he'd gotten his voice.

"He didn't get it from me. Must have gotten it from his mom."

They all laughed.

"He's singing with Opera Colorado now. And before long he's going to be singing with the Metropolitan Opera in New York City."

She remarked on how proud Cecil must be—all the more, she said, because his son was so tall.

"He didn't get that from me either."

They laughed harder.

Father and son talked more basketball and football, devoured their meal, talked about the fishing trip Cecil dreamed of taking one day with all of his boys, and went to the bar for a nightcap.

"Do you know who my son is?" Cecil asked the bartender.

They drove up to Central City, up to eight thousand feet. One thing Ryan was beginning blurrily to see, beyond how much his father loved him, was how easily his father connected with people, joked with them, charmed them, broadcast things about himself. The tamale pants were part of that: he was a chef, a barbecue expert, running a restaurant. It had only five tables, but he was in charge. Ryan noticed a link. He traced his own comedic, over-the-top performance of arias like "La calunnia" to his father's playfulness and antics and habit of self-announcement. He tied the ability he recognized in himself, the ability to pull people in, to what he'd seen with the waitress, his father's quickness at winning people over. The link elated and soothed him at the same time. The realization spread within him physically, like something pumping through his blood vessels.

They reached Central City and collapsed, his father in the room next to his, and late in the morning, when Ryan awoke, Cecil was gone. Ryan phoned; his father was in a casino. He'd been up since four, he said, playing the slots. When he'd taken a break for a drink, he told a guy at the bar that he was here because his son was an opera singer, and he'd learned that the guy was cooking in a barbecue festival that afternoon. They struck a deal to collaborate on the guy's grill and smoker.

That evening was Ryan's opening, a performance of *La Bohème*. Putting on his costume backstage, he thought to call his father, to make sure he was getting ready. The last he'd seen him, Cecil and his new friend were serving ribs and bacon jalapeño poppers on Main Street to the longest line at the festival. They were talking about how they should really rent an eighteen-wheeler and start a roaming restaurant, cooking across the country.

On the phone, Cecil said that he'd lost track of time. He was still barbecuing. Ryan told him to leave—now—to hurry. Cecil made it to his seat in time. He was there: there when Ryan walked onstage, and there for Ryan's aria as the opera ascended to its desperate climax. Afterward, it was Ryan who watched. In Ryan's room, his father fed seven singers from the cast, served them the food he'd put aside from earlier at the festival. They gorged on his poppers, feasted on his spicy ribs and wings, and praised the chef to the skies.

THIRTEEN

T ERRENCE COLEMAN," RYAN said. He leaned with the heels of his palms on the thin red blanket that protected the top of the piano in Mark Oswald's studio.

"Terrence," Oswald echoed.

"Terrence, Terrence, Terrence, Terrence," Ryan repeated.

They were taking a break from singing runs of notes on particular vowel sounds—up to and down from Ryan's uppermost E on an *ah* vowel, up to and down from his highest E on an *aw* vowel. They were taking a break, as they sometimes did early in a lesson, so Ryan could tell his voice teacher how things were going inside the program. The Met paid Oswald's fee; he wasn't on the Met staff. His studio was a few blocks from the opera house and he worked independently, but he knew the Met from the inside, having sung as one of the Met's leading lyric baritones, performing with Pavarotti and Domingo, before vanishing from the stage a decade ago, when he was thirty-five. For Ryan, he was teacher, counselor, and confessor, and this afternoon there was something Ryan needed to pour out.

"I've been hearing a lot of Terrence talk. Pretty much since I got into the program. Pretty much half the Met people, I mean the Met people with power, are like, 'Terrence is a singer you should keep in mind.'"

Oswald sat at his baby grand. Scores crammed the shelves at his back. A box of tissues, piles of music, Post-its and scraps of paper for scribbling notes cluttered the surfaces of the piano; the scraps encroached on the highest and lowest keys. Oswald's presence was a counterpoint to the chaos. His body, clothed elegantly in a plum-colored dress shirt and black slacks, was compact; his posture was composed; his face formed modulated expressions of sympathy as he listened.

Growing up in a town amid Pennsylvania farmland, Oswald had sung gospel in the old stone Lutheran church his family attended every Sunday, had sung up front for the congregation of two hundred, harmonized with his father, mother, and sister. "Not rip-roaring gospel," he said. "It was white-folks-style, dumbed-down gospel, close to the sound of a barbershop quartet." He'd gone on to a top conservatory, to win the Met contest, to a spot in the Lindemann Program, to being cast as Figaro at the Met, to being selected to sing at a Met gala honoring Maestro Levine in the mid-nineties, priding himself all along on his technical control, on delivering exquisite tones with unerring consistency. Yet he confronted a crushing lack of control over certain things. Asthma plagued him, and he grew more and more fixated on protecting his health, guarding against any inflammation along the pathways of his voice, so that his singing wouldn't be compromised. He felt that he hardly had a life. "There's gossip out there that says I was a nervous Nellie, but I believe they don't understand. My health caused the nerves. It wasn't that the nerves were a problem on their own." And he perceived his natural gift as "meager." Yes, his singing was beautiful, and yes, he had a following among opera buffs, followers who were full of expectations and imagined hearing him sing arias for another twenty-five years, but his repertoire would always be restricted to parts that were lyric, light. No amount of technical acumen was going to expand his proscribed roles. Facing the constraints of his health and his range, Oswald retired, rescaling his life here in his studio.

"Yesterday was the worst," Ryan said. He wore a gray T-shirt that read "Talk Nerdy to Me." He was bent, wilting, propped against the piano, biceps stretching the T-shirt's sleeves. "Yesterday's meeting was rock bottom. 'Can I be brutally honest with you?' That's how it began. And then they"—two of the most influential people at the Met—"spent twenty minutes telling me how Terrence Coleman is what we at the Met don't want you to be. 'Terrence has a Met-sized voice. Terrence had great potential. But his pronunciation is awful. And his voice is woofy.'"

Terrence was African American, in mid-career, a bass, a graduate of the program.

"'Ryan, you want to bring your sound forward—it's too far back. Ryan, you have to fix your pronunciation. Terrence in Italian, Terrence in German—Terrence's pronunciation is so poor, he's singing words that don't exist.' They kept giving me all these examples. Terrence's problems in this role, Terrence's problems in that role. The terrible things they'd heard after Terrence's performances in Europe. 'We're not saying you're like Terrence. No one's saying that, but there are things to watch out for. No one wants you to be another Terrence.'" Ryan forced out a laugh. "*We're not saying you're like Terrence*—but we're going to tell you about him so many times that when you look in the mirror you see his face."

Oswald winced at what Ryan was reporting, the messages of his first several months as a trainee. Yet he kept the wincing minimal. He steered the conversation to technical solutions. On whether Ryan was generating his sound from too far back, too far from the facial bones, and so failing to sing with the ideal overtones, failing to blend the right degree of operatic brightness into his darkly shaded notes, failing to give his singing enough clarity and brilliance, Oswald promised they would tinker with things together. It was a matter of balance, Oswald believed. "Woofy" and "too far back"—these were ways of describing a sound that seemed lodged too heavily in the throat. Yet the risk was that in brightening the sound, richness would be lost. And a rich timbre was the essence of Ryan's voice; it was a major part of why he'd made it this close to success.

"Spacement," Oswald reminded Ryan, trying to calm him with a word that Oswald had coined. The idea was that a singer had to find and familiarize himself with the sonorous spaces within his anatomy, bones and pockets of resonance from the hard palate to the brow, from the nasal cavity to the region above the soft palate to the chambers farther back and down. The singer had to use these sound-producing structures in just the right combinations. The mixture was different on any given note and differed with every artist. The singer had to learn not only how to locate these resonant spots but how to manipulate them, altering their relationships, their angles, their sizes, and then how to employ "placement" in order to channel the right portions of the voice through the various areas. "Space" and "placement" had merged into one of Oswald's favorite terms.

Ryan remained stooped over the piano.

Oswald assured him that they would add sheen without losing what lay underneath. He moved on to the issue of pronunciation. "If you can simply sing with as legato a line as you can," he began, soothing Ryan first about his Italian, "if you can move from one vowel sound to the next with as little interruption as possible—if you can treat the single consonants almost as though there is *no* consonant, you will have won more than half the battle." He pledged to help him accomplish this, though pronunciation was more the domain of the Lindemann coaches than it was the province of a voice teacher. He asked which aria Ryan wanted to start with today.

But Ryan had something to add about yesterday's meeting at the Met. "Another thing they mentioned to me, they said, 'You know, Terrence has been doing a lot of *Show Boat*s lately. And when someone like Terrence starts doing *Show Boat,* it's not because he thinks it's going to move him in the right direction artistically. It's because he needs the work. You want to apply yourself during the program. You want to take advantage of the program, so when you leave here you're prepared. So you don't end up singing

Joe. So you can avoid the *Show Boat*s. You want to avoid being typecast.'"

Ryan let out a groan. He lifted his hands off the piano and straightened his torso, ready to get back to work.

"Eight five three one," Oswald said.

He played the sequence and Ryan sang.

"Try a little bit of umlaut to the mouth," the teacher suggested. "On that note, the slight alteration of the lips will create the forward resonance."

Ryan hadn't needed the advice about *Show Boat*. The musical and the role of Joe—and Joe's song, "Ol' Man River"—had haunted him for years. White people who heard him sing had been urging him to do "Ol' Man River" since Governor's. "Oh, I would love to hear you sing 'Ol' Man River,'" he'd been told back then by his classmates' parents and grandparents, and he was told the same by well-wishers in the crowd after the Met finals. He'd heard it uncountable times in between, after performances at his conservatories in Connecticut and Florida and at the community centers in Colorado.

"You know, son, when I was growing up—have you ever heard of Paul Robeson? Do you know who that is?"

"Yes, sir, I know who that is."

"Well, I could just hear you singing 'Ol' Man River' the way Paul Robeson did."

Or they named not Robeson, who'd played Joe in the second Hollywood film of *Show Boat,* but William Warfield, who'd played Joe in the third.

"Are you familiar with William Warfield?"

"Yes, ma'am, I am."

"Because he sang 'Ol' Man River,' and I think you're the second coming of William Warfield, and I can't wait to hear you sing that song someday."

"Thank you, ma'am."

But 'Thank you' was not what he wanted to say; grateful was not what he felt. The linking of his voice with two historic black voices wasn't the problem—about that there was pride. The problem was that in these situations he'd just finished performing Verdi or Puccini or Mozart, and here were these people, these opera lovers, these classical music lovers, telling him that he would be perfect for a role in musical theater.

"It's a stab," he said as he and I walked toward the Met after the hour with Oswald. "It's a smack in the face if I've just sung in a recital, sung Liszt, and someone comes up and says they imagine me as Joe, they see me as Joe, they'd love to hear me as Joe. Not that they'd like to hear me sing something in the genre I've chosen. They want to hear me sing something not even in the same stratosphere. It's like being kicked to the ground."

He'd played Joe once. It was during college, with a summer theater company in a beach town in New England. He'd played the black laborer, who toiled on a steamer that paddled the Mississippi River, traveling through the Jim Crow South at the end of the nineteenth century. At stopovers along the shore, the boat's white owner put on plays for all-white audiences. And all the while, as the boat churned downriver or docked at river towns, Joe and his wife, Queenie, hauled and cooked, sweat and slept in the heat of the steamer's lower decks and holds.

The musical, first staged on Broadway in 1927 and in constant revival across the country ever since, was partially a protest against racial divisions. Yet Joe's signature song, about his longing to escape his life and his envy of the river he works and lives on, had been controversial from the musical's earliest productions—controversial because Joe sang the word "nigger," controversial because Joe sang in dialect, controversial for emphasizing the character's resignation to his degrading plight.

> Dere's an ol' man called de Mississippi
> Dat's de ol' man dat I wants to be
> What does he care if de world's got troubles
> What does he care if de land ain't free

> Ol' man river, dat ol' man river
> He must know sumpin', but don't say nothin'
> He jes' keeps rollin'
> He keeps on rollin' along

> He don't plant taters, he don't plant cotton
> An' dem dat plants 'em is soon forgotten
> But ol' man river
> He jes' keeps rollin' along

> You an' me, we sweat an' strain
> Body all achin' an' racked wid pain,
> Tote dat barge! Lift dat bale!
> Git a little drunk an' you lands in jail

Ah gits weary an' sick of tryin'
Ah'm tired of livin' an' skeered of dyin'
But ol' man river
He jes' keeps rollin' along

Niggers all work on de Mississippi
Niggers all work while de white folks play
Pullin' dose boats from de dawn to sunset
Gittin' no rest till de judgment day

Don't look up an' don't look down
You don't dast make de white boss frown
Bend your knees an' bow your head
An' pull dat rope until yo' dead

Let me go 'way from de Mississippi
Let me go 'way from de white man boss
Show me dat stream called de River Jordan
Dat's de ol' stream dat's I long to cross

Before he played the role, Ryan learned about the musical's themes and history. Until then, though he'd known about Joe and his anthem, he hadn't known much about the overall story, about its portrait of a mixed-race couple among the troupe that performed the shows in the riverside towns: a white man and a woman who was passing, a woman with a fraction of black ancestry. He hadn't known much about the musical's elements of protest. He learned, too, about the debates over the song's lyrics. For the 1936 movie, "niggers" had been changed to "darkies." Robeson, in recitals, had gone further, getting rid of "Dere's an ol' man" and singing, instead, "There's an ol' man." He'd insisted on adding dignity by cutting "Git a little drunk an' you lands in jail" and substituting "Show a little grit and you lands in jail."

What Ryan learned—that *Show Boat* was critical of racism and that Robeson, who later became a civil rights activist, had partly accepted those lyrics as accurate to the time and place and character of Joe and partly changed them to honor Joe's intelligence and moments of defiance—had made him eager for opening night. He was going to be using Robeson's version of the song.

Then, in front of the summer theater audience, Ryan's singing of "Ol' Man River" brought the musical to a halt. The immediate applause made it impossible for the cast to go on. The clapping surged in tandem with his final note, swelled, became a standing ovation. For minutes, the clapping didn't subside and the crowd didn't sit.

He didn't credit himself. He couldn't. He knew better. This had been the response to "Ol' Man River" since *Show Boat*'s initial Broadway runs. Stirred by Joe's song, white audiences had risen right away to their feet.

"It disturbed me, to stand there and feel it. It actually shocked me—the extent of it. I've never had longer applause in my life. Not before, not since. We did four or five performances, and every night it was the same. Every night everything came to a stop. White people *love* this piece of music. If I sang it in front of African American people, I can tell you, they might clap, but they wouldn't be yelling for more. They wouldn't be yelling for me to sing it again. That's what those people wanted. And I didn't want to sing it again. I gave them a few lines. But

I'm feeling, *Why?* And here I am, still asking, why are white people so moved by this song? It's about something you shouldn't want to hear about from me. It's about how everything, every day, is so hard because of you. Because of white people putting black people down. It's about being oppressed. It's about being free but not free. It's about a man who's a second-class citizen, who has to live belowdeck, who makes two cents a day. He'll never earn enough money, never earn the respect he deserves, never be treated equally. He'll always have to watch his people get treated like crap. And his only consolation is death. When he dies he'll be free.

"But everyone in that theater, they couldn't get enough of it. They're cheering and crying. I'm belittling myself the whole show to appease the white man. I don't know what Kern and Hammerstein, the two white guys who wrote it, I don't know what their intention was. But Joe was pleasing to the white man in the nineteen twenties. He was pleasing to white people who had separate toilets and sinks for black people. Joe doesn't know how to talk. Everyone around him who is white talks in a completely different way. And 'Ol' Man River' is pleasing white people to this day."

℘

"I'm going to spend the rest of my life getting out from that shadow," Ryan said. He disappeared then, descending to the subterranean levels of the Met for a coaching session on Italian pronunciation.

Ken Noda had warned him. He would be judged more

critically than a white singer. "I can speak to you as a minority," Noda had said. "I can speak to you as a person with a not-white face. People assume you won't be as good. You have to be twice as good. Our preparation has to be twice as strong. Because of my face, because of my Japanese features, people looked at me at first with an expression that was like, *Do you know anything about this art form? Can you possibly know anything?* Even now, after all these years here, I feel like I have to be ready to fight that look. It's something I walk around with. I'm still afraid that someone might look at me in that way."

And Noda said to me, "There's an obstacle. It's not obvious, but it's significant. It's true for Asians as well as African Americans. There are lots of aspiring Asian singers in our field, but very few who are doing well."

He didn't mean that the Met—or the world of opera—was especially bigoted. People at the Met prided themselves on their liberal politics, their open minds. It was probably safe to say that within the opera house nearly every voter had, a few years earlier, cast a ballot for Barack Obama to become America's first black president, and it was probably safe to say that most had celebrated when he'd won. It was a progressive place.

People assume you won't be as good—these words lay within the shadow that Ryan felt looming, the shadow that he was determined to escape: the sense, in this well-meaning, liberal realm, that he would not meet the standards of the art, that he would be forced by his shortcomings to follow Terrence Coleman into the role of Joe, or forced into a career whose mainstay was *Porgy and Bess,* the story of life in an African American slum in Charleston a century ago. *Porgy and Bess* wasn't *Show Boat*. Its music was rated as real opera by the opera world—or it had been since the seventies, forty years after its opening. That was when the composition had been reappraised, elevated. Still, making a career of playing Porgy, the crippled black beggar of Catfish Row, in front of the throngs that inevitably packed theaters wherever the show was staged, would mean being far less than successful in the Met's terms and in his own, far less than what he'd wanted for himself since seeing *Carmen* at fifteen.

℞

I'm going to spend the rest of my life getting out from that shadow. He descended to his session on Italian, his words containing an ineffable weight. It was a weight, a burden, that went beyond preconceptions and Terrence Coleman's failure and Noda's warnings. *I'm going to spend the rest of my life.* It was a burden of identity that I, hearing the reverberation of those words after we said good-bye and he walked downward, could only intuit. It was a pressure that I, being white, would never feel. I existed, white within a white city—no matter that it *wasn't* a white city, that whites were less than half the city's population; it *felt* to me like a white city, which was the point—white within a white culture, white within a white nation, my race irrelevant to my own definitions of self, or seemingly irrelevant. If identity was a series of words or phrases completing a sentence beginning with "I am," how soon, or late, in my series would "white" appear? Would it appear at all? Yet for Ryan, the situation was reversed. There could be no such taking for granted. Instead, there was an inner interrogation. It merely started with the question of whether, despite his resolve, he was doomed to a path like the one Terrence was on. The cross-examination continued from there, zeroing in on whether there was something suspect, after all, about the career he was pursuing, whether opera was, finally, as white as his tormentors on the bus had believed, whether he was rejecting his race, whether he was playing the house nigger in the old scenario that divided house from field, Oreo from black straight through, false from true.

He rejected this line of thinking, spurned it now just as he had back then. But rejecting it wasn't exactly the same thing as being rid of it.

Somehow, he thought, he'd found himself on this road. Somehow, some way, this goal, to sing opera with mesmerizing power, had gotten hold of him, gotten inside him. It had begun, he thought back, with a white singer performing the toreador's aria—but an African American artist had been at the heart of that production. A black diva had cast a spell. And his next steps had been taken under the instruction of a black teacher. And before that, there were the lines he'd learned in Mrs. Hughes's class, the lines she'd made them memorize, the lines from Martin Luther King's speech. "I have a dream"—that phrase, it seemed to him, had carried forward in his mind, giving him permission to harbor a huge ambition and teaching him the importance of declaring his ambition out loud, the way he'd done on the plaza after *Carmen*.

"Not be judged by the color of their skin"—he felt an intimate connection with King's historic crusade. That speech, he sensed, had helped to drive him and went right on pushing him now. He wanted his voice, his artistry, to be perceived so strongly that his complexion became secondary, immaterial. "No one before him," he said one morning, "had ever spoken so eloquently about those ideas. Hundreds of years from now we'll still be reciting and remembering Martin Luther King's words. I feel awesome to try and be a small part of his dream."

℞

Sometimes, listening to Ryan, I thought about the last years of King's life and the book he published a year before he was assassinated. The civil rights movement had split, and as King made his way into a White House–sponsored conference on civil rights, black protesters ridiculed him as an Uncle Tom. His belief that someday Americans would transcend race, that race would no longer be the primary way we perceive and categorize one another, was derided by rival black activists, who not only dismissed nonviolence but championed a purely black concept of identity. King's book, *Where Do We Go from Here?*, was his response.

"James Baldwin," King wrote, "once related how he returned home from school and his mother asked him whether his teacher was colored or white. After a pause he answered: 'She is a little bit colored and a little bit white.' This is the dilemma of being a Negro in America. In physical as well as cultural terms every Negro is a little bit colored and a little bit white. In our search for identity we must recognize this dilemma." The dilemma, for King, was a spiritual blessing, pointing toward the "society of brotherhood" that awaited, in his religious vision. But over the half century since, though King had become universally revered, this conflict between the dream of racial transcendence and the need for racial identity hadn't gone away, not really. It had quieted, become less overt, more complex, yet it still vibrated— vibrated for Ryan in the word "Oreo," vibrated on the bus as his schoolmate grabbed the music from his lap and spat out, "We knew you was white," vibrated as Ryan said, "When you come from a certain demographic, it's frowned upon to talk properly," vibrated right up to the present in the long persistence of a metaphor Ryan referred to, the metaphor of house and field. And recently it had echoed in a different way, after Obama's first election as president, when, for a fleeting interval, some had been willing to speculate—in a state of giddy misapprehension—that America was striding toward being "post-racial." The term had multiple wishful meanings. One was simply that American society was moving beyond racism. Another was that America was moving beyond race itself.

On the night of November 4, 2008, the night Obama was elected, Ryan was in Florida, in Tallahassee, working as a bouncer. This was how he paid some of his expenses as he studied at Florida State's graduate conservatory. He'd done the same in Hartford as an undergraduate. Given his size, the jobs just found him. In Hartford, he had gone with his suite mates to a club, gotten in line, and, on the spot, been offered a job with the security team. His shift ended at four o'clock, four nights a week. Mostly, the only difficulty was that with his classes starting at nine, he didn't have much time for sleep. But the club sometimes booked musicians who came with a rough following. Ryan and his bouncer colleagues tossed out fighters trying to cut each other with broken bottles. One night, as he herded brawlers out the door, someone sprayed him with mace. He showed up the next day for a dress rehearsal without a voice.

In Tallahassee, the bar where he worked was near campus. Crowds spilled onto the sidewalk from happy hour till last call. But by three in the morning after election night, the place was deserted, and Ryan was straightening up on the patio. A straggler stood nearby, facing the other way, talking drunkenly into his cell phone, his voice leaping into a yell. "I hope they're friggin' happy with their nigger president."

Ryan looked over; the student wore a polo shirt, a visor, boating shoes.

"I really hope they have fun with their nigger president." The kid hung up, turned around. He saw Ryan and seemed to grasp, over a slow, inebriated second, that what he'd been saying wouldn't sit well with the person he was looking at.

He ran. And Ryan sprinted after him. A moment earlier, he'd been trying not to hear the student's words. He'd been trying to pretend that none of this was happening. But now something had switched on—or switched off—inside him. He was going to teach the kid a lesson.

They ran past palm trees, past fraternity houses. The student had gotten a head start, and Ryan wasn't fast; the kid receded. But Ryan kept him in view, watched where the boy turned, and trailed him, though he was no longer in sight, past the cannon on the lawn and between the white columns of one of the frat houses. Ryan knocked on the wooden front door. He banged.

"What do you want?"

But before Ryan could answer, the person behind the door told him to go, to leave, told him he'd call the cops.

"No, no. No, I just want to talk to one of your fraternity brothers. One of your brothers was at my bar, and I just want to talk with him about the election."

The heavy door stayed shut. Behind it, the person introduced himself as the fraternity president. "We don't have any brothers who were out tonight."

Through the door, Ryan described the student and what he'd been shouting. He warned that he knew someone at the university newspaper, and that the writer would be happy to come over for an interview about the incident. "Or you can come out as president and hear what I have to say."

The door opened.

"You know, people shouldn't use that word," Ryan began.

"You don't have to say that."

"He has a name. His name is Obama."

"It won't happen again."

"Tell your friend he's not welcome at the bar. I don't want to see him there, ever."

"I apologize for what happened."

Ryan had one more thing he needed to make clear. There was a lot inside it. There was his mother's service in the military, the best job she'd had, which made him appreciate Obama's war hero opponent. There was his anger about all kinds of assumptions. But he couldn't explain everything.

"And tell your friend," he said before walking away, "I voted for McCain, too."

FOURTEEN

Ryan's voice is dark and rich and velvety. And long."

Brian Zeger ran the training program. Across the street from the Met, he also directed the vocal division at Juilliard, where we sat in a rehearsal room with tiers of empty seats rising at one end. And as a pianist, he'd performed throughout the world in recitals with the best singers in opera—Anna Netrebko, Marilyn Horne, Bryn Terfel. Now that he was nearing his sixties, he still performed, but he was aware that his fingers were stiffening slightly. He needed to put himself through protracted exercises to get them limber enough to draw the sounds he wished from the keys. And new music, which he'd once memorized effortlessly, took much longer these days to imprint in his mind. Nothing pathological was at work, nothing more than age and the administrative demands of two jobs, and the decline of hands and brain was imperceptible to anyone listening to him play. Yet the difference whispered to him, foreshadowing an end to performing. "I see a time coming when I won't do it anymore, and I don't know what that will cost me," he said, his gray hair full and hazel eyes steady, unwavering from the truth. "I love getting up on-stage. I love the whole process of being on tour. In a way, it's an infantile mode of existence; everything is about the performance—everything else becomes minimized. And I feel a sense of authority in front of audiences. I don't know what it will be like to stop, but I feel there's a knee-jerk reaction from anyone I talk with about it. 'Oh no'"—he imitated their voices—" 'there's no reason you should stop. You have to keep going. You must.' But why? Because I once was good at it? Because that was my life? Our lives are finite."

As we detoured from talking about Ryan, he touched on music he was recording, an adaptation, for voice and piano, of Keats's "Ode to a Nightingale."

...for many a time
I have been half in love with easeful Death,
Call'd him soft names in many a mused rhyme,
To take into the air my quiet breath

He spoke about an ascent in the music, a flight that ap-proached freedom, accentuating the "emotional opening up" in the word "easeful." He spoke about the way the per-manence of his recordings would, and would not, counter what was beginning to ebb from his fingers.

Then we returned to Ryan. "It's a large voice, yes—and the size of his sound alone is a gift. But the *length* is re-markable. It's one of the first things I noticed. It's one of the things we dream about. Sometimes with low voices the range is restricted. The artist, over a career lasting decades, will explore and develop the beauty of his voice within a somewhat narrow span of notes. And in a small set of roles. Even so, it will be a memorable career. But Ryan, with his strong bottom and strong top, his climactic top—he can thrive up there, live up there—Ryan could be a shape-shifter."

Zeger's eyes, sober as he'd talked about his own aging, seemed to quiver as he invoked this magic-laden phrase. If Ryan's career unfolded the way it should, his repertoire would be wide and unpredictable: romantic, comic, de-monic, mythic—Zeger named an array of roles. Perhaps the Dutchman, Wagner's tormented sea captain, or Wotan, Wagner's god of gods, would become signature parts. "These roles are like playing Lear," Zeger said. "The stamina, the emotional demands, the demands on the bot-tom and top of the voice. Wotan has this tremendous Oedipal struggle. He has to kill his own son. In opera, these roles are like Olympus." Singers capable of the music Wagner had written—merciless for the artist, rapturous for the audience—came along so rarely, appearing, with luck, once in a generation. Perhaps Ryan would be one of them.

But the characters Ryan might one day inhabit weren't the only reason Zeger's eyes danced as he talked about the expansiveness of Ryan's voice, from the lowest note he could sing without struggle to the highest he could hit without strain, a range, found and fostered in increments over the years since high school, that covered more than twice as many notes as an average person's. Zeger thought, too, of individual musical moments. "The longer the voice, the more colorful and more interesting any one note can be. You know the term 'chiaroscuro' from art history?

From *'chiaro'*—clear and bright. And *'oscuro'*—dark." He evoked religious paintings of the sixteenth and seventeenth centuries, their shadowed figures illuminated by shafts of divine light. "We use the same term to describe voices. It's the mix of tones, of bright and dark, that a singer can incorporate within each note.

"Every instrument produces this mix. If you play the A above middle C on the piano, you will hear a wave frequency of four hundred and forty cycles per second. But as you strike that one key, there will also be a series of frequencies, of harmonics, of partials, above four forty. Something similar happens with the human voice. And it's the prevalence and ease and richness of those harmonics that make for the distinctive colors as an artist sings.

"It's about options. One of the principles of vocal production, whether you're a soprano or a bass, is that the higher the top you have and the lower the bottom you have, the more options you're given in the coloring. You might be singing a note near the middle of your range, but you can tinge your voice with the levels of brightness above and the levels of darkness below."

At the center of the rehearsal room, Zeger sat at the piano, and though the tiers of empty seats seemed to press inward on the space, his words, and the scattered passages he played to help me understand his points, filled the room gracefully. He had an air of elegance that was an antidote to the frenetic desperation of all those singers, at Juilliard and in the Lindemann Program, who strove to cure the ills their teachers and coaches perceived in their technique. "It's all so subjective," he said. "And each singer hears so many perspectives on what he is and needs to be. On his

flaws and how to fix them. The teachers, the coaches—
we're like blind men trying to talk about an elephant. One
of us is touching the trunk, and one of us is touching the
flank, and one of us is feeling the tail. We're each grasp-
ing at our area, whatever we ourselves are best trained
at, whatever we think is most important, and we're all
tugging. We're describing, we're prescribing. We're laying
claim to the finite hours in a singer's day. And the singer
has to deal with all of us."

Subjectivity had gripped and pulled at Ryan maybe more
than most. Because of his vocal range—a range that elevated, these days, from a basement D to an F-sharp or
G two and a half octaves higher, and that encompassed
this vertical distance almost effortlessly, with no suggestion, especially at the upper end, that he had yet extended
himself as far as he could go—his teachers and coaches
had been debating over the most basic aspect of his voice
since his undergraduate years in Hartford. They had been
telling him one thing and another about whether he was
really a bass or a bass-baritone or a dramatic baritone or a
lyric baritone or, moving upward in range, a baritenor or a
heldentenor.

He was classified and reclassified, identified and reiden-
tified. The categorizations could sound abstract to an out-
sider, but they weren't for any singer of opera; they
controlled how you trained, the roles you were considered
for, the repertoire you prepared for your auditions. But
it was more than that. For the singer, the sound was the
self, propelled directly from within, put into the world.
Your category defined you. Disagreement over your identity was tolerable only to a degree. Close differences of

opinion were bearable; bass or bass-baritone—this was a common uncertainty. But to be called a bass one month and a heldentenor the next was to be spun into a state of panic.

Back in Hartford, it didn't help that his voice sometimes slipped into periods of complete turmoil. One week he sang notes higher than anyone would have predicted, no matter how they identified him, and the next it seemed he couldn't sing anything, regardless of where the notes lay on the staff. Since then, his voice had settled, but the memory of never knowing what it would and wouldn't do, never knowing where on the staff it would and wouldn't comply, unnerved him. And though the disagreements over his classification had faded, they still lingered. One of his coaches at the Met believed he was destined for a historic career, if only his other instructors and Ryan himself would acknowledge that he was born to be a baritone, and that he must concentrate more thoroughly on nurturing the glorious upper register he'd been given. Ryan refused to hear it. He couldn't afford to. The judgment of this coach threatened to leave him unanchored, drifting, not knowing what or who he was.

The rest of Ryan's Met guides had resolved that he was a bass-baritone, but he felt a constant dim fear that their certainty would loosen, or that his own would falter, doubts that joined his louder worries, worries that he heard and absorbed from just about everyone around him and that Zeger shared as he and I sat at the piano:

"Ryan and I have spoken about this, that his lower and middle registers tend to be a bit opaque, a bit cloudy." Listening within the tight confines of Mark Oswald's studio,

Zeger said, I wouldn't notice the trouble, because there, he explained, "to a layman's ear, it's just a big, warm, beautiful sound, a blanket of sound." But even within a small space, someone like Oswald, with a career of teaching built upon his decade of singing at the Met, would recognize the cloudiness that would pose unmistakable problems in an opera house. In the 3,800-seat house at the Met, the sheer size of Ryan's voice wouldn't be so omnipotent, and the audience would hear that an element was missing. They would sense a lack of luster. They would long for a shimmer atop the fathomless vocal depths. The less educated listeners wouldn't be able to specify what was absent, but just the same, they would know that the singing wasn't quite as beautiful as it should be.

The solution was to borrow from his upper layers of sound, from the brighter segments of his spectrum, and to brush a suggestion of brilliance into even his most somber notes. "A teacher like Mark Oswald will know how to pinpoint those harmonics no matter how dark the music becomes. Mark will try to build those overtones permanently into Ryan's singing."

If Oswald couldn't teach this, if Ryan couldn't learn it, the trouble would be worse than a missing sheen. Orchestras would devour him, leaving him intermittently inaudible, despite his natural volume. Hard as it was for a soprano to be heard over so many musicians, it could be harder for a bass or a bass-baritone, though the soprano's anatomy, her lungs and throat and overall heft, were dwarfed by a body like Ryan's. A soprano's main frequencies flew above the orchestra's. A bass-baritone's sound waves were slower, lower; they could get lost amid the mass of instruments. The singer with the low voice needed to add the right harmonics, on each note, to form a sound that would "cut through the texture of the orchestra," Zeger said as he struck a series of keys on the piano so I could hear how these overtones might marshal themselves together. For Ryan, the upper harmonics were not only for luster. They were not only aesthetic. They were functional. Without them, on some measures, he would be muffled. He would be mute.

&

"One way to think about Ryan's voice," Zeger went on, "is that he was born with a trombone. He has to work on making his trombone a little more of a trumpet." This was the riddle Ryan needed to solve. And the almost infinite intricacy of the riddle was that it had to be approached linguistically as well as musically. The two were intertwined. When Ryan was hounded about his pronunciation, it was not simply because butchered Italian or German or French might render his portrayal of a character ridiculous, the same way, Zeger said, that an actor playing Happy in *Death of a Salesman* would seem absurd if he had a heavy Latino accent and no one else in Willy's family did. "You might even feel that it was impossible to watch the play." Not everyone in a Met audience would wince at Ryan's botched syllables, it was true, but plenty would, and European audiences would rebel, and most crucially, the people in charge of casting at the Met and across Europe wouldn't consider hiring him. Or if someone from an important house did persuade himself that Ryan's pronunciation could be amended quickly during rehearsals and hired him with that hope, Ryan would be fired when he kept mangling the libretto. If Zeger had any doubts about his judgment, he received confirmation from a scout who visited the program and heard Ryan sing in Italian. She told Zeger, "I couldn't possibly put *that*" in front of her conductor.

Yet pronunciation mattered for more than the libretto; it mattered to the *music;* it was a key to combining trumpet with trombone; it was essential to the melding of harmonics. A vowel pronounced one way would help to produce a different chiaroscuro, a different blend of brilliance and shadow, than the same vowel pronounced with a slightly different shape. An *ah* would be brighter than an *ah* with some *aw* added in; the position of the lips and jaw and tongue, and the arrangement of a dozen other anatomical parts, affected the music of the voice. A singer had choices to make: decisions that could transform the artistry of a note, decisions that sometimes determined whether he could hit and sustain a note at all—and whether he would come to it with confidence or trepidation—for the shape of a vowel could render a difficult note easier or more daunting to generate. He couldn't make these subtle choices, though, if he didn't understand how the language was supposed to sound in the first place. He couldn't alter vowels if he didn't know the boundaries beyond which adjusting a syllable garbled a word. With scant rudimentary knowledge, he couldn't include nuance. Or he could—but at the cost of creating a mess.

"But nobody responds to any singer purely aurally," Zeger said. "There's always a visual component. And this discussion raises questions about how we see one another, about race. About how race affects how we hear. Can we talk about Ryan without talking about that? Can we talk about race without stating that every American conversation about the subject has a charge to it? It's very vexed. I think about race a lot. About the goal of color-blind casting. About how we're perceiving race always. I think we're unconsciously surprised, in the theater, when an Asian actor is sexy, because we expect him to be reserved. I think we're surprised when a Latino actor is intellectual—I bet if Raul Julia came back to life he would have some stories. How many black actresses will have Cate Blanchett's career?

"I find some of my colleagues in opera appallingly unaware of their reactions. I can't tell you how often people will compare a young minority singer with another singer of the same race who's come before. It's extremely limiting. And then the questions: Is this singer not well educated? Will there be an issue of professionalism? No one would ask that about a bespectacled Jewish kid, about a singer with a last name like yours or mine. No one would ask, is he serious enough? Is he smart enough, quick enough mentally, refined enough intellectually? People wonder about Ryan in a way they never would if he wasn't black. When he makes a mistake, if he wasn't black, they would just think he'd been misinformed and that he would get the problem fixed."

It was all tangled—the preconceptions were real, but so, it seemed, were Ryan's shortcomings. A further entanglement was the possibility that some of the cloudiness in his vowels was due to physical attributes found more

217

frequently in African American singers, pockets of resonance whose geometry enhanced warmth and richness but worked against gleam and precision. Zeger wondered about this, guessing that the theory might be right. But he emphasized that his thinking was based on his own listening, that there was no substantial science to support the idea. Oswald spoke along similar lines. Yvette Wyatt had said much the same: that the racial distinctiveness she heard in the young black singers she taught—in most of them, though not in the girl who'd refused to follow Wyatt's advice that she model herself on Denyce Graves rather than Alicia Keys—was a matter of nature at least as much as nurture.

Yet always there was the issue of expectation. To what extent did we hear—in African American and white singers—what we expected to hear?

I asked Dr. Paul Kwak about the roles of nature and nurture. He was the accompanist and ENT specialist who'd talked with me about the mystery of why big voices like Ryan's take longer to mature. About race and the physiology of tone, he said, "You can't do that study." Political objections would rain down on any researcher who tried to compare the vocal anatomy of blacks and whites. He surmised that nurture—the influence of black popular vocalists and church singers—played the heavier role, but that inborn aspects of the pharynx, the region running from the back of the throat to the back of the nasal cavity, might well have an effect. "Part of it has to be what you're born with, but we don't have the data, and then singing is so multifactorial that it would be extremely difficult to isolate causes."

Zeger, at the piano in the Juilliard rehearsal room, turned to another topic. He played a chord in three-beat clusters. The measures were from Banquo's aria, a piece that Ryan continued to practice. He planned to use it when the time came for auditions. The chord was menacing, the rhythm disturbing, and Zeger played it to illustrate something more that Ryan needed to work on. His rhythm was "flabby." The clusters of three were from the orchestral accompaniment; they formed an unsettled heartbeat, a fearful pulse, and Ryan's cadence as he sang, though not intended to be matched with the throb of the music, should align with it in a relationship that would add to the emotion of the aria. He wasn't getting this right. It was about more than following the notations in the score. He should be listening more acutely, "contextualizing the vocal line, responding to and using everything around him in the music."

The list of Ryan's weaknesses seemed limitless. Zeger mentioned something basic: Ryan too rarely sang less than forte, less than loud. He boomed without regard for a composer's modulations, for the fact that Verdi's markings for Banquo dropped as soft as triple piano. Then Zeger returned to things more sophisticated and elusive, to "harmonic listening," to "internalizing everything that's happening in the orchestra as part of the psychology of the character."

℘

"You're frustrated with me, aren't you?"

In a Met studio belowground it was sometimes Hemdi

219

Kfir who awaited him. She had an angular face and an Israeli accent.

"No," Ryan said, "I'm not frustrated."

She had once trained as a singer. She had been told that she had a lovely voice for Renaissance and early Baroque music, the type of repertoire that was sung in recitals in cozy venues with ensembles of period instruments. It was another way of saying that her voice was small. And meanwhile, her parents let her know that small wasn't good enough. She had abandoned the ambition to perform.

"Madamina." She spoke the first word of the aria.

He uttered the word back to her, the sixteenth or twentieth time they'd gone back and forth on these four syllables in this session, as she tried to make his vowels more purely Italian and suffuse brightness into his singing. His attempt, she told him again, was a disaster.

Lots of Americans, she knew, tended to take unstressed vowels and turn them into some version of *uh*. "Ab-*suh*-lutely." "Terr-*uh*-tory." Ryan couldn't seem to tear himself free of the habit: "*Mad-uh-min-uh*." The *uh*s wrecked the word and darkened his voice.

"'*Maaah-daaah-meen-aaah*,'" she exaggerated. "You're not too frustrated?"

"No. No way."

"'*Maaah-daaah* . . .'" she demonstrated yet again.

At last, he confessed that he could no longer hear the distinction between the vowel sound she wanted and his own failed efforts. They'd been concentrating on this single word for a quarter hour, and he felt he was going deaf—or crazy. But no, he assured her, they shouldn't stop.

When she said that she was satisfied, not pleased but satisfied, they continued on to the next word, in which he encountered a *c* and a *t*. She told him he was aspirating too much on both.

He admitted that he didn't know what she meant. He'd vowed to himself, when he started the Lindemann Program, that he wouldn't fake comprehension and lose out on learning; he was going to ask questions. "People might think I'm stupid," he told me, "but the only thing that's stupid is not to ask what I don't know."

She defined "aspirating" and pronounced the consonants, adding and subtracting air, mispronouncing and pronouncing properly, directing him toward the desired delicacy, the ideal Italian smoothness, the sensation, as the singer glided past the consonants and lingered on the vowels, of riding up and down gentle hills, of legato.

But excess air kept hopping from his mouth in microeruptions. "Maybe I'm not made for Italian." He smiled apologetically. "Maybe my mouth's not a lover. Maybe it's more of a fighter."

He struggled to replicate what she did, struggled until he felt like his teeth and tongue and hard palate were turning to stew.

⅋

"Our job," Oswald reminded Ryan one afternoon in his studio, "is to figure out how to sing thirty pitches on approximately twenty vowels, so six hundred combinations."

The thirty pitches referred to the notes in the two and a half octaves Ryan was capable of spanning. The number of vowels referred to the International Phonetic Alphabet and its coded system of vowel sounds, from æ to ʊ. It was a system covering the building blocks of more or less every language whose pronunciation a successful singer needed to master, from French to Russian, though the twenty sounds Oswald spoke about were just a start, a subset that wouldn't take him into Russian territory. The six hundred combinations were an accounting of the vocal adjustments a singer needed to make—many of them instinctual but many of them learned—in order to hit every pitch while producing the æ's and ʊ's, ɛ's and ɔ's and Ø's.

"And let's not forget the various dynamic levels," Oswald said. Some of the combinations required a shift in technique, depending on whether the score called for forte or pianissimo. He smiled, laughing for a second at the scope of the task. He relished the specificity of the work. He also liked to keep things upbeat. "That's it, in a nutshell," he summed up. "That's all there is to it."

"In a nutshell." Ryan laughed for a second, too.

The move to teaching had felt natural, Oswald had told me. "Singing always took such a toll. In teaching, the highs aren't as high, but I get to feel the highs almost every day."

They began studying a Verdi aria that was new for Ryan, the cry of an elderly aristocrat betrayed by his young fiancée.

Ah, perché l'etade in seno
giovin core m'ha serbato
Mi dovevan gli anni almeno
far di gelo ancora il cor

Oh, why has age kept my heart
   youthful in my breast
The years should have turned
   my heart to ice

Ryan sang, halting on an early note. "That was not good."

Oswald didn't disagree but didn't dwell on what had gone wrong. He moved swiftly onward: how to get the note right? "More reverse megaphone," he said, and instructed his student to lift one hand to the side of his head and bring the other close to his nose and mouth. He told Ryan to try the note again in this stance, a way to broaden the chamber back by the uvula while still manufacturing enough of his sound near his face—against the facial bones and in the cavities just behind them.

Oswald judged some of the advice Ryan was receiving at the Met to be misguided: Ryan was being bombarded with too much talk about pushing his voice forward. Not only might this steal the richness from his voice; it would also fail to provide the very gleam that the Met wanted. The correct method for adding luster, Oswald believed, could be paradoxical in some singers. Placing the voice forward, placing it "in the mask," was supposed to infuse brightness and clarity, but to his ears as he listened to Ryan, too much mask had an inexplicable result; it had an inverse effect; cloudiness returned. The key was to augment both front and back, both trumpet and trombone.

This wasn't the only split between the instruction Ryan got in Oswald's studio and at the opera house down the street. To cure his mispronunciations, Oswald insisted that he should concentrate mainly on the suppleness of his legato, in Italian or any other language, that this would be a panacea. Oswald didn't want him obsessing over each separate letter and syllable. In the subbasement rooms of the Met, the coaches told him that he'd better obsess.

Ryan didn't feel in any position to balance the points of view. The only solution seemed to be to divide himself, to work one way in this studio and a different way in others.

He sang the tricky note with his hands next to his head and face, Oswald applauded him, and they paused to talk about how gestures affected singing: half consciously, by suggestion.

"Like Sam Ramey's claw," Ryan said, naming a well-known bass. Sometimes the gestures were only for practicing, as with Ryan's two raised hands; sometimes, as with Ramey's covertly crimped fingers, they were encrypted prompts, and singers took them onstage and hoped that no one caught on.

"Certain artists are doing this or that with the hands, always," Oswald said. "They need to have a hand in a particular spot for a particular note, but they will never tell anyone what they're doing."

Teacher and student went back to the aria. "Up the middle of your head," Oswald said. "Verticality. Dome." He elevated a palm above his scalp, and Ryan did the same. "Superdome. Think Superdome." They were both football fans; the Superdome was the New Orleans stadium, and Oswald was searching for images of the shape that he wanted Ryan to picture, the shape that might aid him in vaulting the soft palate—the rear of the roof of the mouth—by a fraction of a millimeter and making better use of the anatomy nearby. This bordered on shamanism; these were involuntary or semivoluntary areas. Yet singers swore by these methods.

They had to. Somehow they needed to take the prosaic buzz of sound that rose from the vocal cords—those two oscillating flaps of tissue that stretch across the throat— and transform it into music, transfigure it by channeling it to flow and bounce in calibrated ways around all the internal chambers above the cords, and off the soft membranes and the hard surfaces, and through the lips and out into the world.

"Why don't you come over to the mirror?"

Ryan squeezed alongside the piano and faced his reflection in the mirror on the studio wall.

"On this note, let's try showing a little teeth." Oswald returned to the voluntary. "Just a little front teeth, so you can hardly see them in the mirror. It will give this note the brightness. But keep anchored and dark in the back. And let's think about the diaphragm, about support. We have to engage the abdominals below the belly button; you want that angled support."

Oswald had noticed something about Ryan, something he hoped to relieve through all his directions about teeth and diaphragm and dome and anchor: a look of bewilderment and helplessness when Ryan heard a note go awry. "It can last for five seconds," Oswald told me, "which is a long time. You can see how concerned he is. You can see him thinking, *I can't fix this—I'm standing in front of someone important, and I can't fix this.*"

℞

"It's melancholy," Noda said about the mood of a Michelangelo poem set to music by Wolf, one of the pieces Ryan was learning.

"Sorry, I don't know what 'melancholy' means." Ryan was faithful to his vow, obeyed his own edict: "The only thing that's stupid is not to ask what I don't know."

Noda and another coach who'd joined them in the practice room, a German specialist wearing knee-high black suede boots, attempted a definition. "Reflective and—"

"Dejected."

"Downcast."

"Tell me more," Ryan said. He never forgot a definition once he'd taken it in.

"Heavy in feeling."

They read through the text, the German specialist, her silver hair cropped short and black jacket cut tight, correcting: "The *ch* in *'flüchten'* is too thick. Bring it forward. And the *ü* must be more open." Ryan's mind was a vault for definitions, a sieve for enunciations. She repeated herself, and finally they decided it was time for him to sing the piece. Noda played the quietly churning introductory measures, and Ryan came in. Noda cut him off.

"Remember what the mezzo said in the forum last week, that she never sings loudly when she's first learning a piece, because she wants to fully take in the accompaniment. There's so much to pick up subliminally in the music if you let yourself hear it."

Ryan agreed, then said he was curious about something in the text. One of the lines seemed to imply that Michelangelo had been a singer—was this right?

"No, a sculptor, a painter," Noda said. "An architect, a poet."

"Okay, I'm not going to lie. I didn't really know who he was before I looked him up online. I read a lot about his art. The Tristine, Chistine—"

"Sistine Chapel."

℞

Pristine Italian vowels, the note-by-note repositioning of invisible anatomy, the capacity for subliminal listening— the necessity of uncountable elusive skills was preying on Ryan one day when his cell phone rang.

He was a year into the program. His progress so far had been reasonable, if unremarkable, to Oswald's ears; it had been sluggish to Noda's and Zeger's. Yet there was one exultant moment. As part of the program, he'd had his Met debut. He was given a few lines of singing in a production of Puccini's *Turandot,* a love story set in a Chinese royal court. Ryan didn't have much to do vocally, but his costume was an amalgam of the Oriental and the surreal, with a stupendous cloak and gilded talons that doubled the length of his fingers. The costume stood out even among the other figures of the palace, and for this, it seemed, the audience awarded him with an uptick of applause when he took his bow. Or maybe they clapped heartily because he looked so happy to be on that stage, and so unsubtly pleased by their approval.

Both Valerie and Cecil were there for opening night, proud but reticent, Cecil's gregariousness quelled by the aura of the Met, though he did wear a flashy cutaway jacket and silver vest, as if to advertise his connection to his son, the star. There was a stiffness, a chilliness between Ryan and his mother. They didn't talk much by phone these days, and he rarely initiated the stilted exchanges they did have. He had spoken to me, a year earlier, of the wall he felt that his mother had built between the two of them, after he'd threatened her life, a wall that remained standing and that he yearned to bring down, bit by bit, with his singing. But now he seemed willing to leave the wall between them or, tentatively, to be putting up a wall of his own.

With his father, he'd been talking regularly by phone since their time together in Colorado. Cecil had described an idea he had, a dream for both of them. He'd made Ryan a proposition. He and Ryan should go into business together. They should combine his barbecue catering and Ryan's singing. It was scarcely relevant to Ryan that this didn't exactly match his own dreams for his future. What mattered was how his father always ended their calls. "I love you, son," he said.

When his cell phone rang—as he stood in an area of the opera house with glass-walled offices and a tiny lounge—it was toward the end of the *Turandot* run, which spread over four months. Ryan could see on the screen that the call was from his father. A jolt of guilt ran through him. It was his father's birthday—he'd forgotten to call.

The area where he stood was a kind of home to him; several Met staffers had desks there, and Gayletha Nichols, the motherly director of the contest, had her office there, and Lindemann faculty and trainees wandered through. Between coaching sessions, Ryan liked to spend time in this corner of the Met, chatting with anyone who might be available for conversation. He seemed compelled to do this, inexhaustibly eager to bond.

"He's a special guy," Nichols said. She hadn't been able to help but keep watch over him since the competition. "He puts himself out there, so people are drawn to him. You can tell he's sought out a feeling of family here, even with all the pressure and judgment."

"He has to know everyone. He knows the stagehands, he knows all the security guards," Noda said. "When he's late for a coaching, it's because he's talking. He's like this wide-open heart. He's like a walking heart with a face and a voice."

Now Ryan said hello into his phone and waited for his father to rib him about his forgetfulness. But it wasn't his father. It was the woman Cecil had been with for the past few years, who'd become his fiancée, a woman Ryan knew as Miss Lonna.

Seconds later he was kneeling. "You're joking, you're lying, it's his birthday."

He straightened, reeled into a hallway to be alone, sank down again. "You're lying. No!" he howled. "That can't be true." He could hear only half of her words over his own insistence, but it was plain that there was no joking or lying in her voice. His father had gone back to bed in pain that morning and hadn't woken up. He'd had a heart attack.

One of the Met staffers tracked him into the hall. Sobbing, Ryan tried to answer his question, to communicate that his father was gone. He fled along the hall and lunged through a yellow-and-black-striped door. He was in a parking garage. He hurried past numbered pillars and stop signs, his vision a blur, and out onto the sidewalk. He slowed in front of a Met loading bay. It was a giant mouth, rimmed by concrete and corrugated metal, dark inside. He lost all strength and stopped, as if he wished to be swallowed by it.

Nichols, alerted by the staffer about what had happened, trailed Ryan and saw him up the block, bent over next to the loading zone. The skeleton of an unfinished building rose above him, sheets of orange plastic flapping. He was fighting to slow his sobbing breath. She put a hand on his back, and he pulled himself up partially, hugging her, propping his weight against her girth, crying. "I'm sorry, I'm sorry," he said.

She asked what he needed, her arms enwrapping what little they could of his upper body. "Do you want me to take a cab home with you?" she asked.

"No, I'm okay, but thank you. I'm sorry."

"Make sure I know whatever I can do."

"I'm sorry, I'm sorry."

℘

He traveled to Bakersfield for the funeral a few weeks later. The Met paid for his flight—another singer in the program offered to do this, too—and condolence emails came in from his fellow trainees and from Levine and Oswald and Noda and Zeger and the Met administration. "You're in my thoughts." "If there's anything you need at all..." The emails consisted of the standard phrases, but for Ryan they signified family.

At the funeral, Adrian wore a sleeveless T-shirt, muscles and elaborate tattoos on display. He was with a woman who was seven months pregnant with his second child. He didn't really know his first child, his eight-year-old son, at all. Ryan hadn't seen Adrian in a number of years, hadn't heard anything from him in over two. Cecil's stepson, Ryan's stepbrother, was still serving time, and wasn't there.

Over the last week, Ryan had rehearsed and rejected twenty songs till he resolved on one that expressed the way he felt.

Hear my cry, hear my call
Hold my hand lest I fall

He barely made it through without disintegrating. Adrian didn't make it through "When Tomorrow Starts Without Me," the poem that Cecil's fiancée had chosen for him to read.

I wish so much you wouldn't cry the way you did
   today
While thinking of the many things we didn't get to say

The ache that was Adrian's life, the ache that was this moment, overtook him, rattling his naked shoulders, forcing him to stop again and again, to wait for his violent shaking to subside. His and Ryan's half brother, Greg—the son Cecil had before Adrian, with a woman he'd known before Valerie—held Adrian as the shaking slowed to trembling.

Ryan had never seen Adrian so defenseless. Maybe, he thought, he and his brother would be able to connect before the weekend was over. They hadn't spent a minute alone, he realized, in nearly ten years. A few years before that, Adrian had punched through the wall of the trailer and basically disappeared from his life.

The service was splendid. A photograph of his father as a child, clowning and smiling, glowed on the wall above the podium. It was the same smile Cecil still had at fifty, Ryan could see. Friends and relatives told stories: Cecil as a hapless fisherman with a sense of humor, Cecil as an agile dancer with exuberant moves, Cecil as goofy, Cecil as someone with a gravitational pull, someone people wanted to be near. For Ryan, the likeness he felt in Colorado was confirmed. He was his father's son. "From the way everyone talked about him, you could see he had such a zest," he told me. "I didn't grow up with my dad, but a lot of people's personalities—it's genetic. So much of me is his soul in mine."

The weekend that followed was a series of high-piled plates and boozy concoctions. There was a restaurant with all-you-can-eat catfish; there was glass after glass of Baileys Irish Cream poured into dark beer. At a diner, at two in the morning, Ryan looked across the table and said, "I need you to get your life together. I need you to do that for the child you have on the way. Adrian, I need you to do it for me, for me as your little brother." It wasn't just the two of them in the booth. It wasn't the private situation he had imagined. Two of their cousins and the mother of Adrian's unborn baby were squeezed in with them. But the others remained quiet, and Ryan lurched on.

"I looked up to you as a kid because you're so strong. And when I think about it, I think one of the reasons I got into opera, it was because you were so different.

You were the greatest artist in the world. You drew all those dinosaurs. Those superheroes. All that artwork. I thought you were so cool. You're my big brother. When you left, when I never heard from you, I wondered why you hated me. But I never stopped worrying about you. I never stopped wanting to hear from you. We need to be better brothers to each other. We're made of the same genetic material."

Ryan kept expecting someone to interrupt him as he recounted and pleaded. No one did, not his cousins and not the woman who stroked Adrian's back. Adrian said nothing. He stayed silent even when Ryan wound down. Yet Ryan could tell he was letting the words flood through him. And he felt Adrian's silent listening flooding back.

But before he boarded his flight to New York, he had one more drunken conversation. Greg, his half brother, who hadn't known Cecil for much of his childhood but who later became close to their father, told Ryan there was something he should know. Cecil hadn't believed that Ryan was his son.

FIFTEEN

I ASKED HIM if he was serious," Ryan told me, "and he said he was. And then he kind of went dead. I went dead, too. I didn't push the subject. I didn't delve any deeper. I didn't ask him when our father said that or how it came up. I didn't think about it till I was back here. Then it hit me. I was—"

Ryan was about to say something about the feelings that came when he thought about his half brother's revelation. He cut himself off. We were alone in the apartment he shared with a roommate. In the small common area off the kitchen, there was an electronic keyboard on a folding stand, where he plunked out notes to help himself practice, and a television for watching football. Sitting on a leatherette couch, he paused for quite a while before continuing: "I don't know. My brother and my half brothers have my dad's complexion. I'm my mom's complexion. I know he was unfaithful. I don't know about my mom. I—"

Again he stopped himself. He yawned. It was a long, oversized yawn, but there was nothing theatrical, nothing exaggerated about it; the reflex seemed to overtake him, to shut down his mind and break off his thought. When he resumed speaking, it was on the same topic but with the focus turned upon his half brother. "I just feel bad for him. It sucks that he had to hear our father say that. It sucks for him."

Ryan didn't doubt that his half brother was telling the truth about his father's words. "He wouldn't lie to me about that kind of thing." Then his voice lifted: "I believe my dad died knowing that I'm his son. I know he loved me, and that he passed away knowing how much I loved him. I talked to him in the weeks after he died and before the funeral. I know he's in a better place, watching down on me."

I asked whether he'd spoken with anyone, besides me, about what his half brother had said, about the emotions it had stirred. He hadn't. I asked whether he thought he should, whether he thought a therapist might be helpful, whether the Met program might put him in touch with one or whether he'd like me to do that. I had a sense of foreboding. He'd lost his father three times: lost him as a child, for twenty years; lost him to death just as he'd reclaimed him in the contest and in Colorado; and lost him now to the doubt his half brother had planted. It seemed too much.

"No," he said. "I don't think I'm ready for that. It could make me go backward. I want to think of my father the way I think of him. I don't want to think of him as the person who didn't call me for years, who forgot my birthdays. I, me as a child, desperately wanted to know him and for him to love me. Desperately. I wanted *him*. But that's something I've tried to teach myself—forgive; don't blame people for being human." He laughed slightly, coughed, and groaned in quick succession. "There's probably a lot of things I should see a therapist about, but I've built myself up mentally by always pushing forward. Seeing a psychologist might make me fall apart—and what would I do after that?"

℞

The same sort of fear—of falling apart—stalked him during acting class in the program. The sessions were essential to the training; acting was becoming a crucial part of opera. There had long been some singers who found it a distraction, who felt it was beneath them. Lately the Met was making it clear that it mattered for casting.

The program's acting coach led the trainees through exercises. They recalled private scenes, memories that would connect them to their characters. Ryan admired how the others seemed to hold these memories in their minds as they sang. No one was permitted to share the recollections aloud, yet he felt he could see them at work in the trainees, permeating their bodies, their faces. He couldn't do this himself. Once, working on an aria from *The Marriage of Figaro* that he was considering adding to his repertoire, an aria about the dangers posed by women—"These you call goddesses...are witches who enchant"—he pictured what led up to his being locked away: the frenzy of rage his mother had stoked in him; his threat on her life; her calling the cops; their carrying him down the stairs. But he couldn't hold on to the images as he sang in class. Right away they fragmented, faded, cleared. This was lucky, he was sure. It would have been impossible for him to get through even the opening lines of the aria with that in his head.

The scenes he was drawn to using all centered on his family, but they were too powerful. He had to ignore the exercises; if he didn't, the vocal techniques he was learning with Oswald would be obliterated. Maybe in the future he would try what the coach was teaching—maybe in the future, when the musical techniques were rooted within him and the memories weren't so consuming.

For now, there was a divide between his dramatic and his comic arias. With the dramatic characters, he ventured further than he would have before starting the program, pushing himself to understand the men he was playing and to let his understanding spread through both voice and body—but with limits. He wasn't going to risk the coach's methods. With the comedic characters, though, no method was required. His immersion was immediate, complete, natural. His acting was manic in the right way, enthralling, charismatic. It had been full of flair in the contest; it was more so as his time in the program went by; everything that he kept in check emotionally seemed to spring out sideways in comedy. And the link he'd discovered with his father's personality, a hereditary tie he didn't question consciously for more than a few scattered seconds, impelled him.

℘

Ryan's second Met role, given to him as a Lindemann trainee, was in Wagner's *Parsifal*, and rehearsals were under way at the time of his father's funeral. The Met asked if he wanted to be released from his part, because of all he was going through. He did not. His father's death only made him more determined.

The role was like nothing else he'd done; it was neither comic nor dramatic; Wagner had probed psychology through myth. *Parsifal* drew from a legend of King Arthur, and Ryan was cast as an unnamed knight who reported briefly to Amfortas, the king. "I have the biggest part of the small parts," he told me. "I move the plot forward." He studied his few lines and found artistic reasons to sing them with great emphasis and flourish. There was, as well, something familiar about Wagner's world, a place of super-heroes, like the Schwarzenegger figures he and his brother had stolen and cherished as kids. When he addressed the king, he was going to make the moment his own, singing with grandeur.

During their coaching sessions, Noda chided him for his mispronunciations of Wagner's libretto and for the waver-ing aspect of brightness in his voice: "We will do this over and over.... That note is way too dark.... I don't care if we don't get any further today.... Please apply yourself, please, because you know I don't have endless patience." But his patience did seem almost endless. He was growing ever more fond of Ryan, and he liked his stylistic choices for the knight, his demonstrative singing. Ryan was also making sudden strides technically. To Noda's ears, the flaws were diminishing. As he coached Ryan for the role, he pumped him up even more than Ryan was pumped up on his own, reminding him that this was Wagner at the Met, and that this production of the opera was new—new sets, new stag-ing, new directorial interpretation—meaning that it would get even more attention than Wagner usually would, and always Wagner was an event. There were Wagner junkies who traveled the globe for his operas. Noda told him that he had a chance to make an impression, and Ryan hatched a fantasy that edged toward an expectation. Someone involved in casting at Bayreuth—the house Wagner himself had helped to design in Germany in the eighteen seventies, so that his operas would look and sound just as he imagined them—would be in the Met audience, would be struck by Ryan's singing, and would think, *We need to grab this kid.* On the Met stage, Ryan would be exchanging lines with two of the best singers on the planet, René Pape, who was playing Gurnemanz, and Peter Mattei, who was singing Amfortas. "It's huge. When Amfortas enters, I'm the one who changes his mood to anger. I change his emotional direction."

"No, no, no, no," the conductor, turning his thoughts to Ryan during a rehearsal late in the process, said. The musicians silenced themselves. The conductor told Ryan that he was a lowly knight, that he was singing to a king, that he must not be so loud or expressive; his manner must be more deferential. The musicians played their instruments again, and Ryan resumed. Again the conductor interrupted. He looked at Ryan, lifted one hand with two fingers dangling downward, and moved his fingers across the air in a quick stepping motion. His message was plain. Though the score gave Ryan some leeway in his pacing because of the way several measures were written, he should pick up his cadence. He was keeping the focus too much on himself.

"It was definitely a chip, or more like a chop, off what I thought of my role," Ryan said after the rehearsal. "But he made a good point. I'm a subcharacter. Anyway, being told

239

that isn't necessarily a bad thing. It just means I have to be more special with less."

To be certain he was ready, Ryan asked Oswald to make time for an extra session on the day of opening night. Because Ryan was going straight to the Met afterward, he wore his Brooks Brothers tuxedo, wore it with his own touches, a purple cummerbund, a black shirt. He walked into the studio, a trickle of sweat already creeping toward his jaw, shut the door behind him, and muttered, "My mother."

Outside the studio, in Oswald's cramped vestibule, Valerie sat on a wooden bench. She kept her black wool coat on. Her face was expressionless. She'd taken time off from a job she'd gotten as a dispatcher with the Navy and flown up from Norfolk at dawn; she'd hardly slept the night before. And now she'd been trailing Ryan through his day. I asked if she was worried about staying awake through the five-hour opera. "I'll be all right," she said. "It'll keep my interest." To this understatement, this declaration of pride in her son, she added the faintest smile.

In the studio, after his two words, Ryan rolled his neck, stuck out and stretched his tongue, and emitted a note of anguish. The neck and tongue were part of his normal warming up, the note wasn't. Having his mother in tow was taking its toll. He'd had misgivings about having her here; he hadn't mentioned *Parsifal* to her until just recently. He'd known it would be taxing to have her close.

It was more than taxing. Her presence felt both domi-

nant and horribly weak. "She is my past. So much of who
I was and what I'm moving away from is all mixed up with
her, growing up with her. She's still the person who can
push my buttons. Twist me up. She doesn't even have to say
anything. All she has to do is stand there."

Yet at the same time, he felt that she was deteriorating.
This weakness was new, or at least he hadn't noticed it
before. It took him by surprise. She was short of breath
as they walked together on the street. She was fifty and
called herself old. She complained about her legs and her
heart. He felt he was losing his sanity; he couldn't fit the
feebleness together with the power she held, and, too, the
feebleness itself unsteadied him. Though he maintained his
guard, though he'd spoken with her only occasionally by
phone since moving to New York, he told me, "I love her. I
get upset at myself for being so cold. But I have to be. I try,
I really try to be better about her. But it's really hard. One
thing about always pushing myself forward is that it makes
me very distant from her. And then her being so run-down,
I don't know what to feel. Walking with her huffing and
puffing, I thought, *I know you—you're the woman who
faced down the dealers when I was about to get jumped.
You're the woman who made sure she got her community
college degree.* Her being weak, I could never imagine it.
But she's not the same."

As his mother sat on the other side of the door, he ran
through arpeggios with Oswald and, after warming up, ran
through the knight's lines. Ryan placed a finger against the
flesh between his nose and upper lip to make sure there was
enough vibration in that area, a sign that his sound wasn't
too far back, that he was creating enough luster.

"That's not too loud, is it?"

"You're allowed to be confident," Oswald said.

"Remember, the maestro wants it soft," Ryan said. "And what the maestro wants the maestro gets. Even if there is an exclamation point there in the score, and even if an exclamation point equals *exclamatory*. But the good thing is, when I respond to Gurnemanz, they told me I can make a gesture to let everyone know I'm about to sing, something not too much." He asked Oswald for a suggestion, and they resolved on a restrained movement of his right arm.

"Now if it were up to me," Oswald said protectively as the session ended, "you wouldn't do any vocalizing at all between when you leave here and when you're onstage. I know your schedule at the Met. You've done enough singing today. Hopefully no one will come into your dressing room asking you to run your lines."

Valerie was still in her wool coat when Ryan emerged. She stood slowly. His face, usually so open, calcified instantly and closed off. They walked through the lobby and outside, wordless.

℘

Soon it was time to get into his costume, a white shirt and gray pants for this stark, postapocalyptic production. He shared a dressing room with another singer from the program, a Korean American tenor a foot shorter than Ryan. He was cast as a sentry. Between the red couch and the black upright, they buttoned their shirts while a humidifier gurgled and sent steam into the air. "Did you bring Uno cards?" Ryan joked nervously. The remaining hour till the curtain's rise seemed insufferably long.

"I might play Star Crash." The sentry named an online game.

"Toi toi!" people called in the hallway. It was an opera singer's equivalent of "break a leg." No one was sure what it meant or what its origins were; maybe it was a distortion of the German word for devil. "Toi toi toi!" rang up and down the corridor, and two of the top people at the Met, who kept tabs on the progress of the trainees, leaned in to wish "toi toi" to Ryan and the sentry.

A tall woman with blond hair tapped on the open door and walked in. "Do you want to run that line for me?" It wasn't a question. In one of the final rehearsals he'd forgotten his words. Ryan stood face-to-face with her and sang the phrases. She nodded and was gone.

"Thirty minutes" came the announcement over the intercom. "Thirty minutes."

In half an hour, the overture's first notes—delicate, wounded—filled the house, and twenty-five minutes after that Ryan went down on one knee, kept his shoulders and head lowered, sang to the king for twenty-five seconds, and made his way offstage. Except for one later line, this brought his performance to an end.

Valerie and I shared a snack at intermission. She descended the red-carpeted stairs doggedly, cautiously, in black pants and a formal blouse, and we stood at a high round table. I mentioned a trip that Ryan might take to Berlin during the coming August, with the Met paying the bill, to help him absorb the sounds of German. She said that she knew nothing about it. "Ryan does not speak to his mother."

Her voice was flat and her words were clipped, not sharp but tight, partly because of fatigue and partly, perhaps, because an extreme reserve had replaced the volatility that had crouched close to the surface in an earlier time. "If you let him tell it, he got everything good from his father. That's his belief now."

℘

Der Mensch liegt in größter Not
Der Mensch liegt in größter Pein....
Der liebe Gott...wird leuchten mir bis in das ewig
  selig Leben

Man lies in great need
Man lies in great pain....
The good Lord...will light the way to an eternally
  blissful life

"Jessye Norman sang this," Noda said, telling Ryan to find a recording of Norman, the African American diva of the nineteen seventies and eighties, performing this piece by Mahler. He'd chosen it for Ryan's upcoming recital, to be held in a small auditorium around the corner from the Met. Annually, each singer in the program gave a recital along with one or two other trainees, an exercise enacted in the hope, however slender, that someday the public would flock to hear them both in concert and on the opera stage. The recitals were also a chance, beyond the minor roles in operas, for the singers to be heard in formal performance by Lindemann and Met staff. This concert was scheduled for the week after *Parsifal*'s closing night. Noda had picked the Mahler song as a way for Ryan to honor his father and help himself to heal.

"I'm going to play it for you," Noda said, and for two or three minutes he compressed all of his talent as a soloist into this basement performance for his student, so that Ryan could hear, as Noda heard, all the emotion, all the compositional genius, that had gone into Mahler's music. For Noda, the instrument under his fingers was unfriendly, unalive; he rued the years of learning the piano to fulfill his mother's dreams. But these feelings were impossible to detect in the sounds he produced in the underground room. It was as if his regret and pain about the instrument were transposed into the artistry of his playing. On the first measures, he allowed each chord to fade almost yet not fully into oblivion before he struck the next. Those measures alone were enough to open any listener's rib cage and leave him exposed, aching.

"I think it's the most beautiful piece of music on earth," Noda said when he was done.

Ryan agreed without speaking.

Noda read aloud Mahler's notation above the first line, *"Sehr feierlich, aber schlicht,"* and translated it: "Solemn and ceremonial, but plain and simple." He instructed Ryan to look up more translations that evening—he wanted to be sure that Ryan understood everything that was embedded in the music. Noda led him onward into the song's passages of crystalline suffering, and into the music's frantic quest for rescue, and toward the quiescence, the redemption, of the end.

Ryan brought the piece to Oswald the next time they met. "Ken chose it because of my father. So I could sing it for my father." He handed the pages across the piano. "And Jessye Norman sang it." He'd listened to Norman's recordings of the song, fallen into the folds of despair in her voice—"feelings," he said, "way beyond language."

With Oswald, he was anxious to begin. "But I definitely need your help warming up today."

"How late were you up last night?"

"There's nothing I can do. I'm onstage in the third act," he said about *Parsifal,* "so I think I got to sleep by three in the morning." He was feeling hints of a cold, maybe a sinus infection, maybe the flu. He plucked a tissue from the box on the piano and blew his nose in the staccato way he had; it made a half squeak, half honk that seemed to come from an aquatic mammal. "If I start seeing yellow crap, it's two or three weeks."

They discussed singing through sickness, when it was possible and when a lack of rest could risk disaster. A bad cough could be a nightmare—as you expelled mucus from the lungs, the pressure of air shooting through the larynx caused the vocal cords to slam and slam and slam against each other. They traded thoughts about steroid medication. "Steroids bring the inflammation down," Oswald advised, "but then you'll re-swell to a worse state. And steroids can dry the membranes."

They talked about getting vacuumed and how hideous that process could be. Ryan had gone through this a few times with Dr. Youngnan Cho, an ENT specialist whose practice was full of Met singers. She'd pried open his nostrils with her speculum, probed his sinuses with tubing, and switched on a suction machine, and he'd watched globs of mucus and blood, mustard-colored, green, dark brown, spurt and slide from within him, out his nose, and through the tubing for ten minutes at a stretch.

"Slowly, then." Oswald cut off the conversation and laid one hand on the keys. Gradually they worked their way into Mahler. "Go for more dome. That note sat too low. That's why the grit came into the voice."

Da kam ein Engelein und wollt mich abweisen
Ach nein! Ich ließ mich nicht abweisen

"That vowel—you want it to be bright but not overly bright. You want it *roundedly* bright."

Ich bin von Gott und will wieder zu Gott

"Good. The legato is getting better."

I am God's creation and want to return to my Lord

On the subway ride home he recited the piece in his mind, and in the room off his kitchen he stood at the keyboard and tapped out the measures with one finger, singing syllable by syllable, note by note, penciling reminders into his score and scolding himself in a heated mumble.

"No."

"That's the A-flat."

"No, shit no."

"It's your passaggio."

"Cover."

"Go a little higher."

"Oh, shit."

"Roundedly bright, roundedly bright."

Weeks later, with the recital only days away, Oswald said, "That's masterful," about the song's closing phrases. He praised the intermingling of tones, of throat and mask, dark and light.

"Gorgeous," Noda exulted that same week, raising one hand, thumb pressed to fingertips in a sign of tribute. "I think *Parsifal* was a great experience for you—being around those great singers. Now please, I want you to practice every schwa. But it's incredible hearing you. It's like hearing Jessye as a man."

A diffuse light reflected off the pale wood of the recital stage.

"This piece is dedicated to my father," Ryan said in front of the audience of Met insiders and fellow trainees and donors to the program. He lifted his hands to the level of his rib cage. His palms, partially upturned, floated in the air, as if he was gathering something in.

Parsifal, the recital, a concert of scenes performed by the trainees—these were all steps in the sudden progress that Ryan was making, to ears like Noda's and Oswald's, in the aftermath of his father's death. It was as though the distance made permanent by his dying was an expanse he could cross only with his voice and only if he mustered more and more artistic strength.

Like other trainees, Ryan, during his second year in the

program, was offered a spot in the company of a summer festival, with dates coming in June and July. In the smaller of its two theaters, the festival, outside Washington, DC, staged a little-known opera by Rossini—composer of *The Barber of Seville*—with a cast of young singers. The opera was a romp about a group of European grandees who converge at a spa before attending the coronation of the new French king. And Ryan, playing a scholar tagging along with the nobles, had an aria that mocked each character in turn.

He prepared for months before arriving at the festival. His aria contained an abundance of patter, line after line of high-velocity libretto with bursts of repeating staccato notes that tended to toss him off pitch. And there were leaps into falsetto and plunges down the staff. But the worst problem was that the patter put an emphasis on language, and the language was Italian, and while Ryan's Italian pronunciation had been improving, the improvement had been at a crawl.

Hemdi Kfir was no longer his Italian coach; he felt that he was always failing her, that his mouth turned to mush during every session. He switched to her mentor, Bob Cowart, who'd been with the program for thirty years and who taught in a cell even more monastic than the Met's other underground vaults: the lighting was dim, the piano unpolished, and the unadorned cinder block walls especially close. Cowart looked like he might live there, like he never sought out the sun and seldom bothered to straighten his clothes or comb his tufted gray hair.

He kept with him, at all times, a laminated page from a Japanese encyclopedia, a gift from a voice teacher he'd met while coaching in Japan years ago. The drawing captured the surfaces of bone within the head, the plates of reverberation and cavities of resonance, and it accentuated a parallelism between structures, a relationship of arches; the interior of the head seemed to have been designed by an inspired architect. "Isn't it wonderful?" He revealed the drawing to Ryan, shared it like a glimpse of ancient treasure, and shared his theory that Italian was the ideal language for classical singing, because it took such advantage of this internal amphitheater. "I'm obsessed with this picture. I sleep with it. I show it to my nephews and nieces. Isn't it glorious?"

Ryan found Cowart's eccentricity soothing. Together they laid a foundation. But Italian was only the beginning of the pronunciation he needed to learn; the grandees he mocked in this aria came from all over the continent. There was a Russian, a Spaniard, a German, a Frenchman, a Pole, and as he poked fun at them, he adopted the quirks of their versions of Italian, with the Russian's Italian vowels sliding backward and rolling around like marbles in his mouth, with the Spaniard caressing his *j*'s, with the German employing his lips and tongue like weapons. It was an aria of linguistic slapstick, and by the time Ryan arrived at the festival for rehearsals, he was on the brink of making it a piece of bravura.

During rehearsals, he applied some finishing touches to his enunciations. He added some physical comedy, miming and posing. He devised a dance, a swaying two-step that channeled lots of his father's comic dazzle and a little of his moonwalking skill. And on opening night, when he performed, the festival audience laughed aloud, with big guffaws here and there in the crowd. They yelled "Bravo!" at the curtain call. Some got carried away, dispensing with opera convention and letting out whoops of appreciation. The *Washington Post,* in a review by its chief classical music critic, gave him one sentence: "Ryan Speedo Green, who sang Don Profondo with a warm mien and sound, seems fully ready for a big career."

Brian Zeger—the head of the Lindemann Program, who sometimes envisioned Ryan becoming an artistic "shape-shifter"—traveled down from New York for the third night. He told Ryan afterward that he would arrange for him to sing the aria for Maestro Levine when the program started again in the fall, that Levine would love it.

"I feel like the sky's the limit," Ryan said, driving away from the festival grounds, folded into his economy-size rental car.

SIXTEEN

Ryan bowed his head over a plate of eggs, potatoes, and biscuits, and thanked God for the food, as his mother had taught him to do when he was a child. He and I sat in a chain restaurant in Staunton, west of Richmond and almost to the West Virginia border. The restaurant had a rustic theme, with rough beams overhead and old rifles mounted on the walls. In his prayer, he used his customary words, then stopped, shut his eyes more tightly, hunched his shoulders, and said, "Lord, please Lord, help me to help at least one or two of these kids today."

Months earlier, I had spent some time in and around the facility, and the director had asked if I thought Ryan would be willing to speak to the kids. Despite all his fear about revisiting the past, he was more than willing.

On the afternoon before his breakfast prayer, we had driven toward Staunton on the route he'd taken in the back of the police car, through the forest that clung to the edges of the road. "I had no idea where I was going," he said. Otherwise he was quiet.

We exited the highway and wound to the top of the knoll and parked in a lot surrounded by a patchy field. There was no one outside on the grounds. A scattering of crows seemed to own the expanse of rough grass and gave out isolated caws to confirm their possession. Below, in the distance, an industrial plant emitted a steady hiss and a percussive clank, but the noises were far-off and faint. Staunton wasn't a big town, yet it was spread out, and the existence of the center at the top of the hill, the center that had finally shed DeJarnette's name, felt like it would be easily forgettable.

"Cell Phones Are Not Permitted Past This Point," read a sign in the waiting area, and another stated, "No Weapons." Ryan struck up a conversation with the receptionist, mentioning his past, his present. She told him she'd worked on the wards of the old center, the boarded-up pair of mansions with pillars and balconies on the opposite hill, then quit before the new facility was built, quit before Ryan's time. Turnover among the ward staff had always been high, then and now. She'd returned to this safe position behind plexiglass. "It is so heartwarming to see someone like you," she said. A heavy door opened, and the director, Jeffrey Aaron, ushered us into the facility.

The plan was that Aaron, who'd been a psychologist at the center for over a decade and had just taken over its leadership, would give Ryan a tour, so he could look around privately, without being the object of everyone's attention, and then, the next day, Ryan would deliver a presentation to the kids and another to the staff. Aaron was in his late forties; he had a goatee and wore a gray tie and casual gray pants. He led us along an immaculately clean corridor. A harsh cry—crow-like, though louder and more protracted—came from somewhere within the building. He swiped a card and tapped a code and unlocked another heavy door, this one to Ryan's old unit, and from the moment we proceeded forward, Aaron was no longer Ryan's guide.

Ryan's memory of the layout was immediately so precise, and the force of emotional gravity so strong, that he went directly toward one of the two seclusion cells, as though pulled there by a chain. The cell was empty, and he stepped inside. He touched the cinder block.

"The walls weren't blue," he said to Aaron.

The director replied that the color had replaced off-white sometime between then and now.

"And there weren't any of these fish." Ryan's tone was flatter than usual, not accusatory but not friendly either. He stared at the few big tropical fish, yellow and red, painted onto the blue.

"No," Aaron said.

Turning in every direction, Ryan scanned and inspected the surfaces of each wall. "Being here at the center," he said to Aaron, "it feels like every minute you're living on glass, and the second you break that glass, you're in seclusion." He spread the fingers of both of his large hands over the cinder block, removed them, returned them to the wall, and walked out of the room. He spun and went back inside. "This cell felt like a torture chamber."

He pressed his fingertips to the blue, dragging them two or three inches, as if searching for something. "The walls don't feel the same. They weren't like this. I remember the texture so clearly. They were so much more rough."

Aaron said that they'd received a lot of repainting, a lot of layers. Ryan wondered to himself about the stains that had been covered over, and I thought about some of the scenes that the director had recounted to me, the kids pounding their heads against these walls and the staff having to decide whether to intervene, maybe just by standing there and holding a pillow between a kid's head and the wall if the worker didn't feel too endangered.

Ryan drifted out, reluctant to leave. Another shriek resounded from beyond the unit. His pod of twelve kids was empty. The kids were elsewhere, the unit peaceful for the time being. Somewhere, someone began banging, the noise violent enough to reach us. Ryan walked with purpose, ahead of Aaron, again as though pulled.

"This was my cell."

Aaron knocked to be sure that no one was inside. The room, it turned out, had no one assigned to it; the shelves and cubbyholes were devoid of belongings. Without pausing, Ryan lay down on the thin mattress and remained on his back, rigid, unmoving.

℘

The director took us to the gym, where Ryan would give his talk in the morning, and there Ryan met a few teenagers having their recreation time. He tossed a football to a stocky girl in sweatpants, the ball wobbling and falling at her feet, and chatted with two boys. The eyelids of one of the boys sagged, and his posture was vaguely skewed; he gave off a hint of mental illness. The second boy's stance and speech suggested nothing abnormal besides a barely contained readiness to erupt. The second boy was probably five eight, with broad shoulders. Ryan had been around this kid's size when he'd been here. The kid had a short Afro and wore red leather high-tops and blue jeans decorated with a pattern of silver studs. The two boys struck Ryan with a visceral recollection, a memory not new but newly physical. Half of the recollection was that when he was here, he'd been revolted and terrified by the mentally ill, afraid that he might be as sick as they were. The other half of the memory that knifed through his body was that, like the second kid, he'd been a threat to everyone.

Aaron introduced Ryan, saying nothing about his past, only that he would be singing opera and speaking to them tomorrow.

"You a singer?" the second boy asked.

"Yes."

"I'm a rapper. That's what I'm going to be."

"Hey, all right!" Ryan smiled and offered an excess of enthusiasm.

"I'll check you later," the teen said, all but sneering, and walked off.

In Aaron's office, Ryan told the director how badly he wished to have an effect on the kids.

"You will—though they might not thank you right away."

Ryan and I went for coffee after the visit, and he kept our conversation focused on the rapper: how much he hoped to reach him. "He was the first one I saw when we walked into the gym, the first one my eyes went to. He's going to be the toughest nut to crack."

Then the afternoon, the walls he'd touched, the bed he'd lain on, assaulted him. "My brain hurts," he said. "I better sleep."

&

In the morning, after the prayer and the breakfast, we returned to the top of the knoll, the field of crows. "I'm not going to lie," he said before we got out of the car. "I'm nervous. *Nervous*." He laughed in a way I'd never heard from him before, a choked falsetto. "I don't want to say the wrong thing, I don't want to mess up. I want to make an impact. The people who said I was worth something, Mrs. Hughes, Mr. Brown—that's so rare in this world. I would give anything to be that person for someone."

Aaron took him straight to the gym so that, before the kids came in, he could run through the two pieces he would sing with the accompanists Aaron had lined up. He'd found them among his staff. One administrator would play the show tune Ryan had chosen to include, and before that, because the administrator had arthritis and couldn't manage sixteenth notes—apologetically, he lifted and displayed his crippled hand—a part-time music therapist would play "La calunnia." A keyboard was set up along one sideline, in front of an elevated alcove that Ryan would use as a stage. He asked the pianists gently for three or four adjustments of tempo, and told them both, generously, "That was amazing."

The kids filed in and sat in rows of plastic chairs. Some were in slippers, some in high-tops, some in T-shirts, some in hoodies.

"This gentleman is named Ryan Speedo Green." Aaron stood before them, near a short set of steps leading up to the alcove. "And he's a star. And he flew down here from New York City just to be with you—that's actually the truth. He sings at the Metropolitan Opera House, which is one of the most important opera houses in the world. Things are going pretty well for him. But they weren't always going so well, and he decided to come down here to tell you about his journey."

During Aaron's speech, one of the younger kids, around ten, perched himself on the railing of the alcove steps, above and behind the director. Intermittently, he spat down on Aaron's head. The rest of the residents looked on without reacting, as though the spitting was too common and trivial to draw much attention. Ryan was reminded of himself, ungovernable, as a child. The spitter slid away.

"Good morning!" he began. He wore a charcoal-gray suit. "Or, in Italian, it's 'Buongiorno.'" Staffers stood at the perimeter of the chairs, their walkie-talkies crackling, but he seemed to be aware of only the kids. He spoke only to them. "You know, I've sung in front of thousands of people, but nothing is more nerve-racking to me than coming to sing in front of you guys. It means more to me than you can possibly imagine. So thank you—thank you for letting me sing and talk to you."

He smiled, seemed to lose his direction, and repeated, "'Buongiorno.' Can you say that? 'Buongiorno.' Try it. 'Buon—'"

The staffers must have tensed, wondering if the group would go along with this hokey exercise. He waited in the silence, his smile stiffening into a grimace.

" '*Buon*,' " most everyone called out finally.

" '*Giorno*.' "

They responded.

" '*Buongiorno*.' "

" '*Buongiorno*.' "

"Yes! That sounded great! Now you can say 'Good morning' in Italian! Okay, how tall do you think I am?"

Back at breakfast, he'd asked for advice about his presentation, and now I wished I'd done more than assure him that the kids would be moved by whatever he was compelled to say. He was flailing, foundering.

"Six five" came the first guess. The game ended with the accurate answer.

"Yes, that's right." His eyes skittered this way and that; he was lost again, but collected himself. "I wasn't always this size, though. I was five seven and one hundred and forty pounds, and I was where you guys are. I was here. Yes. I was here in this facility. I came from a single-parent household, and I lived in the kinds of places maybe some of you come from. My siblings have been in and out of the system. My stepbrother's in prison right now. Where I lived in high school, the kids around me were selling drugs bigtime, and it was scary. I really didn't feel safe until I left for college. But being here was one of the scariest experiences of my life.

"I felt so alone. I was the kid who fought everyone around me. I was the kid who cursed everyone. Whenever I got upset, I wanted to harm somebody. Somebody needed to feel how angry I was. Everybody needed to feel it. I spent plenty of time in seclusion. And in that cell, you know, at first you're furious and then it's all despair. You are *so* alone. But here's one thing I remember, here's one thing about my time here. It's something I want to tell you. I had a favorite possession. I had a radio that for some reason someone here gave me. I don't know why they did it, but I'm sure I didn't deserve it, and I wasn't any kind of musician. I wasn't a singer; back then, I didn't have any idea I could sing. But in my room, I would listen to the songs that were playing that year, and I would mouth every word. I would sing to myself, for myself."

Abruptly he stopped talking, climbed into tenor range, and crooned a couple of lines from hits of that time. They were songs the kids recognized, and they laughed with pleasure.

"I think that radio helped me start to realize something, even though I didn't know it till later. And one of the things I want to say to you is to try and find something that matters to you, something you're interested in. Really try."

He walked over to a boy whose tattoos covered both of his arms. "Like, maybe you have an interest in art," he said to the kid. "Maybe you didn't know this, but ancient cultures used tattoos to describe memories of the past or to put good fortune into the future." He went on, veering from one tattoo-related topic to another, talking about a famous fashion designer who'd started as a tattoo artist. He attempted to somehow transform all the ink embedded in the kid's arms into something that would save him.

He stepped over to others in the crowd, naming interests and careers that fit with anything he noticed or sensed about them. One kid could be a sports referee, another could be a social worker. He didn't see the rapper anywhere. "Okay, enough of my talking," he said. "Do you know what opera is? When I was your age, I thought opera was a ginormous obnoxious Viking lady with horns and a sword, screaming and breaking windows." Before he sang, he explained his character and translated some of the words: "*Terra...sotto voce...cannone...* Now you're learning more Italian!"

Then he performed from the raised alcove, his makeshift stage. Mid-aria, he hopped down dramatically. But meanwhile, the spitter, who had left the railing earlier, returned and reclaimed his perch. It seemed that Ryan's size wasn't going to dissuade him from showering his scalp, until Ryan incorporated him into his act, pivoting and leaning toward the boy and booming into his face. The boy scurried in retreat; Ryan sang to the audience. The kid scampered back up the railing, poised to spit; Ryan turned and bombarded him playfully with his voice.

Finished with the aria, he asked if there were any questions. A teenager in a hoodie put up his hand and demanded, "When are you done?"

"I'll be done soon, don't worry. If you want to stroll around, it's okay. It really is. It won't bother me."

He pushed for more questions, answering everything that came his way—"What's your favorite basketball team?"; "What helped you the most when you got out of here?"—talking at great length and with all sorts of tangents, refusing to relinquish any chance to connect, until Aaron signaled that it was time to wrap up. Ryan sang the show tune, "This Nearly Was Mine," a ballad from *South Pacific,* and staffers knuckled away tears. When he was through, he said to the kids what he most needed to say: "I believe in you, I believe in you, I believe in you."

They stood and drifted out of the gym while employees surrounded him, hugged him, thanked him, had their pictures taken with him. The kids passed by, saying nothing.

"It's such a privilege to meet you guys," he called out to the backs of their heads as they disappeared. "Thank you for listening to me."

Then he extricated himself from the employees and, with a staff psychologist for an escort, walked hurriedly down a hall and entered one of the units.

℘

A girl, sixteen or seventeen, sat alone in front of a small TV in a room off the communal area, a cloth tied over her head, her dark face obscured by a horde of darker blemishes and scars. For a reason the psychologist didn't specify, she hadn't been able to, or hadn't been allowed to, attend Ryan's event. She turned only partway from the screen when Ryan introduced himself and summarized his story. "I just want to ask if you have any questions about my time in this place or my time after, to see if there's anything I can say to, you know, inspire you or help you. Do you have any questions for me, any questions at all?"

"How did you feel?"

"How did I feel? You mean here?" He spoke to her impassive profile about his solitude and fear. The psychologist switched off the TV. "Was that the History Channel?" Ryan asked the girl. "Do you like history?"

"I like TV."

"You like TV?" He was straining to engage her. "What do you like to watch? Do you like reality shows?"

"Yeah, reality shows."

"Like what?"

She named a program, and he answered with his thoughts about the show. "Anyway, if you like reality TV, there's so much involved in that. There's so much you could do. You should look into production. Whenever you get back to school, you could start by volunteering—lots of schools have a newscast team. When I was here, I listened to the radio, the same songs over and over, memorizing. I had no idea at the time, but music was my passion. Your interest in TV might be the same, or it might lead to other interests."

She listened stoically. A cacophony rose from close by within the pod, a thudding on one of the doors, a howl that hit an excruciating note, while Ryan kept on. "Do you have any other questions for me?"

"No."

"Okay. It is such an honor to meet you."

Another teenage girl came in, hair black and skin pale, a bandage on one arm from her elbow to her wrist, and she mentioned, in a slight accent, the Middle Eastern country she was from and that she had trouble with her family. She remained standing, her body petite, her voice tiny yet animated, her eyes downcast but eager. She said that she liked to sing.

"Do you know any Arabic songs?"

"Yeah."

"Can you teach me one?"

She hesitated, shifting uneasily, but fleetingly her dark eyes met his. "This song, it's about the end of sadness. It's about we all make mistakes in our lives, like you were saying in the gym." She prepared herself to sing, stilled her fragile body and seemed to wait for her mouth to move and for sound to emerge, but nothing happened. She laughed— the laughter no louder than a whisper. "Oh," she said, lowering her head.

"That's okay. When I first got onstage in high school, I froze and forgot my line. I just stood there. You can imagine what a blow that was to my ego. But you have to think about performing like this: when you go to sing, the people who are there, they want to hear you—it doesn't matter how good you are or bad you are, they want to take in what you have. They want to absorb it. It's okay to be scared. Can you teach me how to say 'hello' in Arabic?"

" 'Marhaba.' "

" 'Madahabah.' "

She giggled and slowed her pronunciation: " 'Marhaba.' "

" 'Marahabah.' "

She slowed some more. " 'Maar-haba.' "

" 'Marhaba.' "

"Yeah." Her voice frayed with sentiment.

"What are the first words of the song you were going to sing for me?"

She recited them.

"Wow, that sounds so cool. Sing the first line for me."

She ventured a line, then three more, progressing from the flatness of shy speech to the rhythms of a chant to— with the last phrases—an ascent of notes followed by an artful bend and a simple, unself-conscious fade.

"That is so beautiful! Brava! Brava!" He was beaming, clapping. "I've heard singing in Russian and Spanish,

English and Italian and German—you're the first person
I've ever heard sing in Arabic. I will never forget that, *never.*
Brava!" He became both solemn and light-headed: "You
know, I might not be able to be wherever you are to talk
to you and encourage you and sing for you, but you can
always put my name in on YouTube, Ryan Speedo Green,
and hear my voice and remember how happy you made
me today—you have no idea how happy you made me by
singing for me."

She held out a small notebook. "Can you sign for me
somewhere?"

"Of course." He asked how to spell her name. "Can you
sing me more of the song while I write?"

Confidence crept into her answer. "Yeah, sure."

She sang the ascent, the bend, an ascent yet higher, a
plaintive syllable that she maintained and maintained until
her voice skipped nimbly downward before rising again to
the plaintive cry. She sang for a full two minutes. "That's
the whole song," she said.

"Brava! Brava! And in case you can't read my handwrit-
ing, this says, 'You are an amazing talent. You are my hero.
Thank you with all my heart.'"

&

The psychologist took Ryan toward another pod. A
shout of rage penetrated walls and filled the corridor,
the words unintelligible. The psychologist apologized to
Ryan for his having to hear this. Quickly, tightly, Ryan
said, "No problem." He stared through a long window
into an empty high-walled pen, one of the areas where

uncontrollable kids went outside, alone, for exercise. He let out a groan.

In the pod, he sat in a side room with soft chairs and a beanbag cushion on the floor. The rapper walked in, the red leather high-tops impeccably clean, his blue-and-white plaid boxer shorts on display above the studded jeans he wore more than halfway down his hips. "Y'all want to talk to me?"

"Hey, what's up, man? How you doing, man?" After the presentation, Ryan had said to Aaron that he'd like to speak with the kid. Now something close to a stammer invaded his effort to make conversation.

"*Shiiit.*"

"You can grab a seat."

"I'm about to race."

"You're about to race? You can chill, man. Just grab a seat. Red your favorite color?"

"Yeah."

"Why is it your favorite color?"

"Huh?"

"Why is it your favorite color?"

"Ever since I was a kid, it was. The Game was my best rapper."

"The Game. I remember when I first heard The Game." The Game was an L.A. rapper known for his crew's gun battles, for getting shot, for his ties to the Bloods, who advertised their gang with red accessories. "You ever heard of Q-Tip?"

"He's old-school."

The talk sputtered. The rapper leaned far back in his chair.

"You weren't there this morning in the gym."

"I think I was 'sleep."

"Hey, man," Ryan said, sympathizing, "I should have told them. Singers, we don't get up that early. I don't usually get up till eleven thirty."

"Yeah."

"You know, a while back, I was a resident in here."

"Whoa. Shit."

Ryan gave some details. The rapper didn't respond directly, but he shared some of his future plans. These involved his cousins, who were "in and out," he said. "I used to be on the path they is. But they say they just going to help me get back on my feet. Take me to their clubs."

"Did you know that rap is a form of poetry?"

"Yeah."

Ryan talked about Langston Hughes. "He put his life on paper, he put his empowerment on paper." Then he redirected the conversation. "We think we know hard times, growing up in the neighborhoods we grew up in. But fifty, sixty years ago, our people couldn't drink at the same water fountain as white people. Couldn't eat at the same restaurant."

"Oh yeah," the rapper slurred, slouching lower. "Like Martin Luther King."

"Right. Like Martin Luther King. People then, they put their anger and their sadness to use for good. You don't want to be around people who are going to pull you back. I know you think, *I'm the only person who understands me, I'm the only person who cares about me.* Those are exactly the thoughts that I had. You know Arnold Schwarzenegger? He was my hero. He could lift cars, he could rescue kids—he was like God. All I wanted was for my father to be like Arnold. I thought if my father cared like Arnold, I wouldn't be here."

"I know what you mean."

"You should read poetry. Imagine if you could really learn how to put your emotions on paper."

"How long is this meeting going to last?"

"It's not a meeting." Ryan hurried: "Things do get better, man. If you could have seen me. But you should never expect things to change overnight. It takes your will. Every day can be progress. Jay Z didn't do it overnight."

The mention of Jay Z didn't regain the rapper's interest, not in the way Ryan intended. The kid remarked that he needed some sex.

"Chill, man. Worry about what's important. Just chill. Work on this and this." Ryan touched his head, his chest. "You got to get those straight."

"'Chill,'" the rapper said. His voice had a quiet spite. "That's what I *am* doing." He'd had enough; he stood and sauntered to the door. "I'll holler at you."

_____

"I've read a little bit of my files, but I couldn't read any more," Ryan said to the staff later that afternoon. "I thought, *This is awful, this is awful.* The things I did, the things I said. My right-wrong meter was very skewed." In the meeting room, he sat at a beige table with Aaron to one side and the staff like a class in front of him.

"Yesterday," the director said, "when you stood in the seclusion room, you used the word 'torture.'" Aaron had a mission: to move the staff incrementally away from methods that relied too heavily, he thought, on rewards and punishments.

"Every time I got put back in there, I got crazier and crazier. Because it was this cell at the bottom of my existence—the bottom in this place where I thought I was being put for life. I've spent my whole life since then trying to forget it. It's true, the staff, in my mind, they tortured me. They had a system, and if you screwed up, all your points got erased. And I would screw up—I made people fear me. That's what I did, being physical when I was upset, that's the way I was raised. And I would get erased, and I would get pissed, excuse my French—"

"We do hear worse," Aaron said.

"And I would think, *I'm not good enough,* but also, *It's* your *fault,* you *don't care about me.* And my mother didn't want me. And *pock pock pock.*" He devolved, losing language; he had only the sound and insistent rhythm of torment.

"But there was one lady, she would talk with me. I've spent so much energy trying to forget, I can't remember what we talked about, but I believed she liked me. And she would give me a point when maybe no one else would have, and she wouldn't erase everything when I probably deserved to get erased. And when I got put in seclusion, I thought she would quit liking me for getting put there. I thought she would stop, because I was so awful. I revved right back up again, but I felt—I can't express it—because I worried she wasn't going to like me anymore. I felt a lot of emotions for her. I remember thinking about her when I left here. She wasn't afraid of me. That was one thing. I got here because I threatened my mother, and the law thought I was capable of doing what I said, but I remember feeling like this lady wasn't always waiting for me to snap, like even when I had to be restrained, she wasn't scared of me, because she thought I was a kid."

Ryan had spoken briefly about her to Aaron and a few employees since the day before; no one seemed sure who she was. Now, as he answered staff questions, a woman in black slacks and a white blouse, with light brown skin and her dark hair clipped back, walked into the meeting room, paused along the side, exclaimed something in Spanish, and said, "You're a little taller than I remember."

He recognized her right away. "How did they get you here?"

"I got a little call today."

An employee had solved the puzzle of her identity.

Ryan felt obliged to finish up with the staff, and returned to the answer he'd been giving, but soon the two of them sat in a conference room adjacent to Aaron's office. This was Priscilla Jenkins, the Cuban staffer.

"Holy moly," he said. "I couldn't remember your name. I can't believe—"

"I'm so proud of you."

"It's—it's very nice to see you. I've wanted to—I'm living in New York City. I have my own apartment. I have a steady girlfriend. I'm an opera singer. I was just talking about you in there, how you helped me."

"Children create stories to make themselves feel better."

"No." He stopped her. "Thank you. Whatever relationship you created with me, it helped me."

"Oh, you were so angry. To see where you are today, it's only what one can dream of."

"Being here, meeting you, meeting the kids, it inspires me to do awesome things so I can come back and tell them nothing is impossible."

She recounted that she'd retired from the facility after being injured by one of the residents, that she'd become a Spanish interpreter, that she had a teenage daughter.

"I know you're a great mother," he said. "Oh my gosh, I didn't think I would meet you, but when I get home I'm going to put my words together. I was the worst of the worst on that unit. You're one of the reasons why I'm—why my life isn't ruined."

"You had to do it."

"I know. Believe me, I am one prideful person. But I am blessed, because there were people who put themselves in my life even if I acted like I didn't want anyone in it."

SEVENTEEN

I don't have anything to sing," he said at the party. He stood beside the piano. He'd already performed one song. The hostess and her husband lived a few blocks from the Met in a grand apartment building with a facade of ornate stonework. Their living room ceiling rose two stories, and the double-height walls were covered with European tapestries from centuries ago and a huge painting of a parlor scene and miniature portraits of Napoleon and his family. The hostess was a great fan of opera; she loved to fill her home with opera singers; and now, toward the end of his time in the program, a roomful of her guests stared expectantly at Ryan.

"Oh, you should do 'Ol' Man River,'" the pianist, an elderly African American, suggested.

※

There were moments when Ryan seemed utterly alone. It didn't matter that he was cheerful and charismatic, that he drew people toward him, that he had a steady supply of people to socialize with, that he'd sought out an approximation of family within the Met and found it in the protectiveness of coaches like Noda and in Nichols when she had chased him through the garage and onto the street and held him after he got the call about his father. None of this altered his underlying solitude. His father was gone, glorified but infinitely beyond reach; his mother was near enough but unbearable for him to be next to; and he'd talked with Adrian only twice since their father's death. It had been over a year now since the funeral. The first of the two talks had been a call from Ryan, the second a call from Adrian on his younger brother's birthday. Afterward, Ryan described how that second call had felt: "The person in me who is pursuing achievement, trying to be a success, to that person maybe it's not so important to have him remember my birthday. But to the little brother in me, the little kid in me, the human being in me..."

Once, Valerie had shown me a photograph of her two sons from around the time of her split from Cecil. Ryan, about four years old, wore snug gray gym shorts and a tight orange T-shirt that had been scissored off above his belly, a style that his father favored to show off his abs. The positions of Ryan's and Adrian's bodies were telling. It seemed that whoever snapped the picture had said, "Turn this way." Adrian's entire body faced the photographer. Ryan had tried. His lower body was almost turned in that direction. But immediately he had been distracted by his interest in his big brother; his hips and shoulders angled toward him. Ryan's head was in profile. The snapshot captured the glow of one plump cheek as all his attention fixed on Adrian's wide smile. Ryan's mouth was open; he was not smiling. He was doing something more than smiling. His mouth and gaze were full of attachment and wonder.

Neither of the two calls since the funeral had lasted long. "We don't know how to talk to each other. It takes time, I guess. I was trying to figure out what to say, how to extend the conversation." The intimacy of the late night at the diner, when Ryan had implored, "We're made of the same genetic material," was gone. Following the birthday call, he checked his phone log and saw that the conversation had lasted two minutes and thirty-four seconds. They hadn't spoken in the many months since.

♊

The girlfriend he'd mentioned to Priscilla Jenkins was the exception to the profound isolation I sometimes sensed. Irene Fast hadn't known anything about opera when she and Ryan met online half a year after Cecil's death, but they had something in common. It kept them talking by phone and texting and emailing for two weeks before they met in person.

Irene and her older sister had spent their early years in Kazakhstan, under Soviet rule, in the nineteen eighties. They had lived in poverty in a country that could be cruel to girls and crushing to women, and their mother was determined to rescue her daughters from the lives that awaited them. At last she managed to get them into West Germany. But the price was that she stayed with her husband, who was Irene's sister's father but not Irene's own. He had relatives in West Germany and helped them all to

immigrate. The price was that she and the girls continued
to live with him. The man was a drug addict. He screamed
and splintered furniture as he scoured their apartment for
the money she tried to hide from him, cash he took for his
drugs. She ordered the girls outside whenever he began to
explode, so they wouldn't have to hear and see.

Irene's biological father was a Russian soldier stationed
in Kazakhstan, a man her mother had fallen for, and had
an affair with, years before they immigrated. The soldier
had offered a refuge from the addict's abuse, and for a
time Irene's mother had accepted that refuge, that affection.
Irene had never met him. She knew only what her mother
had told her: his name, the year he was born, that he was
from Moscow, that he had been kind. Irene dreamed of lo-
cating him somehow, contacting him, seeing him, talking
with him.

Irene had landed in America three years before she and
Ryan met. She had slept on the couch of an acquaintance
in a Hassidic neighborhood in Brooklyn, found a job as
a clerk with a jewelry company, weighing and measuring
stones, then gotten herself hired as a paralegal by a law firm
that made use of her fluent German. To Ryan, her lack of
knowledge about opera was irrelevant. There was her past,
and there was her dream of finding her father, and there
was her beauty—these were more than enough.

She was there at the party, at the back of the room, when
the pianist suggested "Ol' Man River," proposed it heartily,
his voice ringing out.

The hostess and host and their guests, a celebrated Met
tenor among them, formed a white chorus:

"Yes!"

"'Ol' Man River'!"

"Sing 'Ol' Man River'!"

℘

He was surely alone at that moment. He wanted to be *seen*.
He wanted to be *heard*. And here he was in a room packed
with well-meaning people who did not see him, who perhaps were incapable of seeing him, who possibly refused to
see him, and who were eager to have him inhabit an object
of pity, to hear him *be* that pitiable object with every note
that rose from behind his ribs and from within his throat,
to gather around the big brawny black man and listen to
him lament his oppressed and thwarted and minuscule life.

"I am the epitome," he'd said in the months before that
party, "of 'Don't judge a book by its cover.' Everything
I did when I was younger, everything I was around, everything I was, gave you only a cover to look at. I was
another number, another statistic. I was a stereotype, another kid going worse than nowhere. And *I* was only seeing
the cover. A few people were trying to read the book, and
then I started to read it and started to create new chapters
in it. But earlier, the cover was what I was looking at." And
here, beneath the tapestries, he was surrounded by people who longed to have him shrink back behind a cover—
not the same cover, but a similar one—and the threat he
felt was not only in how they would see and hear him but
in how he would see and hear himself, in what he would
sacrifice, in what he would betray of his ambition and accomplishment as he sang each note.

He would feel reduced, confined, simplified, compressed,

concealed—while a crucial part of what he aimed for as an artist was an expansion, a wrestling against assumption, a defying of definitions, a tenacious embrace of complication when it came to being African American. Beyond that living room, in the city and in the country, those were keenly troubled times on the topic of race. The Trayvon Martin killing, and the trial of his killer, George Zimmerman, still hung in the air. Race—and stop-and-frisk policing—had dominated the campaign for New York's mayor. And things were about to become far more painful. A spate of police killings of African Americans, from Missouri to New York to Ohio to South Carolina, was on the way. Ryan and I talked sometimes about the Zimmerman trial, about the acquittal of the neighborhood watchman who testified that Martin, a black seventeen-year-old, appeared to be casing houses for burglary. Zimmerman had confronted the kid, who was unarmed but who, Zimmerman insisted, made him fear for his life and fire his gun in self-defense. In the aftermath of the trial, President Obama had given a televised address that began by touching on the experience of young black men who were presumed to be criminals, who were trailed by security guards as they shopped in department stores, who, as they crossed the street, heard the locks click on car doors. The president said that he himself, as a teenager, might easily have been perceived as a criminal and wound up shot.

"That took a lot of guts," Ryan said. He kept his vote in Obama's second election private, but added, "I think he probably pissed off a lot of people with that speech. It was amazing. He spoke to the African American community, because when he talked about being followed in malls, and about women holding their pocketbooks tighter when you're near, that's what happens. What happens to me. On the street, all the time, women will look back and walk slower and stop so I'll walk past. I know the signs. Or when their boyfriend is there, he'll grab her hand to let her know he's protecting her, like I'm an evil homeless animal. I'm numb to it. I'll say to myself, *My music is me, just let me get home.*"

He recalled a drive he'd made from Colorado, when he'd moved his belongings to New York after being accepted into the Lindemann Program. He made the cross-country drive with a black friend, and in Nebraska a cop pulled them over. He couldn't give Ryan a ticket; Ryan hadn't been speeding. He peered into the car and asked to search it. "Don't you need paperwork for that?" Ryan answered crisply, restraining himself, taking in the cop's hostility.

"Honestly, though"—he returned to the subject of Obama's speech—"I wish he'd also said more about how we need to do better. How we can't have this generation of African American men calling women bitches and men niggaz and throwing up gang symbols and going around shooting each other, being just what society builds up about us. What the videos on VH1 and Black Entertainment TV build up. That's not what Langston Hughes or Martin Luther King or Thurgood Marshall wanted us to be."

Not long ago, he'd moved from an apartment in Washington Heights, near the northern tip of Manhattan, to an apartment in Harlem, and Harlem thrilled him, reminded him of the Black History Month essays his mother had assigned, made him think about the African American luminaries, from Hughes to Malcolm X, who were part of this place where he now lived. They were in the air he breathed. "This is a neighborhood of significance," he said, and on 125th Street, where tables of merchandise lined the sidewalk, he bought a set of chunky wooden beads to wear around his wrist. He bought a wooden medallion of the African continent to wear around his neck.

But he tried to avoid the subway stop three blocks from his building, because it let out on a corner he couldn't stomach. There, toward the eastern end of 125th, a few blocks from the section of the street with the tables of beads and Africa medallions, around a series of steel side-walk benches, addicts and drunks spent their days and nights. There were a lot of them, sitting or standing, inert or milling—a gauntlet. At varying hours they occupied the entire block. It was an unusual sight in the city where Ryan had come to live, a city that had undergone a two-decade transformation, and it was unusual in Harlem, which had its rough edges but was part of the transformation—and Ryan, though he was a recent arrival, was acutely aware of the anomaly. It pained him. "Why do they let them do it? There's a police station right near. But no one does anything about it. There are so many crackheads. They smoke their rocks right behind the supermarket. There are so many prostitutes. Just hanging out in the open air. I feel like it's the twilight zone. I feel like this might have been what New York was like twenty years ago. But for some reason they allow that to happen here. It's a major intersection. It's 125th Street!

"When I watch the kids getting off at the bus stop there after school and seeing those guys drinking their forties and walking around wasted and going through the trash bins—

what does an African American kid think, taking that in? It blows my mind. This is Harlem. It...When I have to go to the supermarket, I walk around the long way, so I don't have to see that block. When I'm on the subway, I'll get off at 116th, so I can walk home from the other direction. I resent those people for displaying their inability to fix their problems and do something with their lives. For openly displaying their giving up. They represent every stereotype you can come up with. *Acchh,* it's not okay. It's not okay."

♋

He had already been to one of the hostess's parties, a year earlier. She had a position at the Met; she was entrusted with making sure that European stars felt at home during their stays in New York, that they had everything they needed. She'd met Ryan in the opera house and asked him to one of her gatherings, an honor she was known to extend to only a few in the program. Excited, he had gone, not knowing that a song would be mandatory, that all the singers obliged. After mustering up a show tune on the spot, he was besieged by cries for "Ol' Man River." He smiled and said no, smiled and demurred again, and angled his way swiftly from the piano to the food table. He remained at the back of the crowd, praying that he wouldn't be asked again for the song. Then, for a year, he had declined the hostess's invitations. But recently he'd run into her at the Met, and lightly she'd demanded to know what he was doing on a certain date. He found himself trapped into attending this party.

He went with a strategy. He would volunteer to sing first,

before anyone else. He would perform the Broadway song he'd done at the center, "This Nearly Was Mine," and after that, because there would be many singers left to fill the evening, he would be allowed to drift away without any more attention. He was fairly confident this would work. Instead, though, everyone shouted for an encore; he said he had nothing prepared; the silver-haired African American pianist, in his reading glasses and jacket with a handkerchief in the pocket, made his loud proposal; the guests agreed avidly; and Ryan was stuck standing at the piano, perspiring and saying, "I don't really want to sing that."

Even the clothes he'd chosen for the evening emanated his reluctance about being here and his dread of this request. The rips in his jeans and the slack, stretched neck of the undershirt he wore with a blazer were stylish—but not in this formal crowd.

"Please!" the hostess called.

"Everyone wants you to sing it!" someone bellowed.

"Please, sing it for me. Sing 'Ol' Man River' for me."

The food table, to which he'd fled the last time, seemed a long distance away, and the apartment door was just as far. The pianist was smiling up at him, glad that his idea was so well received. He motioned for Ryan to lean down and murmured into his ear, "Do the PG version."

"PG version?"

"Yes, you know. Don't say 'white boss.' Say 'big boss.'"

Ryan laughed softly, furious. So he was supposed to sing woefully about the oppression of black people while taking care not to make white people uncomfortable? His mind swirled, his body straightened. He saw a mob of desiring faces. He dropped his eyes to the piano. He stared at the surface of brown wood, as if at a sheet of music. No music lay there. He didn't need any. He only needed to direct his gaze somewhere other than where he was. Two minutes ago, performing his first song, he'd stepped away from the piano, wandering this way and that in front of the guests, swaying, relishing the emotion of the romantic ballad from *South Pacific* and singing into their eyes. Now, his torso stiff, he stayed tight to the instrument and avoided any glimpse of the hunger in their expressions. He lowered his head slightly. He wished to float out of his body, out of this room. He felt a kind of death claiming him.

There's an old man called the Mississippi
That's the old man that I'd like to be
What does he care if the world's got troubles
What does he care if the land ain't free

Enunciating, he got through the first verse, but as he neared the PG substitution in his half-dead state, he lost his way entirely. He sang a contorted word that didn't belong to any language or dialect, and realized how disoriented he was, that he had no idea what verse he was in. He hunched down for help from the pianist, who cued him, and he continued, his pronunciation shifting.

Don't look up
And don't look down
You don't dast make
De big boss frown
Let me go 'way from de Mississippi
Let me go 'way from the —

His voice stumbled; he looked perplexed. Was this another spot for the substitution or was he someplace else in the song? Haltingly, he forced himself onward.

—the big boss man

His eyes flitted across his audience. He heard how incompetent he sounded, and he attempted, with a twist of his face, to turn his broken rhythm, his botched notes, his mangled verses, his breakdown into a joke. He didn't succeed. There was a moan of disappointment or disapproval from the crowd. He bent toward the pianist, bent almost double, getting his ear close to the elderly black man's mouth, seeking some word of guidance that would get him through the rest of the song. The man said nothing. He kept his fingers moving on the keys and chuckled.

Ryan recoiled from the piano player, pulled himself up. He pivoted gradually to face the nearest wall, the wall on the opposite side of the instrument. He faced away from the audience, partially away from some, completely away from others, and sang the final verses. Flawlessly. With the hostess and the host and the guests at his back or at his shoulder, shut away from him, he sang the climactic phrases—sang with almost enough ferocity, and with almost enough beauty, to crack the wall in front of him and make it disintegrate.

EIGHTEEN

H<small>E LEFT THE</small> party quickly afterward, explaining to Irene why everyone's plea for the song—and why the old African American's proposal of it and instruction about the word he shouldn't sing—had rattled him to the point of falling apart in public.

He would perform the song again; he was sure of that. The song was, it was true, a stunning piece of music with a shattering story to tell and a past that included Paul Robeson, the greatest African American bass of the last century. And Ryan felt that his voice did own those final verses or that somehow they possessed him, that he couldn't and shouldn't escape them. But Joe and "Ol' Man River" would have to be part of something much, much larger, part of a career consisting of Verdi and Rossini, of Wagner and Mahler, of everything that had somehow taken root within him since he'd seen Denyce Graves in *Carmen* and told Mr. Brown what he intended to do, of everything he now was.

There had been signs lately that such a career might happen—and not merely on lesser stages, not merely in the cobbled-together way that awaited those who were selected for the program but never fulfilled their promise or never had luck flow in their direction. There had been small signs, uncertain signs, of something more. The *Washington Post* had written that one spectacular line about him. Then again, that single line had come within a list of compliments for other singers who'd been onstage alongside him that evening, and it had come within a review of a summer festival production whose purpose was to nurture young talent. After the euphoria of reading the critic's words had worn off, he'd understood that her standards that night weren't the highest.

Within the program, Maestro Levine—whom Ryan called "a musical Gandhi" for the wisdom of his appraisals and the delicacy of his baton work—had listened to him one afternoon from his elaborate wheelchair. At the end of the aria, the maestro lowered his baton at the pace of a falling feather. He declared in front of the other trainees, "Well done, sir. Well done. Your voice is in great shape." And these days, whenever Levine, in his gray sweatpants, motored into a room to preside over the group, he seemed, in Ryan's mind, to bestow on Ryan an extra bit of attention. Levine and the program's coaches also seemed to trust him in a new way, to believe that he could make meaningful interpretive decisions, that he could absorb the music of an aria and study the libretto and arrive at nuances on his own, a confidence that they'd never shown before. And one of the most important people at the Met had called him into his office and advised him about potential managers.

Ryan had spoken with two. One of them managed Renée Fleming.

Then again, the Met tended to cast singers far in advance, and the house had booked two of Ryan's fellow trainees for prominent roles in coming seasons. For Ryan, this hadn't happened. If he let himself think about this, he sensed that he was being left behind. The evidence piled up. Despite the enthusiasm that both managers conveyed about his voice and his prospects, and despite one of them saying that he'd heard talk around the Met that Ryan might be "something special," neither of them had presented him with a contract and offered to make him a client.

He'd won two prestigious grants from opera foundations. Then again, both were for emerging singers and had been given more often to artists who wound up failing than to those who went on to first-rate careers.

The program had been putting him on the list for lots of auditions whenever casting directors or their assistants flew in from overseas or from American cities to scout singers for their companies. Numerous times, he'd waited outside the Juilliard rehearsal rooms where the auditions were held. He'd shuffled and paced with the others who were scheduled for a ten-minute slot near his own, traded audition horror stories, and stared at the lapdog one of the accompanists insisted on wheeling everywhere she went in a screened case.

Only one of these auditions had worked out. He was booked to sing a somewhat significant role, a few years in the future, with a fairly insignificant company in northern France. "If I prove myself there..." he said. But it wasn't at all clear what, if anything, proving himself there would mean.

Then, through the program, he was scheduled for an audition with the Vienna State Opera, Austria's main company. Along with the Met, it was one of the five most revered companies in the world. The program arranged auditions at this high level partly in the hope of bookings but mostly so that its singers could at least be heard by the most elite decision-makers in Europe. Serious consideration for roles might only come later on, and this was especially true for basses and bass-baritones. So when Ryan woke up early that morning, having felt congested all week and feeling sicker now, he decided not to cancel his ten minutes. He reminded himself that the audition was only an introduction. He told himself that he didn't have to sing perfectly.

He didn't consider how badly things could go.

The problem was a combination of a waning cold and surging allergies. Ryan contracted more than his share of colds no matter what the season, and was assaulted by pollen every spring and fall; he was a regular in the chair of Dr. Cho, the Met's ENT. But the day before, when he could have scheduled an appointment to receive one of her assortment of temporary cures, and maybe had his infected mucus and blood vacuumed out, his sinuses hadn't felt as clotted as they did this morning. His throat hadn't felt so tight, his ears hadn't been so clogged. Now it was too late. His audition was at 11:10 a.m.

In his bedroom, he marched his voice through arpeggios, testing his limits. He could get close to his usual top and typical bottom, but both high and low were a strain, and he had little sense of how the notes sounded because the passageways leading to his ears were filled with fluid. He emailed the program's administrative assistant, telling her to take one of his pieces, a vaulting Mozart aria, off the repertoire list that the auditioner would pick from.

He coughed, hacking a yellow-green globule into a paper towel. He reread the directions on a box of decongestant pills, sneezed out tusks of snot, and reread the directions again. There was no question: he wasn't supposed to take another dose so soon. Resisting, he put aside the box and blew his nose until he felt that he was about to propel frontal bits of his brain through his nostrils. He poured green powder into a glass of water, guzzled, attempted more arpeggios, heard the hoarseness clinging to his voice, sipped chamomile tea, and decided to quit warming up and stay silent.

He got himself into a purple dress shirt and black vest without sneezing on the fabric of either, and got himself onto the subway. Riding downtown toward Juilliard, his hacking ceased and his nose cleared, but his throat felt as if someone had stuffed it with cotton balls, and every cavity and passage behind his nose was plugged. He took the elevator up to Juilliard's third floor and was glad to see one of his favorite trainees, the Korean American tenor who'd shared his dressing room for *Parsifal*, outside the audition room door. "Tell me you have a cough drop," Ryan said, needing to get rid of the cotton.

The tenor didn't. Ryan wandered down the hall, emitting notes with various vowel shapes, trying to shift the placement of resonance this way and that on one pitch and another, forward or back within his head, a tad higher or lower, searching for unclogged spots. He put his forefinger on the flesh above his upper lip to check for the proper vibration. He felt nothing. The door opened; it was his turn.

The piano sat deep in the room, below a strip of windows set high in the wall. The windows didn't admit much light, and the walls and floor were dark gray or black. To Ryan's left as he stepped toward the instrument, Brian Zeger, who ran the program and who'd been so kind lately, sat next to the auditioner from Vienna at a fold-out table. The auditioner wore all black. He had a notepad in front of him, to be filled with commentary, with verdicts. Ryan kept his eyes on Zeger's generous face, stilled himself, listened to the hush of the room and then to the piano filling the quiet. He sang.

Within a few phrases, he could hear the raspiness stealing into his throat and adhering to his notes. But it wasn't only that. He realized that his voice was spreading amorphously, that it was fuzzy and unfocused, that he was producing the kind of low pitches that would wallow inaudibly beneath a world-class orchestra like Vienna's. His mind manufactured two runs of words simultaneously, the lyrics of the aria and a litany of reproach: *This is the worst audition you've ever sung, they're not even going to let you sing a second piece . . .*

Zeger's face was unreadable. When Ryan finished the first aria, the auditioner did request a second, but added, as Ryan reached for his bottle of water, "Take as much time as you need. Don't worry." He spoke in a tone of consolation that summed up everything.

Ryan proceeded through "La calunnia," flitting his

hands in a facsimile of his usual clownishness. Between congestion and despair, he could hear himself only distantly. He pushed himself arduously, traversing a sequence of alternating eighth notes, Cs and Bs, that led to a high, elongated E, one of the song's comic peaks, a note that was well within his range and that he could hold with ease. After a particular C and B he always took a breath, filling his lungs for what followed. But this time, in his agitation, he forgot. He recognized his mistake two notes farther on, too late to inhale before the extended, mock-heroic climax. His voice climbed upward toward the E, hit the note, and immediately gave out. The comedic culmination was, instead, an absence, a void, a zero.

As the aria wound down, he surrendered to what felt like an omnipotent force of self-destruction. He relinquished all will, attempted no artistry, no recovery. He let the notes drag him to the end.

The audition was over.

"Thank you," the man from Vienna mumbled.

Ryan smiled and hustled out of the room and past the tenor and into the elevator and out the revolving doors and onto the sidewalk. He fled past Lincoln Center, fled across the intersection where Broadway and Columbus converged, fled through the chaos of traffic, fled down the block toward Oswald's studio. He had a lesson scheduled; he was late but wanted whatever minutes he had left— for Oswald's sympathy, for any solace he could give, for his advice about how to avoid being written off as an embarrassment, as hopeless, by Zeger and the program, if avoiding that was even possible.

He buzzed and was let in. He reeled through the building's lobby and into the studio. He stood in front of Oswald's piano. He dropped his neck, let it loll, and from his height he wilted in stages until his forehead rested on the crimson blanket that covered the piano top. After a long moment, he straightened partially, leaning. He reported what had happened, in words punctuated by guttural sounds of shame and self-recrimination. Oswald kept his reaction modulated but looked worried—more than worried. He helped Ryan to draft an email, an effort to limit the damage.

Hello Mr. Zeger,

I was sick earlier in the week with bad allergies and I ignored my gut instinct to cancel today's audition because I wanted to give my all. I apologize for the result this morning.

Two hours later, Ryan opened a message from the program's administrative assistant. He was wanted for a callback the next morning.

Was this a mistake? A message meant for another singer? Had they heard the same crippled E, the same complete anticlimax, the same eight-minute disaster he'd heard, dimly through all the fluid, with his own ears? Soon after the message from the administrative assistant, he received a second email. This one was from Zeger.

"They liked you tho I knew your top was not all there." He went on, "These auditions are about the future— it's not too soon to be heard." This wouldn't be his last chance to audition for Vienna, Zeger reassured; he should just go to the callback tomorrow without fretting about his allergies.

In three days, Zeger sent another message. This one was full of capital letters and exclamation points. Ryan was going to Vienna.

NINETEEN

Sparafucile in *Rigoletto,* the Egyptian king in *Aida,* the Commendatore in *Don Giovanni,* Basilio in *The Barber of Seville*—these were some of the midsize roles Ryan was given in Vienna during his first year after the program, the first year of his two-year contract with a company once led by Mahler, in a house where Norman and Callas and Ghiaurov and Pavarotti had performed, in a city where Mozart had composed. Outside, winged horses pranced atop the arched entryway, and fountains and statues and ornate stone columns surrounded the Viennese who sat on the square, watching the operas on a giant screen, while those who watched from inside passed between gilded walls adorned with tapestries and beneath golden cornices and into boxes whose balconies of red velvet seats hovered above the stage.

This story is unfinished, just as all of our stories are. When I last saw him, Adrian was staying with a few friends on a rutted, half-paved street where the sand and scrub of the California desert met the outskirts of a town whose

293

main economy, he said, was the meth trade. The house was tiny and looked like it could be swept away by the winds that came off the Mojave. During sandstorms, dust blew through cracks and joints, coating the furniture.

We went to a restaurant next to a freeway on-ramp. He said he was trying to keep on the right side of the law, trying to get back into cage fighting, and trying to find a job. He talked about Spawn, a superhero who'd been a favorite of Cecil's. In the movie, made in the late nineties, about his demon-killing exploits, Spawn had been the first superhero to be played by an African American. And we talked about dinosaurs. He told me that scientists had found sites with fossils hinting that dinosaurs had been covered in feathers rather than scales. "They were bird-like," he said.

All the while, he fed his baby, who sat next to him in the booth. He spooned bits of mashed up Mexican food tenderly into the boy's mouth. His relationship with the baby's mother was over, but he divided the child care with her. When the baby puked up a good amount of his meal, Adrian wiped him down thoroughly, gently.

Then I drove him back to the cramped and cluttered house at the edge of the desert. Much of the living room was occupied by a giant TV screen filled with the other-worldly fighters of a video game. His friends would take care of the baby while I drove Adrian into town to a potential new job. To get around, he either got rides or walked a fair distance to the nearest bus stop. That afternoon and evening was his trial shift at a restaurant. He may have been living an existence as far as it was possible to imagine from Ryan's, but they shared a resilience: He was going to stand by the side of the road with a sign that read "All-You-Can-Eat Riblets."

$\mathscr{L}$

Valerie was married again, to a diminutive man from the Ivory Coast who worked at one job or another during almost every waking hour. She still had the dispatcher's job she'd found a few years earlier, and together they had left the besieged little house with bullet holes below the eaves. They rented a compact apartment with a sliver of a balcony in a complex near a military air base in Virginia Beach. Fighter jets roared overhead on a regular basis, but otherwise the apartment was pleasant.

As we sat at her dinette table, she wanted to show me various things. There was an invitation card, with fancy gold script, that she'd made in honor of Ryan's senior-year recital at the conservatory in Connecticut. And onto the table she placed a birthday card he had given her several years ago. It said, "Love You Forever."

They hadn't spoken much during the months before he left for Vienna, and they communicated only slightly more now. She wrote sometimes on his Facebook wall. He avoided the sound of her voice. For him, the past continued to be too close, her voice too charged. Yet he was formulating a new understanding about his childhood, one that had been slow to take shape.

I'd heard the change sharply after we visited the center. We were walking toward the parking lot, walking along the red-and-yellow exterior wall of the facility, leaving behind the Middle Eastern girl and the rapper, leaving behind

295

all the kids on the other side of that wall, leaving them to their cells and to futures scarcely in their control, and we fell silent.

"What are you thinking about?" Ryan asked.

I told him I was thinking about what it would be like for my son if he was locked inside.

Ryan's features seemed to flatten. He looked at me with enmity, as if my answer missed the point, as if I lacked all empathy. "Maybe you should think about what it would be like for your son if his mother was the one who put him there."

His anger faded quickly, but it was searing, and I asked him about it during a call to Vienna. I said that the words he'd spoken—"if his mother was the one who put him there"—seemed a long way from what he'd told me when we first met, about singing to wear down his mother's wall and win her forgiveness. "Exactly," he said over the phone. "One of the things I've thought about, especially after that visit to the center, is that it took a lot of emotional karate-chopping, a lot of damage, to get me to the point where I got put there. That doesn't happen naturally to a kid. Knowing me, knowing me as an adult, that wasn't me. So maybe she should be wanting me to forgive her."

He didn't expect, he said, that she would ever apologize for anything that had happened; he would have to do the forgiving on his own. He didn't know if their relationship would ever become easy. But lately he'd done something that was like a shout through the silence.

He knew that his mother had a wish. "It will happen if it is His will," she liked to say, "and I believe it is. It can be a fixer-upper. That's what they call it, and I'm willing to fix up." She wanted, someday, to own a home, and she envisioned children within it: Adrian coming to stay with his new son, so she could help to raise him, though Adrian talked with her even less than Ryan did; Ryan visiting with the babies he would eventually have.

And as Ryan sang in Vienna, her wish seemed to be coming closer. He still had a heavy balance on his student loans, but when she asked, he contributed, and Valerie and her husband made a down payment on a condo near where they now lived. "I feel good as a son knowing that I gave her what she asked me. I love her—she's my mother." The condo didn't exist yet. The developer hadn't broken ground on the complex he promised to build. But he sold to early buyers, buyers who put their faith in him, at a discount. Valerie had studied the plans and fantasized over the photos of staged kitchens and bedrooms. There she would cook for her grandchildren, and there they would sleep.

℘

Irene had moved to Vienna with Ryan, and she tried to shield him from his first reviews. *Rigoletto*—Verdi's tragic opera about a hunchbacked and lonely court jester who hires an assassin to take revenge on a callous nobleman, but who, unwittingly, winds up having his own beautiful daughter killed instead—was not a resounding success for the Vienna company. It was not a success for Ryan. The company had given him some coaching for his role as the assassin, but mostly he was on his own now; the constant instruction he was used to receiving, from masters like Noda and Oswald, was over. Irene translated the *Rigoletto* reviews for him, since he couldn't read German. She altered and adjusted the sentences. But he guessed what she was doing and resorted to translating online. Critics called the production "a disaster." They called Ryan's performance tepid, describing him as a "vocally harmless hit man."

Yet people at the company encouraged him; they seemed to withhold judgment. The man who'd heard his first-round New York audition and been involved in hiring him praised his singing in *Rigoletto,* as if the reviews didn't exist. And it was as if, given all the condemnations he'd once endured, the assault of dismissive and damning reviews couldn't penetrate him deeply. He fretted over the critiques but didn't dwell on them. When I visited him a few days later, he was much more interested in giving me a tour of his favorite sausage stands and taking me to cafés specializing in chocolate tortes than in seeking whatever reassurance I could offer that his initial reviews wouldn't harm his career.

He had the comfort, too, of waking next to Irene every morning. Together they had created a kind of cocoon in a one-bedroom apartment that seemed to them a stroke of good luck—for its modernity, for its heated bathroom floor, but also for its balcony looking out on the cupola of a three-hundred-year-old church. Irene had chosen a light fixture that suffused the living room with a supposedly medicinal and becalming shade of blue, and on their flat-screen TV they often played a video of logs burning in a fireplace. They'd taken cooking classes together in New York, and in Vienna, with the fire crackling, they prepared elaborate meals for each other, and sat down to eat under the blue light, and talked about their pasts, their missing fathers, the violence and chaos of their childhood homes, their terror, shame, isolation. "It wasn't something I spoke about," she said, "before I met him. Never. It just was not something to talk about. He was the first person in my life to say, 'Let it out, let it go.' He and I come from such different worlds, but what we have in common makes us such strong people—combined."

℘

At Ryan's insistence, Mr. and Mrs. Hughes came to visit and hear him in *Aida*. They had seen his senior recital in Connecticut, and seen him in two of his summer festival performances and two of his minor Met roles during his Lindemann years, and they sent him birthday and Christmas cards. But in his mind the Hugheses were forever near, their paired heads, covered in brass-tinted curls, suspended over his life as if they were fairy godparents. While he was at Florida State's conservatory, he and the Hugheses had connected only occasionally, yet when he graduated he sent them a plaque engraved with words he'd written. "Be it known that Mr. and Mrs. Hughes, " the engraving began. It went on "to honor and recognize the confidence, guidance, and wisdom freely given in helping me to attain this important milestone in my life."

When Mr. and Mrs. Hughes arrived in Vienna, Ryan and Irene served them cocktails that they'd chosen with much deliberation—champagne laced with an Austrian elderflower liqueur. This was followed by a fireside meal that took more than a day to prepare. It started with a cream-based soup of fresh chickpeas and mushrooms; continued with short ribs that Ryan had marinated overnight—in bean leaves and basil, olive oil, and brown sugar and a host of spices he'd learned about from his father—and then slow-cooked for six hours and surrounded with Irene's Parmesan Brussels sprouts; and ended with a multilayered chocolate cream pie constructed on a coconut-touched crust that they'd made from scratch.

For their few days in Vienna, Mr. and Mrs. Hughes would be staying at a hotel nearby, but Ryan worried that his desire for their attention might be overwhelming. "I just have to tell you," he said, "that I want to be with you as much as you can stand me."

&

The tones of *Aida*'s overture were fragile, spectral, mournful. Then, sitting on a throne and wearing robes of white brocade that spilled over his knees like a waterfall, Ryan sang the role of the Egyptian king awaiting attack by the Ethiopians. He entreated the gods to grant courage and protection—

Unto death deliver our enemy
Egypt they never shall enslave

—and welcomed the war that would spur the story of doomed love into hurtling motion. The grave music of his voice unfurled throughout the house, echoing in militant counterpoint to the helpless, radiant sounds that would rise from the lovers in the final scene.

The early scorn of the critics faded away. Now, and as Ryan performed through the rest of the season, they called his singing "impeccable" and his voice "voluminous and filled with beautiful colors" and his talent "a true win for the Vienna State Opera." As the Commendatore in *Don Giovanni*, Ryan sang to restore order to the world. He sang as the embodiment of morality in Mozart's battle between the forces of impulse and the forces of the spirit, between the forces of dissolution and the forces of transcendence, between the agents of harm and those of healing. He sang the climactic scene in the opera that Flaubert had rated as one of "the three finest things God ever made"—the other two being *Hamlet* and the sea—sang in confrontation with Giovanni, whose voice was a gorgeous celebration of anarchy; sang over and over to Giovanni, "Answer me, you must answer me." Ryan sang with an untiring, unswayable, urgent need to wring repentance from chaos itself, to control and quell harm itself, sang so that "answer me" seemed to replace the very oxygen in the theater.

&

The bass-baritone who'd been cast as the priest in Shostakovich's *Lady Macbeth of Mtsensk* fell ill. The singer who was supposed to step in was lured away by a much bigger role in another city. A key person at the company stopped Ryan in a back hall of the opera house and asked if he could learn the part. It was less than a week before opening night.

"I've never sung in Russian," Ryan protested.

"Never?"

"Never in my life."

A coach spoke Ryan's forty lines into a recorder, enunciating syllable by syllable, and he went home to Irene with the tape and a copy of the score in Cyrillic script. The score had a hand-scrawled transliteration, but the coach warned him that it was flawed. Ryan begged Irene to help him, and she begged him not to ask.

"Baby, I have no idea how to learn this."

"I have no idea how to teach you." She spoke Russian well but couldn't read in Cyrillic, was confounded by the sketchy transliteration, and was stumped by the antiquated liturgical language used by the priest.

"Dress rehearsal is on Friday!"

In his panic, he convinced her. She set about teaching him to half swallow certain letters, to retract and contort the base of his tongue in a way that led to a sound akin to a bullfrog's call, to string together alien syllables: *"yayvope"* and then *"chyayvope"* and then *"ssss"* and then *"ssssch"* and then *"sssschyayvope"* and then *"sssschyayvope yay-moo."* Between hours-long sessions with Irene and hours-long sessions with the coach and hours spent working alone, and by employing the International Phonetic Alphabet and his own invented alphabetical notations, Ryan made painstaking progress. Before the dress rehearsal, he called Irene's mother in Germany and sang to her on the phone. She understood him perfectly, and if he garbled any of his lines on opening night, no one complained in the opera house or in the press.

Since he and Irene had found each other, they'd made a point of celebrating their "monthiversaries," counting back to the date they'd met online. Lately he'd been composing and polishing a letter that he intended to read to Irene's mother, Olga. She didn't speak English, so he planned to

get it translated into German and practice until he could
pronounce the words easily.

I wrote a letter to read to you today, because I want
to express some things to you.... Since your amazing
daughter came into my life, I've learned what it means
to truly love someone and receive the same kind of
love in return. We have our ups and downs, but there
is never a moment when I don't think Irene is the perfect woman for me. I am by no means a perfect man,
but she always finds a way to make me feel like I'm
the most important thing to happen in her life.... I
will continue to grow and look for ways to be a better
man for her.... Since the day she and I expressed our
love for each other, I knew I would never need another
woman.... Olga Fast, will you give me the honor and
joy of asking your daughter Irene Fast to be my rib,
my partner in crime, my muse for life, my wife?

While he worked on the letter, he was looking into lay-
away plans. He had asked a friend of Irene's about the type
of ring she wished for. When he asked Irene to marry him,
he wanted the diamond to be from exactly the store she
dreamed about.

೯

As a singer, his breakthroughs that year weren't only in Vienna. The Met flew him back to New York to sing the part
of a terrorist in a modern opera, *The Death of Klinghoffer*,
a story of Israel and Palestine. The opera provoked accu-

sations that it was too sympathetic to the Palestinians, that it was anti-Semitic. There were protests outside the theater and, inside, shouts of outrage during the opening night performance. Ryan's pivotal role was musically raw and jagged and daunting to master, but he won approval from the *New York Times* and was singled out by *New York* magazine: "Green sang such a convincingly fierce and unhinged Rambo that I feared for his curtain call....He got the ovations he deserved." Even the one reviewer, in the *New York Observer,* who found minor fault with the way he'd sung this particular part, admired his voice and his acting: "Ryan Speedo Green lavished an almost too voluptuous bass on the vicious hijacker named Rambo, but he compensated with an uncompromising acting performance as an unrequited monster."

Just before *Klinghoffer,* the Met, perceiving Ryan's promise more and more clearly, cast him in a production of *La Bohème* that was two years away. A poet, a musician, a painter, a singer, a philosopher—*La Bohème* told the story of a set of struggling bohemians in nineteenth-century Paris and was the Met's most popular opera. Ryan would sing the role of Colline, the philosopher. In the final act, as the group's poverty became unbearable, as the friends could no longer afford food and as the poet's lover lay dying of consumption, the philosopher pawned his overcoat to buy her medicine. Ryan's aria, the penultimate song in the opera, was a surrender. It was the end of the friends' artistic and intellectual dreams. The piece was brief but wrenching, and the Met often used the part to test the talents of singers it believed might be ready for starring roles. "That aria is notorious," Noda said. "It has this heartbreaking, simple melody, with almost no orchestra. It has to be sung with perfect control. And it has a notorious high note that comes out of nowhere and has to be delivered softly. That note has to be drop-dead beautiful, and from that note the phrase goes down in three half steps that have to be sung with seamless legato. The success of the entire role is about those four notes. If he can break our hearts with that one phrase, his stock is going to go up."

But artistically, the best moment of that year may have come with the same aria he'd sung in the finals of the Met competition, the same aria whose culminating note he'd aborted during the Vienna audition, an aria that he now, cast as Basilio in *The Barber of Seville,* sang within a full performance on the Vienna stage. Basilio was a character of comic evil, both absurd and malevolent. He sang "La calunnia" to Bartolo, who was a doctor and a fool. For the right fee, he declared, he would bring down Bartolo's romantic rival.

Ryan began the aria by ushering Bartolo into a drawing room, by sitting civilly beside Bartolo, by crossing his legs, one knee over the other, in genteel fashion, and by placing his hands on his uppermost knee, lightly. He did all this in precise time with a musical shift by the orchestra, from the tame playing of a harpsichord to a darker swelling of strings. The mere crossing of his legs, carried out with showy aplomb and almost in slow motion as the violins, violas, and cellos were introduced, served as an unsung note of musical dissonance, civility displayed while the strings evoked his malice, the contrast making the comedic tension all the more taut.

A few lines into the aria, he stood, strolling away from

the drawing room and singing with rapture about his own powers. The desperate Bartolo was forced to follow him, stumbling as he rushed over to hear how his rival would be dispensed with. The voluptuousness of Ryan's voice was perfect for this seduction. He sang Bartolo into a trance and himself into a frenzy. He soared up to the E he'd had to abandon in the audition, sustained it triumphally, seized Bartolo's hand, wrapped his other arm around Bartolo's shoulder, and drew him into a euphoric dance. Then he bellowed out a phrase so loudly that Bartolo quaked and reeled at the edge of the stage, in danger of plummeting until Ryan caught him and set him upright, the exuberantly executed dance and slapstick calling to his father in the air of the opera house, calling him close. Ryan stepped to center stage. He spread and lifted his arms, a gesture of embrace to a mesmerized Bartolo and a charmed audience. The orchestra raced, then hushed.

Again Ryan climbed to the high, reverberating, rich, lustrous note, which he held.

ACKNOWLEDGMENTS

This book relies on the generosity of all who provided countless hours of personal memories and musical insight. My greatest debt is to one man, Ryan Speedo Green. I am tremendously grateful to everyone who is named in the book's pages. And I am thankful to the many others who were essential to my understanding of Ryan's story, among them Willie Balderson, Jan Boykins, Robert Brown Sr., Adam Cavagnero, Peter Clark, Margaret Nimmo Crowe, David Fisher, Greg Green, Webster Hogeland, Matthew Horner, Vlad Iftinca, Miles Kreuger, Thomas Lausmann, Paul Lombardo (and his history of the eugenics movement in Virginia, *Three Generations, No Imbeciles*), Phylis Milne, Ben Moore (whose beautiful adaptation of "Ode to a Nightingale" is described in chapter fourteen), Sam Neuman, Stephen Wadsworth, the faculty at the Governor's School for the Arts in Norfolk, and the current and former staff members and residents who spoke with me about life at the center but preferred to remain anonymous.

My extraordinary agent, Suzanne Gluck, has guided me wisely and patiently for almost three decades—my gratitude goes to her and everyone on the William Morris Endeavor team, including Scott Chaloff, Raffaella De Angelis,

Tracy Fischer, Alicia Gordon, Clio Seraphim, and Elizabeth Sheinkman.

My editor, Lee Boudreaux, is a perfect master at mixing literary love with deft critique—I am so very lucky to have her on my side, along with Reagan Arthur, Olivia Aylmer, Nicole Dewey, Lisa Erickson, Heather Fain, Elizabeth Garriga, Carina Guiterman, Andy LeCount, Julianna Lee, Carrie Neill, Michael Pietsch, Mary Tondorf-Dick, Karen Torres, Betsy Uhrig, Craig Young, and everyone at Lee Boudreaux Books and Little, Brown.

Ilena Silverman, my ever-precise and forever inquisitive editor at the *New York Times Magazine,* gave this book its start.

Writing would be nearly impossible for me without the counsel, companionship, faith, and simple existence of my friends Paul Barrett, Julie Cohen, Peter Davidson, Samantha Gillison, John Gulla, William Hogeland, George Packer, Ayesha Pande, Laura Secor, Saul Shapiro, and Tom Watson.

My father, Lawrence Bergner, infused my growing up with both music and morality, and my brother, Robert Bergner, continues to lend his musical passion to my life.

And then there's Georgia West, my love, whose spirit I am blessed to be near.

RYAN'S ACKNOWLEDGMENTS

My love and gratitude go out to my mother, Valerie Henley Elloinchi, who gave me the resilience to get up again any time I fall.

I am eternally thankful for the time I got to spend with my father. He lives on in my music.

Acknowledgments

And to my wife, Irene Green: you are my rib, my muse, the center of my universe.

So many thanks to the teachers, mentors, and family who saw what was inside me even when I couldn't: above all, to Mr. and Mrs. Hughes and to Robert Brown Jr. And heartfelt thanks to Alan Fischer and the faculty at the Governor's School for the Arts; David Fisher; Edward Bolkovac, Joanna Levy, Gabriel Lofvall, and the faculty at the Hartt School of Music; Douglas Fisher, David Okerlund, and everyone at Florida State University's College of Music; Ellie Caulkins, Cherity Koepke, and all at Opera Colorado; and the Love family.

The Metropolitan Opera's National Council Auditions and the Met's Lindemann Young Artist Development Program have transformed my life. I am especially thankful to Bob Cowart, Vlad Iftinca, Hemdi Kfir, Camille LaBarre, Maestro James Levine, Gayletha Nichols, Ken Noda, Mark Oswald, Stephen Wadsworth, and Brian Zeger. I am deeply grateful to Adam Cavagnaro, Matthew Horner, and everyone at IMG Artists, and to Thomas Lausmann, Dominique Meyer, and all at the Wiener Staatsoper.

The Leonore Annenberg Fellowship Fund for the Performing and Visual Arts has been immensely generous in supporting me. Also invaluable have been the Licia Albanese-Puccini Foundation; Martina Arroyo, her foundation, and her summer program, Prelude to Performance; the BBC Cardiff Singer of the World contest; the Gerda Lissner Foundation; the George London Foundation Competition; Opera Index; the Palm Beach Opera Competition; and the Richard Tucker Foundation.

ABOUT THE AUTHOR

Daniel Bergner is a contributing writer for the *New York Times Magazine* and the author of a novel, *Moments of Favor*, and four previous books of nonfiction—*What Do Women Want?*, *The Other Side of Desire*, *In the Land of Magic Soldiers*, and *God of the Rodeo*. *In the Land of Magic Soldiers* received an Overseas Press Club award for international reporting and a Lettre Ulysses Award for the Art of Reportage and was named a *Los Angeles Times* Best Book of the Year. *God of the Rodeo* was a *New York Times* Notable Book of the Year. In addition to the *New York Times Magazine*, Bergner's writing has appeared in *The Atlantic*, *Granta*, *Harper's*, *Mother Jones*, *Talk*, and the *New York Times Book Review* and on the op-ed page of the *New York Times*. His writing is also included in *The Norton Reader: An Anthology of Nonfiction*.

LEE BOUDREAUX BOOKS

Unusual stories. Unexpected voices. An immersive sense of place. Lee Boudreaux Books publishes both award-winning authors and writers making their literary debut. A carefully curated mix, these books share an underlying DNA: a mastery of language, commanding narrative momentum, and a knack for leaving us astonished, delighted, disturbed, and powerfully affected, sometimes all at once.

LEE BOUDREAUX ON *SING FOR YOUR LIFE*

Long before I was lucky enough to publish him, I came across Daniel Bergner's mesmerizing writing in *God of the Rodeo,* which chronicled his unparalleled access to the inmates of Louisiana's infamous Angola prison. I followed up immediately with *In the Land of Magic Soldiers,* about the horrific civil war in Sierra Leone. Never before had I read someone capable of going to such tormented places and emerging with such a profound understanding of the humanity that unites us all. In *Sing for Your Life,* Bergner's empathy, insight, exquisite prose, and gift for articulating the complex and the transcendent (whether that's a relationship scarred by violence or the ancient art of coaxing beautiful sounds from the strange physiognomy of the human head) have found a perfect subject in Ryan Speedo Green, a supernova of charisma and talent. I hope his story, one as timely as it is triumphant, will leave you on your feet, cheering for an encore.

.

Over the course of her career, Lee Boudreaux has published a diverse list of titles, including Ben Fountain's *Billy Lynn's Long Halftime Walk,* Smith Henderson's *Fourth of July Creek,* Madeline Miller's *The Song of Achilles,* Ron Rash's *Serena,* Jennifer Senior's *All Joy and No Fun,* Curtis Sittenfeld's *Prep,* and David Wroblewski's *The Story of Edgar Sawtelle,* among many others.

For more information about forthcoming books, please go to
leeboudreauxbooks.com.